Becoming a Teacher in a Field-Based Setting

An Introduction to Education and Classrooms

SECOND EDITION

Donna L. Wiseman
Northern Illinois University

Stephanie L. Knight
Texas A&M University

Donna D. Cooner
Colorado Partnership for Educational Renewal

WADSWORTH

THOMSON LEARNING Australia • Canada • Mexico • Singapore • Spain • United Kingdom • United States

WADSWORTH
★
THOMSON LEARNING ™

Education Editor: Dan Alpert
Associate Development Editor: Tangelique Williams
Editoral Assistant: Alex Orr
Marketing Manager: Becky Tollerson
Project Manager, Editorial Production: Trudy Brown
Print/Media Buyer: Christopher Burnham
Permissions Editor: Joohee Lee
Production Service: Publishing Support Services

Text Designer: Vicki Moran
Photo Researcher: Terri Wright
Copy Editor: Kay Mikel
Cover Designer: Andrew Ogus
Cover Image: © Davis Barber, PhotoEdit, Inc.
Compositor: TBH Typecast, Inc.
Text and Cover Printer: Webcom, Ltd.

Printed in Canada
 2 3 4 5 6 7 05 04 03 02

Library of Congress Cataloging-in-Publication Data

Wiseman, Donna L. (Donna Louise)
    Becoming a teacher in a field-based setting : an introduction to education and classrooms / Donna L. Wiseman, Donna D. Cooner, Stephanie L. Knight.
        p. cm.
    Includes bibliographical references and index.
    ISBN 0-534-55918-2
    1. Student teaching—United States—Handbooks, manuals, etc. 2. Teachers—Training of—United States—Handbooks, manuals, etc. 3. Education—Study and teaching (Higher)—United States—Handbooks, manuals, etc. I. Cooner, Donna D. (Donna Danell) II. Knight, Stephanie L. III. Title.

LB2157.U5 W57 2001
370'.71—dc21   2001017982

Wadsworth/Thomson Learning
10 Davis Drive
Belmont, CA 94002-3098
USA

For more information about our products, contact us:
Thomson Learning Academic Resource Center
1-800-423-0563
http://www.wadsworth.com

International Headquarters
Thomson Learning
International Division
290 Harbor Drive, 2nd Floor
Stamford, CT 06902-7477
USA

UK/Europe/Middle East/South Africa
Thomson Learning
Berkshire House
168–173 High Holborn
London WC1V 7AA
United Kingdom

Asia
Thomson Learning
60 Albert Street, #15-01
Albert Complex
Singapore 189969

Canada
Nelson Thomson Learning
1120 Birchmount Road
Toronto, Ontario M1K 5G4
Canada

Contents

2   Surveying Educational History and Philosophy   31

8   Teaching Lessons in Today's Classrooms   222

9 Outlining School Contexts, Organization, and Leadership   254

10 Collaborating with Families, Businesses, and the Community   289

Preface

Teaching teachers, like teaching children, is not a morally neutral affair. It is the discharging and instilling of obligations, the primary one of which is discovery and growth in what can be termed the learning process. . . . What we owe children, we owe teachers.

—Sarason 1993, p. 135

Teaching in today's classrooms is quite different from what you may remember about your own early school experiences. The profession has changed dramatically and has acquired multiple and complex dimensions. Some understandings will develop as you gain experience and practice new teaching skills. However, experience in the absence of reflection will not guarantee growth. Reflection, both individually and as a shared process, is an important part of your development as an educator. Discussions with peers, teachers, mentors, university professors, and elementary and secondary school students will enable you to reflect on your experiences through different lenses. As you mature as a teacher, reflecting on your experiences will allow you to effectively interface with colleagues and professionals who work with children and families, deliver instruction to diverse learners, use technology in classroom instruction, and create an environment of mutual trust between you and your students.

This text is designed to introduce you to the education profession—its history and current contexts, the complexities of teaching and learning, and the dynamics of the classroom. What you learn about teaching during your university experience is only the first step in becoming a teacher. We cannot give you a set of skills that will assure your success throughout your teaching career, but we have provided some ideas and experiences that will introduce you to the profession.

Your needs as a beginning teacher will be quite different from those of experienced teachers. The first steps of learning to teach are both exciting and daunting. As you become a teacher, you will need to realize that you are not the first to experience insecurities and challenges.

One of the best places for you to learn about teaching is in a school environment, and we hope your preparation program includes several opportunities for you to work in schools and with students. The experiences you have in the schools are planned by university professors and classroom teachers through a partnership that has been formed between the school and the university. The school–university partnership that accompanies your teacher education program connects university- and school-based perspectives. Recognizing the contribution of university-sponsored research and theory while integrating the practical knowledge that teachers have gained from their own classroom experience is the best way to learn to teach (Zeichner, 1992). Sometimes theory and practice collide. The things you read in your textbook and talk about in class may not match what you are seeing in the classroom setting. When this happens, it is important to talk about the differences and establish a balance between educational theory and classroom practice. Some educators ignore the role of theory and feel that practice is the best way to learn to teach. We believe both aspects of teacher training are important. You may become impatient with university coursework and focus more on your field and clinical experiences. But to be a professional, you must understand both the theories and the practices of teaching.

To help you understand the ideas of teachers as you learn about becoming a teacher, we have included examples and descriptions written by beginning and experienced teachers to illustrate the ideas in this text. The Voices sections in each chapter are designed to provide an "insider" account and let you hear the sound of teachers' voices (Shulman, 1992). These classroom narratives evolved from interviews and written responses. When appropriate, the views of children, parents, principals, and others are included. The stories provide clarification and interpretation for some of the topics presented in the text.

You will become a professional by observing, doing, inquiring, and reflecting on teaching and learning. Each chapter has suggested activities and guidelines for discussions with classroom teachers, your peers, and university instructors. Cultivating interactions with others and sharing ideas will enable you to solve problems collaboratively. If you want to know more about a topic presented in the text, the InfoTrac College Edition activities in each chapter provide a good place to begin your inquiries.

The Field-Based Activities in each of the chapters encourage you to become involved in reflecting on what you see when you are in the classroom. Some of the activities encourage development and collection of portfolio artifacts. Your supervisor or university professor will help you select and personalize the activities most useful to your professional growth. The portfolio activities are more than course requirements—they are designed to engage you in the important process of reflection and will serve as a measure of your growth in this important first phase of becoming a teacher.

References

Shulman, J. (1992). *Case methods in teacher education*. New York: Teachers College Press.

Zeichner, K. (1992). Rethinking the practicum in the professional development school partnership. *Journal of Teacher Education, 43*(4), 296–307.

Acknowledgments

We continue to be indebted to the many teachers and principals who collaborate with us as we restructure our own roles to include a school–university perspective. The teachers who work with us in school–university partnerships have made a commitment to preparing new teachers, and their schools are usually changed as a result of their efforts. The ability of teachers to reflect on their own practice, continue their own professional development, and guide new teachers' first attempts at teaching provides many new lessons about collaborating, teaching, and researching.

We owe a special debt of gratitude to Angela Vogeler at Northern Illinois University who patiently worked with our editorial scribbles and helped communications between the three of us go more smoothly. She is now a veteran of both editions of this textbook.

We would like to thank the following reviewers for their suggestions: Janet Byrne, Roane State Community College; Mary C. Clement, Berry College; Mary Dean Dumais, Kean University; John R. Zelazek, Central Missouri State University.

The Wadsworth editors and staff provided support and encouragement to help us complete this project. Dianne Lindsay encouraged us to begin a second edition, and Dan Alpert guided us through the process of updating and making changes to the text. Vicki Moran, who was in charge of the final production phase, deserves a great deal of credit for her efficient guidance. Many thanks to all of these people.

Donna L. Wiseman
Stephanie L. Knight
Donna D. Cooner

CHAPTER 1

Developing a Personal View of Teaching

IN THIS CHAPTER

- **Impact of Personal Biography on Teaching**
- **Reasons for Becoming a Teacher**
- **Characteristics of Good Teachers**
- **Teaching as a Lifelong Learning Process**
- **The Formal Steps of Learning to Teach**
- **Learning to Teach in a Field-Based Setting**

I remember every teacher I ever had. I say this not to boast about my memory but to illustrate just how powerfully my teachers influenced me. Some of them I knew quite well, particularly the ones in the elementary school, because of the intense relationship between elementary school teachers and their students in their self-contained classrooms and because they lived in my community and were a part of my life outside the classroom. Others I knew only as teachers. I had no idea what their lives were like outside the school or even if they had lives outside of school. The story of those I knew well could be the subject of a book unto itself. Memories of the others provoke a series of questions for me. Who were you really? What did you care about? What did you think of me? Did you even know who I am?

—Gloria Ladson-Billings, *The Dreamkeepers**

---

*From *The Dreamkeepers: Successful Teachers of African-American Children*, by Gloria Ladson-Billings (pp. 26–27). San Francisco: Jossey-Bass, 1997.

Good teachers touch learners' lives and captivate their students' attention, motivating them to learn and encouraging them to do their best. They can demonstrate passion about a content area while caring for and respecting their students. At the same time, teachers are capable of critiquing their schools and understanding the impact of state and local requirements on classroom instruction. Teachers interact with parents and community leaders from all walks of life. They play an important role in the community and know how to use the resources available to them to benefit their students. They are able to understand five-year-olds' explanations of important life events or adolescents' defense of their favorite rock music. In sum, they are lifelong learners who focus their varied skills and abilities on working with young learners.

The teaching profession is complex and challenging. To meet these challenges, future teachers need experiences that will help them acquire and later refine their skills and abilities. The reflection encouraged in your formal teacher preparation will serve as a model for learning throughout your teaching career. This chapter will help you consider and answer these questions:

- Why do I want to be a teacher?

- What experiences have shaped my ideas about teaching?

- What is a good teacher?

- How do teachers learn how to teach?

Impact of Personal Biography on Teaching

Teachers' past and present life experiences have an impact on their attitudes and definitions of teaching and create important influences on their identities as teachers (Knowles, 1992). Personal and professional biography becomes a rich source of information that helps clarify teachers' dispositions and behaviors and accounts for some of their ability to be socialized into the world of teaching. Childhood experiences, early teacher role models, teaching experiences, personal knowledge and beliefs, and significant or important people make important contributions to an individual's definition of and approach to teaching (Calderhead, 1996; Crow, 1987; Knowles, 1992).

Teachers explain that they have entered the profession because they want to positively impact young people's lives. Many believe that becoming a teacher is more than a career choice—it is a calling.

Childhood Experiences

Many teachers can recall when, as a child, they set up a school in their backyard and enlisted their brothers and sisters as students. Although not every child who "plays" teacher in his or her early years becomes a teacher, teaching is something that we observe and know about early in our lives. These early observations and feelings about school and teaching contribute to the ways we think about teaching and what we do in our classrooms.

Even those childhood experiences that occur away from the classroom can become a part of how teachers identify their roles. Personality development, socialization patterns, and ways of interacting with others are some of the same traits developed during early experiences that ultimately become integral parts of teachers' identities. For example, our notion of intelligence as a factor that can change (or not) may develop in response to the way our parents and early teachers regarded intelligence.

Family members provide a great deal of input in how we think about teaching. Those who grow up with parents who teach may be influenced by their parents' careers. If parents are teachers and talk about their work during family interactions, their philosophy and framework can easily become a part of their own children's philosophy. Dinnertime discussions about teaching and schools have the potential to remain with teachers throughout their career. Certainly family attitudes toward teaching will have an impact on a future teacher's way of thinking about schools.

In addition, family expectations and rules contribute to teacher identity. Behaviors learned as a child, as well as patterns of interaction and family values, can have an impact on teaching behaviors. Parents and early childhood experiences influence future teachers in other ways as well. Parental expectations about work, learning, play, creativity, and other important issues are reflected in our teaching careers. Such personal attributes as work habits established as a young child stay with the adult teacher.

Role Models

Positive influences from teachers may provide a clear view of what it means to be a teacher. As Kristen, a future teacher shares, "I have impressions in my mind of some of my favorite teachers. I want that same impression of myself in my students' minds." Obviously, favorite teachers can be significant in helping individuals decide to become teachers. Teachers may recognize a particular talent and encourage their students to become teachers. School experiences also contribute to our perception of the teacher's role. Even negative experiences with teachers can result in a clear conception of teaching based on what we do not want to be. If we did not have good experiences in the classroom, then we may have a different view of how to handle students. For example, those who had experiences in very structured schools may have difficulty developing spontaneous instructional patterns and open classroom responses. These early encounters with teachers continue to help us understand teaching. Studies of teachers' biographies demonstrate that positive school environments encourage positive role identification with teachers as well as positive preservice teacher behaviors (Knowles, 1992).

Teachers at the university also contribute to ideas about teaching. These ideas are most influential during the preservice stage of your career. Many of the experiences and interactions you have in your university coursework will begin to form your explicit views of teaching.

Teaching Experiences

Working with children in informal and formal learning environments before deciding to become a teacher also provides motivation for becoming a teacher.

Field-Based Activity 1.1

Develop a biographical timeline that traces who or what influenced your decision to become a teacher. Form small working groups made up of classmates and identify common themes and factors across the data. Categories can be established by writing group responses on three-by-five-inch cards and organizing them in themes that share similar features. After agreeing on common characteristics, each card grouping can be labeled and discussed by the group.

Experiences in church school, baby-sitting, and summer programs are ways future teachers discover that they have a special talent or preference for interacting with young learners.

Specific lessons are learned in these first encounters with teaching. Early teaching experiences provide frameworks for dealing with children, planning instruction, selecting strategies, and feeling comfortable in the classroom. Teachers' early experiences using small groups or discussion activities in church school might influence the use of some of the same techniques in their own classrooms. Tutoring experiences teach future teachers how to use one-on-one strategies effectively in classroom settings. Early experiences with teaching help individuals understand and use interpersonal skills related to teacher–student interactions.

Preservice teachers can easily relate to viewpoints and orientations to practices in classrooms that are like their images of teachers' work. You may find that you reflect on and consider your early experiences as you begin to learn to teach. When faced with difficult experiences or important classroom decisions, new teachers often revert to behaviors they learned during previous teaching experiences (Knowles, 1992). When your university professor talks about a certain strategy, such as cooperative grouping, it may remind you of times that you were involved in such a strategy. Early experiences can be used as a foundation for reflection. However, it is important to do more than remember the experiences. You also should question why a teacher used the strategy, how children responded, and how you might change or adapt your early experiences. Recognizing and analyzing memories of early teaching or learning opportunities can convert past experiences into a strong influence on your response to current and future classroom events and teaching decisions.

The process of becoming a teacher starts long before you enter a formal university program. Many beliefs, attitudes about teaching, understanding about children and learning, and educational values are established by early life experiences. Your university preparation will provide you with the opportunity to reflect and expand on what it means to be an effective teacher in today's schools.

Reasons for Becoming a Teacher

The most compelling reason given for becoming a teacher involves the interpersonal interactions resulting from continuous contact with children and young people. Specifically, teachers mention that they like to work with children and youth, make a difference in their lives, and see the look of joy when a student finally "gets it" (Metropolitan Life Survey, 1995). Reasons such as these are given by teachers who view teaching as a special mission in our society and consider teaching a valuable service and a way to make a lasting contribution to society. One teacher explained her career choice by saying, "I want to be a difference in somebody's life. I want to mean something . . . change something. I would choose teaching again in a minute if I had the chance. It's what I want to do."

Other reasons people mention when discussing the decision to be a teacher include ease of entry, exit, and reentry into the profession, flexibility of time, and material benefits (Lortie, 1975; Metropolitan Life Survey, 1995). The teaching career is accessible to individuals who start their careers in other fields and develop a second career. Parents enjoy the hours that parallel their children's hours, including the time off during holidays and in the summer. Satisfying salaries, job security, and benefits also attract individuals into teaching careers. Nevertheless, without fail, surveys continue to demonstrate that teachers who indicate that they are not likely to leave the profession give "love of teaching" as the reason they will continue (Metropolitan Life Survey, 1995).

Perhaps due to the influences of family discussed in the previous section, teaching often continues as a family tradition. One future teacher in five reports a mother or father who taught at one time or is still teaching. Parents serve as models and have a great influence on their children's decision to become teachers. As one future teacher wrote, "I never had the opportunity to have my Dad as a teacher, but I have always heard wonderful things about him from his ex-students. . . . I guess you could say I am in the 'family' business."

Despite the statistics, some parents may not support their children's decision to become teachers. Many beginning teachers report that family members tried to dissuade them from entering the teaching profession. Future teachers are often aware of the negative perceptions associated with a teaching career but are not daunted by them. One future teacher admitted, "When I made it to college—

graduating at the top of my high school class—my whole family said I shouldn't go into teaching. 'You're too smart to teach,' they said. 'You need to be a doctor or lawyer and make some money.' I was the only one in my extended family to ever get a degree, so everyone was pushing me to do different things. I looked at business, but nothing excited me like teaching."

Characteristics of Good Teachers

Everyone has a vision of a good teacher or can tell a story of an exceptional teacher and the impact that teacher had on our lives. Even as early as first grade, children have opinions on what makes a good teacher and produce delightful responses indicating what makes a good teacher (Figure 1.1). However, what makes a good teacher may vary depending on the perspective taken when descriptions are formed. A review of how young children define good teaching may provide a composite profile of what is honored and regarded as good teaching.

We may be more sophisticated than the first-graders when we describe what makes a good teacher, but it is possible to recognize their views in even the most academic presentation. The document that sets forth the national standards for teaching establishes the fundamental requirements for proficient teaching as a broad grounding in the liberal arts and sciences; knowledge of the subjects to be taught, of the skills to be developed, and of the curriculum and materials; knowledge of methods for teaching, learner development, skills in understanding the diverse needs of students, and ability to employ such knowledge in the interest of students (National Board for Professional Teaching Standards, 1997). The

World Wide Web Site

You may learn more about the National Board for Professional Teaching Standards at this Web site: http://www.nbpts.org/

National Board further explains good teaching by describing five propositions necessary for good teaching. Let's look at each of the propositions in detail.

Commitment to Students and Their Learning

The basic assumption that teachers must possess is that all children can learn. In addition, teachers must be willing to act on the belief. Good teachers internalize knowledge about student development and learning processes. The work of social and cognitive scientists that applies to teaching is integrated with personal theories of learning and development. Good teachers recognize, accept, and rejoice in their students' differences. They demonstrate the ability and willingness to adopt teaching methodologies that take differences into account. An acceptance of differences and an understanding of personal development and learning processes prod good teachers to provide opportunities for all students in their classrooms to receive attention. To do so, teachers repress biases about ability differences, handicaps or disabilities, social or cultural backgrounds, language, race, religion, or gender. A good teacher constantly struggles to meet the needs of all students in personal and social learning, academics, interpersonal skills, and character development.

Knowledge of Subjects and How to Convey Content to Students

Good teachers are committed and enthused about the subject matter they present to their students. They have a general understanding of how the content is organized and can integrate and connect related content areas. In addition to an understanding of the content, they also possess an understanding of the specialized knowledge of how to convey the subject to a student. In other words, it is not enough to know science; a teacher also must know how to present science content in an appropriate way to the learner. Use of materials and resources is also part of knowing the pedagogical content knowledge. Good teachers possess large repertoires of curriculum resources, teachers' guides, videotapes, computer soft-

Figure 1.1   First-Graders Describe a Good Teacher

These are excerpts of what first-graders wrote about what makes a good teacher. Their original spellings add to the charm of their descriptions.

A good teacher is nice, smart, and has good handwriting. And in order. And gets her stuff dun on time.
    —Zach, age 7

A good teacher is someone Who makes good disishons [decisions]. A good teacher is nice.
    —Manuel, age 8

A good teacher helps you lurn!
    —Elizabeth B., age 7

A good techer helps. A good techer has a plan. some techers giv you a good plan. A good good techer love all the cis [kids] in hr clas. A good techer givs you in st stuchins [instructions] all the time. a techer hast to have a room and qostivachin [positive action].
    —Beth Ann, age 7

I think that the qualities of being a good teacher is the importance of the children learning. You really feel good when you are a teacher. The main thing is to help the kids learn. I think being a teacher is a good job. you should try!
    —Dustin, age 8

Teachers sould have a good atutood [attitude] and be a little pushy. The teachers jobs are teaching math and siens [science] and arithmatick, acsedera acsedera [et cetera, et cetera]. A teacher wants to be a teacher because they jost wont to be by kids!
    —Stacy, age 8

ware, and music recordings that can be used to teach their content. Various resources are used to generate multiple paths to knowledge.

Shulman (1987) describes knowledge of content in three different ways: (1) subject matter knowledge, (2) curriculum knowledge, and (3) pedagogical knowledge. Subject matter knowledge is a deep understanding of the content— for example, what a science major would know about plant phyla. Curriculum knowledge refers to a teacher's knowledge about what is to be taught, what materials are to be used in the classroom, and what students already know about the subject. Pedagogical knowledge refers to how subject matter can be presented to students—the strategies used by the teacher. Taken together, knowledge of these three types represents pedagogical content knowledge.

One of the most important contributions of this way of describing good teaching is the concept of pedagogical content knowledge. In other words, good teachers are those who understand the content and also understand the best way to teach that content to whatever age students they teach. Pedagogical content knowledge is often discussed in relation to high school teachers. However, it is equally important to those who are going to be elementary teachers.

Ability to Manage and Monitor Student Learning

Good teachers have appropriately high expectations for all their students and see their job as facilitating students' learning. They are able to use a wide range of methods to meet instructional goals and to help students learn based on their strengths and weaknesses. Teachers encourage student engagement by managing learning in varied arrangements including small groups, large groups, individuals, and pairs. This often requires that teachers control and manage behavior of students while at the same time encouraging social interaction and engagement. As teachers manage and monitor their students' learning, they are regularly assessing learning progress toward their principal objectives.

Ability to Think about Teaching and Learn from Experiences

Thinking about teaching includes understanding the decisions and actions that occur in classroom settings. The importance of decision making is one factor that makes teaching so complex. Good teachers must make difficult decisions that test their judgment, often while engaging in ongoing instruction. Part of the decision-making skill comes from what they know about teaching through their own experiences, but it also comes from the advice of others. In addition, teachers can draw on educational research and participate in teacher research to constantly improve their practice. Through the very act of teaching, teachers model what it is like to be an educated person and how one can practice lifelong learning.

Participation in Learning Communities

Even though much of their work is done in isolation with groups of young people, teachers are not solo performers. Good teachers contribute to school effectiveness by collaborating with their colleagues. They participate in the joint establishment of goals for learners, development of school curriculum, coordination of instruction, interpretation of state and local goals and objectives, and implementation of student services. Good teachers cooperate with their administrators, share their knowledge and skill with others, and participate in the ongoing development of strong school programs. In addition, teachers must work collaboratively with parents and take advantage of community resources.

The knowledge base about teaching and learning is growing steadily and provides an understanding about what it takes to be a good teacher. All the definitions of good teaching include certain common elements, although they may organize or emphasize different aspects of the teaching process. Several ideas can be taken from this review of effective teaching. First, as in any complex endeavor, there are multiple ways to be good or excellent. Although it may not be easy to measure a good teacher, the processes that contribute to good teaching can be described. A review of these processes reveals the enormous responsibility of a good teacher. Often, these descriptions make teaching appear to be an almost impossible endeavor. Teaching will never be simple or easy, but skills acquired by beginning teachers can be refined through reflection on experience. Becoming a good teacher is a lifelong process.

As previously discussed, there are many aspects involved in becoming a teacher (see, for example, Borko & Putnam, 1996). A teacher is molded by both formal and informal experiences in and out of classrooms. Various individuals and experiences contribute to the dynamic socialization and learning of future teachers. However, learning to be a *good* teacher results from conscious reflection on biographical events, professional training, personal experiences, reading, and other contextual contributions.

Teaching as a Lifelong Learning Process

Good teachers are lifelong learners. A teacher's career is influenced by personal life experiences such as his or her personal environment, family situation, positive life incidents, crises, individual dispositions, interests, and life stages. Becoming a teacher involves several years of formal preparation, but the concentrated university training that prepares a person to be a teacher is not the end of understanding about the profession. Successes and failures in the classroom, the adult development that occurs naturally through life experiences, and the continued formal learning that the profession offers contribute to the professional development of teachers. School regulations, management styles of supervisors, public trust of schools, societal expectations, professional organizations, and unions add to teachers' career development (Fessler & Christensen, 1992). As a result of life experiences, maturation, and normal development, teachers will progress through several stages of teaching. Certain characteristics and needs are identified with each phase of a teaching career.

The Preservice Years

Individuals who are involved in formal intensive university preparation are said to be in the preservice phase of their careers. Initial preparation offered by universities involves courses and field experiences planned by professional teacher educators. The characterization of the preservice stage and future stages of teaching careers can be described in many ways. Figure 1.2 illustrates one way for you to think about your future as a teacher.

Preservice teachers typically need to be socialized into the profession, become comfortable with the methods and processes of teaching and learning, develop instructional and interpersonal strategies to cope with the complexities of teaching, learn to work collaboratively in a professional setting, and understand the purposes of schools and how they work. Nevertheless, not all of those in the preservice stage have exactly the same needs.

The period of life when you decide to enter the preservice stage of your career can make a great difference in how you learn and respond to university preparation. If you are a young adult, your family may provide financial support. Older students may have the responsibility of a family and their own expenses. Depending on your age, you may be planning a marriage, raising young children, or caring for aging parents. Some of you may be entering the profession after several years in another career. You may have experienced responsibilities in work-

Figure 1.2   The Teacher Career Cycle

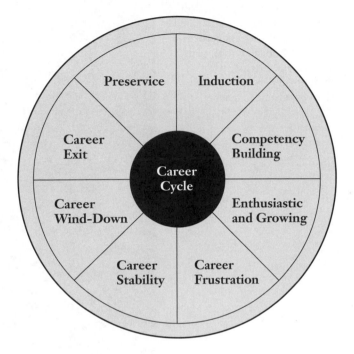

Source: Fessler, R. (1992). The teacher career cycle. In R. Fessler & J. C. Christensen (Eds.), *The teacher career cycle: Understanding and guiding the professional development of teachers* (pp. 21–43). Boston: Allyn & Bacon. Reprinted by permission of the author.

places that may or may not have been related to education. You may want to teach because outside interests connected you with teaching. Working with scouts, clubs, or in childcare may have provided you with experiences that suggested teaching as a career.

Preservice experiences planned by universities often include several common elements, but they may differ in the way that courses and experiences are delivered. Traditionally, courses and experiences have been provided on university campuses. Increasingly, programs include courses and experiences that take place in school settings. Preservice experiences have the potential to greatly influence

Relationships between future and experienced teachers are crucial when one is becoming a teacher. Teacher preparation programs are greatly enhanced when future teachers participate in school activities, plan lessons, and interact with students under the supervision of an experienced teacher.

MARK C. BURNETT/STOCK BOSTON/PICTUREQUEST

the way you think about teaching and the skills and abilities you acquire at this stage of your career.

Societal attitudes, expectations, and needs also may affect your attitude toward teaching. For example, your experiences in dealing with children who are poor, suffer emotional trauma, or speak different languages may affect how you approach teaching. Take time now to complete the Self-Reflection exercise and to think about what you have learned.

Beyond the Preservice Years

Classroom experiences as well as additional learning opportunities and personal development activities may result in different ways of thinking about teaching. One way to think about teachers' careers is to think about progressing through distinct stages (Fessler & Christensen, 1992). As with any suggestion of human

Becoming a Teacher in a Field-Based Setting

Self-Reflection

SHOULD I BE A TEACHER?

Put T for true or F for false in the space provided as you think about each of these statements.

_____ 1. When I think of people I admire the most, many of them are teachers.

_____ 2. A teacher is born not made.

_____ 3. I am really proud of my decision to be a teacher.

_____ 4. One of the advantages of teaching is that I would not have to work in the summer.

_____ 5. As a child, I liked playing school.

_____ 6. If I had to choose a summer job, I would rather work in a store or an office than with children.

_____ 7. I would prefer to teach in a culturally diverse setting.

_____ 8. Teaching is something I can do if other career choices do not work out.

_____ 9. I want to teach even though I was advised to do something more challenging.

_____ 10. All that is needed to teach is knowledge of your subject area.

_____ 11. Liking what I do is more important than making a lot of money.

_____ 12. I enjoy learning about the subject that I plan to teach.

Scoring

Give yourself one point for each true answer on the odd numbered items _____

Give yourself one point for each false answer on the even numbered items _____

Tally the total number of points _____

Six or above. You seem to be comfortable with your decision to be a teacher; however, you may want to look at the items that received no points and reflect on how your response may affect your teaching commitment. For example, if you did not receive points for items 1, 3, or 9, you may want to reflect on your attitudes toward the status of teaching as compared to other professions.

Below six. You may want to investigate the teaching profession in greater depth and plan for ways that you can experience what it is like to be a teacher. Talk to teachers, become involved with children, and read books such as Esme Raji Codell's (1999) account of her first year of teaching.

development, these stages are not exact but only a suggestion of what a person might expect during the progression of a career in teaching.

Induction

The induction stage occurs during the first few years of teaching and is the time when teachers are socialized into the profession. During this time, the new teacher works for acceptance and attempts to become comfortable with teaching on a day-to-day basis. This may be a time when the beginning teacher finds a location or situation where he or she "fits." Teachers may move from building to building or grade to grade until they find a situation where they feel most comfortable. The stress of beginning a new profession may be compounded by other events in individuals' lives (Head, Reiman, & Thies-Sprinthall, 1992). New teachers are usually adjusting from viewing themselves as students to having a full-time job and getting to know a new community. They are dealing with issues related to personal relationships, finances, and activities outside of work. It is an exciting time for new professionals, albeit a busy and stressful one.

During this stage, many school districts provide support in the form of experienced mentor teachers to help induct new teachers into the profession. Mentors provide new teachers with a support system by acting as peer coaches, helping with planning, sharing ideas, introducing school routines, judging appropriateness of assignments, and explaining the context of specific teaching situations (Evertson & Smithey, 1999; Theis-Sprinthall, 1990). Mentors ease new teachers into the profession and increase the possibilities that they will stay in the teaching field for a longer period of time. This is an important role for an experienced teacher because 40 to 50 percent of new teachers leave teaching after seven years or less (Huling-Austin, 1989). New teachers who receive appropriate mentoring during their first year or two in the profession continue to learn, grow, and develop more positive attitudes toward the profession (Head, Reiman, & Thies-Sprinthall, 1992).

Competency Building

The competency building stage is an exciting time when teachers are growing and becoming more secure in their teaching processes. During this time, teachers begin to feel comfortable with teaching and seek out new materials, methods, and strategies. Teachers may continue their professional development by attending workshops, conferences, and enrolling in graduate programs. This stage is characterized by a great deal of experimentation, innovation, and continued learning.

Enthusiasm

As teachers continue to work and gain experience, they begin to develop a high level of competency. The confidence resulting from positive experiences in a classroom leads to enthusiastic support of the teaching profession. Experienced enthusiastic teachers look forward to each day of teaching, enjoy interacting with students, and search for new ways to teach and improve their practice. They often become important contributors to the learning of others in their district and their school by sharing what works for them and by designing innovations to be tried by others.

Frustration

As with most careers, almost all teachers suffer some level of frustration and disappointment during teaching. Although stress may be expected, various strategies can be used to help teachers overcome burnout and view their work with renewed attention, enthusiasm, and excitement. Returning to school, changing schools, or working on an innovation can renew and encourage an experienced teacher who is feeling less than positive about the profession. Overall, today's teachers maintain a positive attitude toward the teaching profession. More than three-quarters of teachers surveyed agreed with the statement "I love to teach," and most would encourage a young person to pursue a career in teaching (Metropolitan Life Survey, 1995). Individuals who are just starting their teaching careers rate having a "satisfying job" as their top reason for entering teaching.

Stability

Experienced teachers achieve confidence and pride in their teaching and enter into a period of stability marked by increased expertise, leadership development, and student success. By this time, teachers have identified those strategies that are comfortable for them, understand their students, and can manage behavior and classroom activities effectively. They continue to refine and perfect teaching strategies and may become "experts" in a particular strategy, approach, or philosophy. This period may be marked by continuing professional education, education and experiences that lead to administration, or involvement in curriculum development and other projects. It is generally during this stage that teachers feel that they can contribute to the development and design of programs and experiences for new teachers by serving as mentors and supervisors in preservice programs.

Winding Down

There comes a time when teachers reach a certain age, develop other interests, or recognize that their life goals have made it necessary for them to move on to other jobs or situations. A spouse's retirement, a parent's illness, or another life event may cause an experienced teacher to consider retirement. Teachers who feel that it is nearly time for them to exit their careers may engage in reflection on different aspects of teaching. They begin to gather information to help them consider what their next career step will be. In the process, they may remember individual students and the stories that accompany their classroom experiences. Some teachers look forward to a career change or retirement, consider it a natural event, and begin to make plans for the future, whereas others struggle with leaving the profession. Depending on the action planned by a teacher who has decided to exit the profession, this stage may take several years or may occur after only a few months.

Career Exit

Teachers exit teaching careers with different plans and patterns. Some teachers leave teaching with the understanding that it may be for only a few years while they are raising children, caring for parents, or exploring another career. Experienced teachers not ready for retirement may leave teaching to become principals or administrators in the central office. Teachers closer to retirement age may avoid full retirement and look for opportunities for part-time teaching and other ways to ease out of the profession they love. Other teachers may close the doors on the classrooms where they have spent many years and never return.

These career stages illustrate that teaching is dynamic and that anyone entering the profession can expect to go through periods of time when they experience different needs based on where they are in the career cycle. At this point, most of you are involved in the preservice stage of your career and learning about teaching is your primary focus.

The Formal Steps of Learning to Teach

Informally, your first exposure to teaching may be working with children in the summer, church school, after-school tutoring, baby-sitting, or various types of childcare that involve untrained individuals. The first formal learning about teaching is usually embedded in the college experience when you enter a teacher preparation program during the last two years of undergraduate study or a year of intensive study after receiving a degree in a content field. The teacher preparation program should extend prior experiences, provide new experiences related to teaching, and give you opportunities to test your teaching ability, receive feedback, and learn to be an effective teacher.

Overview of Teacher Education

The preservice stage of teaching is guided by university curriculum. The goals of teacher preparation include the presentation of a connected and integrated professional program of (1) general and professional studies, (2) observations of practice, and (3) supervised teaching experience (Goodlad, 1990). Training is not a dramatic event in which a preservice teacher becomes confident as an experienced teacher. Rather, it is the beginning of a process that will be ongoing for many years. Preservice professional educational experiences should help you make the transition from being a university student to becoming a teacher. One of the major changes that happen during this transition is that you will become socialized into the profession.

Socialization into the profession means that teachers learn what they should know and be able to do in their profession. Early experiences with schools offer many examples and impressions about schools, teaching, and education. An important part of the socialization of preservice teachers is the opportunity to learn about schools through a guided sequence of activities introducing the culture of teaching. Preservice programs offer a continuous framework for reflection and learning about teaching while experiencing the schooling process. Access to the instructional context of schools during this process is a key element. Formal preservice experiences should be carefully orchestrated between school and university. Ideally, the contexts where preservice teachers are socialized should be positive and represent the most current examples of teaching and learning. Occasionally, however, schools may offer preservice teachers a more negative aspect of school socialization. During your preservice experience, you may observe events and processes that are not the most beneficial for students and that do not fit within the theoretical frameworks discussed in your university classes. When you observe striking and contrasting events, your program should offer you the opportunity to talk with university professors and schoolteachers about what you are seeing.

A future teacher may take many courses in English and understand the content in that subject area very well, but knowing the content is not enough. Teacher education attempts to offer you a glimpse of some of the issues, questions, possible solutions, and strategies needed to move beyond content area proficiency. For example, teacher education helps future teachers learn about society at large—the social, political, and institutional connections that have an impact on schools. Future teachers can benefit from an understanding of the connections between the organizational frameworks of schools and the historical and cultural roots of those schools. Future teachers learn about families, communities, and societies other than their own and how diversity enriches our lives.

One of the striking features of teaching noted in earlier research on schools is the abruptness with which a person must take responsibility for a classroom (Lortie, 1975). Preservice teachers often move from positions of limited responsibility for students during their internship to sole responsibility during their first year of teaching with little attention paid to the demands of the transition. School–university programs provide a logical scaffolding for teacher preparation and provide needed support and structure. Increasingly, early field experiences are being offered that involve practicing teachers in development and implementation of the experiences. In general, teacher education has changed significantly in the past twenty-five years—in practices and contexts as well as in definitions outlining what it means to be a teacher (Griffin, 2000).

Overall, university curriculum goals typically focus on providing opportunities necessary to move teachers into the induction or novice stage of their career. Many professional educators will take part in teacher preparation programs that offer various types of activities designed to prepare and induct teachers into the profession. This textbook and the course you are in right now will help you begin establishing the framework for continued learning during your preservice program. Teacher education programs that are jointly developed and delivered by classroom teachers and administrators and university teacher educators provide an ideal opportunity to link theory with practice.

Linking Theory and Practice

One of the purposes of preservice education is to develop a scaffolding between the content understanding of individuals and the study of pedagogy (Hilty, 1992). To develop stronger collaboration between the schools and universities, many teacher education programs have developed a partnership that provides high-quality preparation for new teachers. Partnerships that focus on teacher education may vary widely in their approach and arrangement. No two partnerships are the same; each partnership has its own personality and character, reflecting the strength and uniqueness of the school's staff and the strengths and diversity of the university faculty. In field-based programs, at least a portion of your preservice coursework will be taught on the campus of a local school by a combination of school and university faculty. You will become familiar with the school and with students, teachers, and parents from a wide range of cultural backgrounds. To take full advantage of the field-based setting, some of your class assignments will focus on meeting with teams of teachers, participating in varied field experiences, collecting data from teachers and students, and becoming comfortable with and using technology in instruction.

School–University Collaboration

Although collaborative teacher education classes are not available at every university, there are elements of school–university partnerships in most good programs. A collaborative teacher preparation program provides opportunities for university professors, public school teachers and administrators, university graduate and undergraduate students, public school students, and others to learn from each other.

The most complex collaboration between universities and schools has produced a concept called Professional Development Schools (PDS). PDS are schools in which a formal written agreement sets forth the methods by which the university and the schools work together. Any number of activities may be

Becoming a teacher is a lifelong learning process. Professional development activities that present new ideas and help teachers learn new skills and abilities are important at all stages of career development.

involved in the agreements, which tend to focus on (1) preparing new teachers, (2) improving preservice teacher preparation, (3) providing opportunities for experienced teachers to continue their learning, (4) changing the curriculum for young people so that they are able to achieve at the highest level possible, and (5) encouraging inquiry and research about teaching and learning. PDS may provide new models of teacher education and development by serving as exemplars of practice, builders of knowledge, and vehicles for communicating professional understandings among teacher educators, future teachers, and veteran teachers (Byrd & McIntyre, 1999; Darling-Hammond, 1994; Holmes Group, 1990).

Partnerships between schools and universities in teacher education tend to provide opportunities for more exposure to schools for a longer period of time. Future teachers become immersed in PDS and will often spend a full year in the schools. The preservice stage of a career may be completed entirely on a public school campus. By definition, preservice teachers will spend a substantial number of hours each week in the field. Public school teachers are usually involved in mentoring, teaching, or supervising a portion of the teacher preparation program.

For many who have experienced teacher education in PDS, it is difficult to think that teacher preparation would be done in any other manner. However, even after a decade of working for the establishment of PDS, there are still only a few hundred such programs across the United States. Many PDS have not been able to incorporate all of the characteristics traditionally associated with school–university partnerships (McIntire, 1995). Establishing partnerships is difficult because PDS involve combining the contrasting cultures of universities and public schools. Interestingly enough, these two settings often use different terms, rely on different funding sources, possess contrasting reward systems, and think about scheduling and workdays in very different ways (Knight, Wiseman, & Smith, 1992). Additionally, teachers and administrators worry that involvement in PDS activities may direct their attention away from students in their classroom when they concentrate on preservice experiences. Often, university faculty resist getting involved in partnership work because universities do not reward them for their efforts (Winitzky, Stoddart, & O'Keefe, 1992).

The University and Public School Contributions

Despite these difficulties, almost all the teachers and university professors who work in school–university partnerships share the common goal of effectively teaching young people in a school setting. They typically find common ground in their love of teaching and learning and concern for students and their learning. But aside from those commonalities, they bring different offerings to the preservice teachers.

University professors generally focus on research and theories about teaching and teacher preparation, learning theory, and content area learning. Although most of them were public school teachers at one time in their lives, they now focus on research and development of ideas associated with learning and teaching. Their schedules are flexible; they may write during the early morning hours, come into work late in the morning to advise and teach adult students and participate in university-based meetings, and teach graduate classes at night. University professors possess expertise in adult learning and spend a great deal of time writing, researching, and reading about education in general as well as in their specific areas of expertise. Areas of expertise may include diverse topics such as metacognitive strategies, mental imagery, children's literature, gender issues in education, social and cultural foundations of learning, and content area pedagogy. University professors are usually experts in a single area of educational expertise and receive promotion and tenure based on how they represent their knowledge in publications, presentations, and research activities. They also focus on the development of preservice and inservice teachers. They will use the knowledge associated with teacher education as they contribute to the blend of activities planned by schools and universities. They may become involved in presenting readings, theories, and research findings connected to what is going on in the schools. Professors may work with teachers to develop research projects that help find answers to instructional issues in the classroom.

Teachers in schools focus on the young people in their classrooms. They possess expertise in such areas as child and adolescent development, classroom management, and motivational techniques related to teaching and learning. In addition, teachers typically have a wealth of practical knowledge about children and young people and the nature of teaching. They know what the state requires of teachers, techniques for organization, and management of classrooms. Their daily routine requires that they walk halls, bend over small desks, supervise lockers, stand on playgrounds, monitor busy hallways, and remain on their feet for long periods during a structured teaching schedule. They work from morning to midafternoon and have little time for any personal business during their workday. If and when they do research, it focuses on classroom issues related to children and young people. Teachers are rewarded by their students' achievement in the classroom, administrator and parental feedback, and other recognition programs in their district. Depending on whether they teach in elementary or secondary classrooms, they are usually experts in child or adolescent development as well as in specific content areas and possess a large repertoire of knowledge linking content areas and day-to-day happenings.

The roles of practicing teachers in preparing future teachers are broad and varied. Experienced teachers serve as role models, provide mentorship, and share information and strategies. They can be crucial to the reflection and learning of future teachers as they plan, discuss, debate, and work together in the school setting.

In the PDS context, university teacher educators and Pre K-12 teachers exhibit different roles and responsibilities related to teacher education. Traditionally, university professors are responsible for planning the preservice teacher curriculum, participating in the delivery of the curriculum, and researching the results of what happens in preservice education. One of their major responsibilities is to increase the knowledge associated with teacher development and preparation and to integrate that new knowledge into the curriculum and experiences planned for preservice teachers. University professors are also expected to disseminate their findings to others in the field of teacher education.

Preservice teachers are heavily influenced by the teachers in the schools where they observe and where they complete their internships. When given a choice, preservice teachers admit to allegiance to their cooperating teachers and

Voice of a Teacher

My work with the school–university partnership is a great deal of additional work added to my duties as a first-grade teacher. I am the person that university teacher educators contact at our school to talk about collaborative activities, field experience arrangements, and other connections that link the school and the university together. I occasionally teach a class on my own or with a university professor who is offering a class at my school. Sometimes my job requires me to do activities that seem to lack professionalism, like sitting on the floor, singing, coloring, and going out to recess. When I work with future teachers and university professors, I feel a great deal of respect for what I do, and I know I am making a difference. I enjoy sharing my teaching practices with future teachers, and they always give me new ideas and help me reflect on my own teaching.

not their university connections (Hollingsworth, 1998). Preservice teachers are quickly caught up in the day-to-day activities of the schools and perceive that they need a great amount of knowledge related to practical aspects of teaching. Both the schoolteacher and the university professor have valuable experiences and knowledge to share with beginning teachers. School and university perspectives offer a preservice teacher a balanced view of education, and the roles of both are important to the beginning teacher.

Learning to Teach in a Field-Based Setting

The formal teacher education program will guide you as you enter the profession. You have different needs as a preservice teacher than you will have at any other phase of your career (see previous section on the career cycle). Learning to be a teacher in a school–university setting will provide you with the opportunity to learn where theory and practice are connected in relevant and meaningful ways. This experience is one of many that will shape your beliefs, prepare you to interact with children and young people, and introduce you to instructional strategies.

Reflection in Teacher Education Programs

Preservice teacher activities should help future teachers build an image of good teaching. This may be achieved by promoting good teaching that is the product of research and theory and providing assisted learning from the range of experiences and involvement of future teachers (Johnston, 1994). Experience is not the only component required when building the image of a good teacher. Analysis and discussion of ongoing events as well as readings and writings featuring alternate perspectives will enable future teachers to focus on a full range of experiences and promote effective learning from those experiences. The reflective processing of experiences, coupled with research and theory, is important to the teacher education program.

Importance of Developing a Personal Philosophy

There is more to teaching than loving children, knowing content, and implementing instructional procedures. The decisions you will make in your future classrooms will have an impact on your future students and will contribute to reshaping schools, families, universities, and churches. Your actions and decisions

---

Portfolio Reflections and Exhibits

You will complete a series of field-based activities in each chapter. The activities will serve as the basis for a portfolio representation of learnings and understandings developed during the activities, readings, and discussions related to the chapters. For each chapter, you may choose one of the field-based activities suggested in the text or develop an alternate exhibit that represents what you have learned. Your responses to the activities or your exhibit can become part of your teaching portfolio, or you may follow the alternate suggestion presented here.

Suggested Exhibit 1: Personal View of Teaching

A portfolio representation for this chapter might include these items:

1. A summary of all field-based activities in this chapter including references to the text and other readings.

2. Identification of one field-based activity in this chapter that was most important to you.

3. A representation of your own decision to become a teacher. Consider the impact of your own biography on your choice to become a teacher. Use the different influences described in this chapter to guide the development of an autobiography of your career choice. Illustrate your childhood experiences, teacher and family influences, and teaching experiences that contributed to your decision to become a teacher. You can develop a portfolio representation of your biography in many ways. A narrative, poetry, music, artwork, or collage can represent your decision to become a teacher.

---

are based on how you know and understand the world (Clark, 1995). Your own philosophy of life and way of thinking about education account for your unique teaching style, educational decision making, and interactions with young learners. Your beginning experiences should help you understand your teaching philosophy and how your beliefs affect your teaching.

Developing a personal philosophy of education involves clarifying educational issues, justifying educational decisions, interpreting educational data, and integrating that understanding into the educational process (Meyers & Meyers, 1995). Although your personal philosophy will influence much of what you do, your expectations for children and young people's learning is an important component of your beliefs. The development of a personal philosophy requires self-examination and honest comparison and consideration of what we are about as teachers. It is a continual process that involves seeking answers to hard questions over a long period of time.

InfoTrac College Edition Extension

InfoTrac College Edition provides online access to hundreds of scholarly and popular periodicals to extend the depth and breadth of your knowledge and to facilitate individual and group projects. To use the feature, log on to the InfoTrac College Edition Web site and type in the password provided on the card that accompanies your text. Familiarize yourself with the search procedures by viewing the introduction and the major search categories described in the Help feature. When you feel comfortable with the system, access these topics through the suggested search mode.

1. Using a subject search, type in one or more of the following topics:

    reflective practice

    teacher effectiveness

2. Using a keyword search, type in the following topics:

    national teaching standard!

    professional development school!

    good teacher!

    (Note that the wildcard [!] enables you to find titles that contain either the singular or plural form.)

3   Using the PowerTrac search, find a recent journal article that the authors of this text published about professional development schools.

Related Readings

The following books provide more information about some of the topics and ideas presented in this chapter:

Bullough, R. V., & Baughman, K. (1997). *"First-year teacher" eight years later: An inquiry into teacher development.* New York: Teachers College Press.
> *This is a description of a ten-year process of Kerri Baughman's struggles and successes in learning to teach. The two authors create a narrative of how beliefs change and the importance of professionalism. This book illustrates the development of an experienced teacher and the role of teacher learning in the professional process.*

Clark, C. M. (1995). *Thoughtful teaching.* New York: Teachers College Press.
> *Dr. Clark believes that what teachers think, believe, and do will ultimately affect the learning of the young people in their classrooms. Teachers' personal and professional development, career paths, relations with colleagues, working conditions, rewards, and the leadership in their schools all affect the quality of instruction teachers deliver. He describes teaching as a syntheses of reason and emotion, feeling and thinking.*

Codell, E. R. (1999). *Educating Esme.* Chapel Hill, NC: Algonquin.
> *This first-year teacher's diary is a rather brutally honest description of the leadership, politics, tears, and joy of a fifth-grade classroom in the Chicago projects. At times, Esme is rather unconventional in her approach to teaching, but there is never any doubt that she cares deeply about her students. This teacher gained quite a bit of attention from the media as a result of her description of her first year of teaching.*

Jaolongo, M. R., & Isenberg, J. P. (1995). *Teachers' stories: From personal narrative to professional insight.* San Francisco: Jossey-Bass.
> *This is a themed collection of stories and anecdotes that will help you understand more about teachers and their classroom experiences. Individual teachers tell stories about how they learn from their students, reflect on their experiences, and resolve conflict. The authors of the book analyze individual stories and expand on the teachers' experiences.*

Sarason, S. B. (1993). *You are thinking of teaching? Opportunities, problems, realities.* San Francisco: Jossey-Bass.
> *Dr. Sarason presents some of the opportunities, problems, and realities of the teaching profession. He presents teaching as a demanding, complex profession and attempts to help future teachers think about their choice of a teaching profession.*

References

Borko, H., & Putnam, R. (1996). Learning to teach. In D. Berliner & R. Calfee (Eds.), *Handbook of educational psychology* (pp. 673–708). New York: Macmillan.

Byrd, D., & McIntyre, D. (1999). Research on professional development schools. *Teacher Education Yearbook VII.* Thousand Oaks, CA: Corwin.

Calderhead, J. (1996). Teachers' beliefs and knowledge. In D. Berliner & R. Calfee (Eds.), *Handbook of educational psychology* (pp. 709–725). New York: Macmillan.

Christensen, J. C., & Fessler, R. (1992). Teacher development as a career-long process. In R. Fessler & J. C. Christensen (Eds.), *The teacher career cycle: Understanding and guiding the professional development of teachers* (pp. 1–20). Boston: Allyn & Bacon.

Clark, C. (1995). *Thoughtful teaching.* New York: Teachers College Press.

Codell, E. R. (1999). *Educating Esme.* Chapel Hill, NC: Algonquin.

Crow, N. A. (1987). *Preservice teachers' biography: A case study.* Paper presented at the annual meeting of the American Educational Research Association, Washington, DC.

Darling-Hammond, L. (1994). *Professional development schools: Schools for developing a profession.* New York: Teachers College Press.

Evertson, C., & Smithey, M. (1999). Supporting novice teachers: Negotiating successful mentoring relationships. In R. Stevens (Ed.), *Teaching in American schools* (pp. 17–40). Upper Saddle River, NJ: Merrill.

Fessler, R. (1992). The teacher career cycle. In R. Fessler & J. C. Christensen (Eds.) *The teacher career cycle: Understanding and guiding the professional development of teachers* (pp. 21–44). Boston: Allyn & Bacon.

Fessler, R., & Christensen, J. C. (1992). Summary and synthesis of career cycle model. In R. Fessler & J. C. Christensen (Eds.), *The teacher career cycle: Understanding and guiding the professional development of teachers* (pp. 249–268). Boston: Allyn & Bacon.

Goodlad, J. I. (1990). *Teachers for our nation's schools.* San Francisco: Jossey-Bass.

Griffin, G. (2000). Changes in teacher education: Looking to the future. In G. Griffin (Ed.), *The education of teachers* (pp. 1–28). Chicago: National Society for the Study of Education.

Head, F. A., Reiman, A. J., & Thies-Sprinthall, L. (1992). The reality of mentoring: Complexity in its process and function. In T. M Bey & C. T. Holmes (Eds.), *Mentoring: Contemporary principles and issues* (pp. 5–21). Reston, VA: Association of Teacher Educators.

Hilty, E. B. (1992). Teacher education: What is good teaching and how do we teach people to be good teachers? In J. L. Kincheloe & S. R. Steinberg (Eds.), *Thirteen questions: Reframing education's conversation.* New York: Peter Lang.

Hollingsworth, S. (1998). Making field-based programs work: A three-level approach to reading education. *Journal of Teacher Education, 39*(4), 28–36.

Holmes Group. (1990). *Tomorrow's schools of education.* East Lansing, MI: Author.

Huling-Austin, L. L. (1989). Beginning teacher assistance programs: An overview. In L. Huling-Austin, S. J. Odell, P. Isshler, R. S. Kay, & R. A. Edelfelt (Eds.), *Assisting the beginning teacher* (pp. 3–18). Reston, VA: Association of Teacher Educators.

Johnston, S. (1994). Experience is the best teacher; Or is it? An analysis of the role of experience in learning to teach. *Journal of Teacher Education, 45*(3), 199–208.

Knight, S. K., Wiseman, D. L., & Smith, C. W. (1992). School-university partnerships: The reflectivity-activity dilemma. *Journal of Teacher Education, 43*(3), 269–277.

Knowles, J. G. (1992). Models for understanding, preservice and beginning teachers biographies. In I. F. Goodson (Ed.), *Studying teachers' lives* (pp. 99–152). New York: Teachers College Press.

Lortie, D. C. (1975). *School teacher: A sociological study.* Chicago: University of Chicago Press.

McIntire, R. G. (1995). Characteristics of effective professional development schools. *Teacher Education and Practice, 11*(2), 36–49.

Metropolitan Life. (1995). *The Metropolitan Life survey of the American teacher, 1984–1995: Old problems, new challenges.* New York: Louis Harris and Associates, Inc.

Meyers, C. B., & Meyers, L. K. (1995). *The professional educator: A new introduction to teaching and schools.* Belmont, CA: Wadsworth.

National Board for Professional Teaching Standards. (1997). *What teachers should know and be able to do.* Detroit: Author.

Shulman, L. S. (1987). Knowledge and teaching: Foundations of the new reform. *Harvard Educational Review, 57*(1): 1–22.

Theis-Sprinthall , L. (1990). *Becoming a teacher educator: A curriculum guide.* Raleigh, NC : Department of Curriculum and Instruction, NCSU.

Winitzky, N., Stoddart, T., & O'Keefe, P. (1992). Great expectations: Emergent professional development schools. *Journal of Teacher Education, 43*(1), 3–18.

CHAPTER 2

Surveying Educational History and Philosophy

IN THIS CHAPTER
- **A Brief History of American Schools**
- **Philosophical Themes**

*P*eople are asking what is the criterion of a teacher. The first requisite and the last criterion of a teacher is to be a true follower of the Great Teacher, not so much in professing as in living . . . it means a right attitude toward the profession, toward each subject taught, toward the home, the community and the child. It means to possess knowledge and the ability to interpret it to right uses so that it becomes a power for good in the life of a child.

To be a teacher, many methods of approach are necessary in reaching the minds and hearts of growing boys and girls: these at the levels of the child's abilities to pursue and achieve. And when such happy team work is obtained the teacher continues to walk beside the developing mind and soul; pressing a little here, guiding, directing thoughtfully, prayerful, ever keeping the goal of a perfected character as the objective sought. . . .

Someone had said to be educated meant to bring forth and train up all the faculties and powers of the mind and body to their highest possible use. To accomplish this makes it mandatory to live in such manner of thought and activity as will make the whole world better for our having lived in it.

—Sarah Gillespie Huftalen, "To Be a Teacher"*

When you are studying to be a teacher, you tend to want to focus on the here and now, learning how to deal with the children and young people in the classrooms where you are learning to teach. It may seem difficult to take time out and reflect on the past, but there are reasons for you to do just that. The foundations of teaching—philosophy and history—are with you in each classroom you enter. Little about teaching, learning, and children was discovered just yesterday. History can illuminate contemporary issues and provide insights into common problems. An understanding of the history of education and how it connects with the present can help us interpret the present and perhaps help us avoid repetition of past mistakes. Cicero (106–43 B.C.) declared that "persons who are ignorant of history will remain forever children" (Power, 1991, p. ix), and educated future teachers have the responsibility to understand what their contribution will be to the continuum of education.

Knowledge of educational history places current educational issues in context, and philosophy provides a tool for educational decision making. Philosophical beliefs have an impact on the way teachers make decisions, interact with children, and approach their careers. Traditionally, well-developed philosophies of education include statements about what education should and should not do: in other words, what the goals, content, and methods should or should not be. Analysis of the aims of education and the dispositions to be fostered in students, determination of the rationale for the dispositions, recommendations about the means of fostering the dispositions, and discussions of the line of argument used to support use of particular means provide a basis for discussing different philosophies (Frankena, 1974). In addition, these elements suggest guidelines for development of more personal definitions of the means and ends of education. As you develop your own philosophy of teaching, you may want to compare your beliefs

---

*From "To Be a Teacher," by Sarah Gillespie Huftalen, Iowa, 1865–1955. In M. H. Cordier, *Schoolwomen of the Prairie and Plains* (pp. 175–209). Albuquerque: University of New Mexico Press, 1992.

Field-Based Activity 2.1

Before you read the chapter, write down your answers to these questions, which will help you build a personal philosophy of education.

1. What should the purpose of education be in the United States? In your classroom?

2. What do you want your future students to be able to do or be as a result of their experiences in your class? Why?

3. What kinds of teaching approaches and strategies will most likely help your students meet these goals?

Share your ideas with another preservice student. How do your philosophies differ? How are they similar?

about what education should or should not do with those of philosophers (past and present).

This chapter will help you answer these questions:

- How are educational history and philosophy interconnected?

- Are there ways to make ancient history and philosophy meaningful in today's classrooms?

- Who are the best-known philosophers in American education?

- What historical and philosophical roots can be linked to contemporary education?

A Brief History of American Schools

The Early 1600s

From the beginning of the settlement of North America during the first half of the 1600s, schools played an important role in establishing the new country. Thrust into a savage new world and working long hours on their new homesteads, busy pioneer parents looked to schools as a way to transmit civilized behavior to their children (Perkinson, 1991). Settlers faced ambiguities related to learning and teaching. On one hand, they wished to protect the culture they were developing in their new country; on the other hand, they were anxious to promote the intellectual, moral, and religious values they had inherited (Power, 1991).

What was happening in Europe had a major impact on early American education. During this period, John Calvin and Martin Luther were active reformers who believed schools should serve many purposes, including teaching as many people as possible to read so that they could read and interpret the Bible. John Calvin's educational approach established mandatory and strict obedience to the church and a belief in God. He stressed civic training and strict discipline for all classes of the population. Luther articulated a plan for education in Germany. As part of the plan, he turned authority of education over to the mayors and aldermen of the cities to educate children of all classes. His theory cultivated future national educational control, and he connected the religious and civic purposes of education. The greatest legacy of this time was the concept of universal education for everyone, which became an important component in the American education system.

Later, in the Age of Enlightenment (1700–1800), European philosophers emphasized the power of the human mind. Philosophers such as John Locke and Jean-Jacques Rousseau believed the way to a better life was through an educated mind, but they differed greatly in their approaches. John Locke challenged both theological and humanistic conceptions of human nature and focused on the importance of learners' experiences (Power, 1991). Locke believed children began as a blank slate, a *tabula rasa* (Smith, 1979). Children subsequently experienced events, developed simple ideas, and eventually replaced initial thoughts with more complex ideas based on experiences. The purpose of education, Locke thought, was to help children to experience a healthy, virtuous, and successful life.

Rousseau believed education should conform to a child's individual needs and that young children learn by acting on natural impulses. "Society," he declared, "should reject any commission to teach persons or direct their scholastic course. Its role should be passive; nothing more than an environment wherein the natural impulses of autonomous persons can find full satisfaction" (Power, 1991, p. 202). He believed all children were good and needed to be allowed to grow naturally. Although Locke and Rousseau held very different views of the role of education, they are considered the fathers of modern child psychology, and their theories are the basis for much of modern-day child development. Their ideas spread to the colonies before the end of the eighteenth century and formed the basis of schooling, but it was not long before the new country produced thoughtful educators and uniquely American educational processes.

Colonial Schools

Early American schools were established to provide young people with the opportunity to study religion. Gradually, religious education began to give way to the idea that the purpose of education was to provide knowledge that would help

TEACHER'S CONTRACT.

It is Hereby Agreed, By and between School District No. *77* .... Township No. *13* ......, Range No. *5* ......, County of *Lincoln* ...., Territory of Oklahoma, and *Ephrem Wall* .... the holder of a Territorial and County Certificate, this day in force, that said teacher is to teach, govern and conduct the public schools of said district to the best of *his* ...... ability, follow the course of study adopted by the District Board, keep a register of the daily attendance and studies of each pupil belonging to the school, make all reports required by law, and such other reports as may be desired by the County Superintendent of Public Instruction, and endeavor to preserve in good condition and order the school house, grounds, furniture, apparatus, and such other district property as may come under the immediate supervision of said teacher, for a term of ...... *3* .... school months, commencing on the ...... *8* .... day of ...*November*............., A. D. 189*7*.. for the sum of ...*Twenty seven*......... Dollars per school month, to be paid at the end of each month; PROVIDED, That in case said teacher shall be legally dismissed from school, or shall have h*is* ...... certificate legally annulled, by expiration or otherwise, then said teacher shall not be entitled to compensation from and after such dismissal or annullment: PROVIDED, FURTHER, That the wages of said teacher for the last month of the school term shall not be paid unless said teacher shall have made the reports hereinbefore mentioned.

And the said school district hereby agrees to keep the school house in good repair, to provide the necessary fuel, school register, and such other supplies as may be necessary.

IN WITNESS WHEREOF, We have hereunto subscribed our names, this *13* ...day of *September*..... A. D. 189*7*..

.... *W. C. Yoder* ......Director or Treasurer.

.... *Ephraim Wall* ...... Teacher.

ATTEST: *Henry Bergdorf* ....Clerk or ~~Treasurer~~.

REMARKS:—This Contract shall be made out in duplicate, and one copy given to the teacher, and the other placed on file in the District Clerk's office. The law does not authorize the Board of Directors to make a contract with a teacher, or to pay his salary, for any time during which his certificate is not in force.

Teaching has changed a great deal since the late 1890s. Individuals who were teachers may have attended only eight years of grammar school, and the responsibilities outlined in this contract were quite different than those of today's teachers.

future citizens uphold democracy. As the young government was established to rule itself, the role of education of all its citizens became more and more important. Laws were passed requiring that everyone become literate and that communities be responsible for establishing schools. As early as 1642, Massachusetts had a compulsory education law that held parents responsible for the education of their children (Perkinson, 1991). Other colonies replicated the Massachusetts law. Even colonies that had no laws requiring schooling established schools and put schoolmasters in place to educate their children. The first laws passed in Massachusetts supporting compulsory education mandated that all children be instructed in reading, although it did not matter if that occurred at home, in school, or elsewhere. The Old Deluder Satan Act of 1647 required towns of fifty households or more to hire a schoolmaster capable of teaching reading and writing. Common elementary schools were established in Massachusetts to provide basic education in reading, writing, and math. Children usually attended the one-room schools from about ages five through fourteen.

Attitudes of elitism and who should be educated were transported with the colonists' European roots. During the early days of the colonies, education was based on the social class system (Timm, 1996). Those who were poor could not afford for their children to attend schools, and at first there was almost no educational opportunity offered poor children, children of slaves, or young girls. Slowly, educational opportunities became available to more and more children. Young women and a few boys attended the dame schools taught by women and held in private homes. The students would study reading, writing, religion, and the rudiments of arithmetic. Boys from higher socioeconomic status levels would continue in Latin grammar schools and learn from the classical system as they prepared for religious or civic careers. The Latin grammar schools were essentially the first secondary schools that prepared colonial boys for colleges—usually Harvard or Yale. A small percentage of children attended grammar schools, and, of course, there was no need for girls to attend because colleges of that time did not admit women.

During colonial times, African Americans were treated as property and their education was limited to technical skills needed for the contribution to the economy of their owners (Timm, 1996). Some owners did provide opportunities for African Americans to learn to read the Bible, but this did not continue after the American Revolution. The Puritans provided a few of the slaves with an opportunity to be tutored, but for the most part African Americans were left out of early colonial educational endeavors.

Contributions of Jefferson and Franklin

The ideas of Locke and Rousseau and the attitudes of the new country helped Thomas Jefferson (1743–1826) and Benjamin Franklin (1706–1790) frame the views of American education to focus on freedom of expression and universal public education. Franklin was a Puritan whose first writings, *Poor Richard's Almanac*, became popular reading for colonists in the early 1800s. In addition to writing, Franklin was a scientist, inventor, philosopher, and educator. Franklin accepted Locke's philosophy of education but extended educational ideas to include all classes and those who had not been involved in the system thus far. As early as the 1760s, Franklin wrote that African Americans were equal to whites and appealed for better treatment of the Native Americans.

Franklin supported the study of basic skills, classics, and religion and the development of high moral character, logical reasoning, integrity, and self-discipline (Smith, 1979). In an essay outlining the academy he had established, he called for a "well-stocked library (complete with maps, scientific instruments, and diagrams); a frugal diet and regular physical exercise for the scholars; training in such practical skills as penmanship, drawing, accounting, and gardening; and courses in arithmetic, geometry, astronomy, English grammar, and modern foreign languages" (McMannon, 1995, p. 17). Franklin's Puritan background influenced his ideas about school, and he wrote that spending too much time with the classics was wasteful and that the core of educational studies should be derived from what is useful and should meet the practical needs of the local communities. He viewed schools as a way to prepare young Americans for business or professions. One of Franklin's major contributions was his attempt to establish a permanent school, an academy, that would reflect stability (Perkinson, 1991). Imagine his disappointment when his academy eventually became a Latin grammar school, embodying many of the aristocratic and wasteful studies he abhorred.

Thomas Jefferson was educated in America and demonstrated great personal abilities in languages and literature. He was also highly talented in music and the arts and was an inventor, farmer, scientist, and architect. He was a student of Locke and Rousseau and believed there should be a government-sponsored educational system so that all citizens could have equal educational opportunities (Smith, 1979). Jefferson envisioned schools as a way to produce future leaders for democratic society, and he believed it was the government's responsibility to provide a system of education. He founded the University of Virginia based on this belief and worked to propose a system of schooling that would provide the most basic schooling to all children in the state. His plan, which was presented to his state legislature but was not successful, provided three years of elementary school. He envisioned an educational system designed to preserve the democracy through well-educated, capable leaders and citizens. Schools were to create a populace that would advance the common interest and protect the young democracy from tyranny or dictatorship (McMannon, 1995).

The 1800s

In the beginning of the 1800s, schools refined the force that shaped U.S. society, and connections between education and government became more explicit (Perkinson, 1991). Americans began to argue for an educational system that was common across the states, standardized in content and duration, and offered to all children equally. By 1860 almost all states had some form of public school system, and some of the ideas that we see in our schools today began to evolve.

The first schools were identified as common schools because they were designed for all children. The common schools of early colonial times were influenced by the ideas of educators in Europe and the United States. The famous Swiss educator Pestalozzi felt that men were neither good nor evil but shaped by their experiences (Button & Provenzo, 1989). He argued for child guidance based on caring, nurturing, and providing children opportunities to be actively involved in learning, as opposed to learning by rote memorization. Pestalozzi honored the role of mothers and believed affection was the basis of obedience. A good teacher was like a good mother. He believed women were well suited for teaching, especially because of their nurturing, caring attitudes and natural affinity for teaching, especially for young children (McMannon, 1995).

Other educators of the early 1800s began to establish characteristics of our educational system that are still in place. Horace Mann, crusading for common, or public, schools, proposed a state board to exercise control over public schools and insisted that the purpose of schooling was to educate the citizenry, not to focus on religion. He supported a practical curriculum aimed at developing moral character and effective citizenship. One of Mann's lasting contributions to the U.S. educational system was to transfer Prussia's graded school levels to the United States. Classification of students was seen as advantageous over the one-room schoolhouses because it provided the teacher with the opportunity to address all lessons to one level.

In the decades before the Civil War, educational efforts were almost all focused on elementary schooling. Schools provided free and universal elementary education to all children, particularly those who were poor, with the hopes that education would improve their lives. In 1820, fueled by the belief that democracy could not be totally run by those educated in common elementary schools, secondary schools began to emerge. Secondary schools were more comprehensive than the early Latin schools, which concentrated on classical education. History, bookkeeping, geometry, surveying, and algebra curriculum began to evolve from the first secondary schools. During the last half of the century, the clamor for a more practical curriculum led to manual training courses in existing secondary schools and new manual training high schools.

With the rapid expansion and experimentation with curriculum, high schools were very different from each other. Educators were split on questions defining the purpose of secondary schools. Should they offer curriculum to prepare students for college or to train youth for jobs? In the wake of this controversy, in 1892 the National Council of Education appointed the Committee of Ten to study secondary school curriculum and make recommendations. The committee called for efforts to ensure that all students take a similar core of academic courses. As such, it was one of the first "back-to-basics" movements in education (Angus & Muriel, 1995).

Initially in the 1800s, a great deal of attention was given to common schools and secondary schools, but colleges began to gain attention. In particular, the evolution of state colleges was strong during the 1800s. Colleges began to add professional, technical, and scientific curricula to their traditional focus on religion and social graces. By the mid-1880s, an entire component of new learning emerged with the establishment of agricultural, industrial, mining, and engineering units. At first, colleges did not admit women, but women gained access to university in private schools, and examples of coeducation soon became representative in both colleges and universities. By the beginning of the 1900s, nearly one-fourth of the students in college were women (Power, 1991).

The 1880s signified a growth in U.S. school systems. Theories of teaching and learning began to grow. Nevertheless, education was still not available to all citizens. Secondary schools did not encourage attendance by women. When women enrolled, they were offered different experiences and less academic content than that offered to their male counterparts. Even though there was some movement to include African American students in formal educational experiences, children of slaves did not have equal access to education. In Boston during the early 1800s, African American parents began to establish separate school systems for their children and requested integrated educational systems. Abolitionists were in favor of education for African Americans, and a school opened to educate black Americans in Philadelphia in 1820. Education for slaves was still opposed in the South.

Some African Americans, albeit very limited numbers, had access to higher education during the 1880s. Oberlin College was one of the first universities to admit both black and white students (Timm, 1996). Soon, African American educators began taking leadership roles in the educational process. Booker T. Washington, who was born into slavery, was educated at Hampton Institute, and he founded Tuskegee Institute, a showplace that provided vocational training for blacks. He viewed Tuskegee as a way for blacks to win acceptance in the white world. His philosophy was to encourage educated blacks to do good work and win the approval of the white world by helping others.

A very different approach was taken by the educator W. E. B. Du Bois, who sought a liberal education for African Americans. He was born a freeman and, after becoming the first black Ph.D. in the United States, taught at Wilberforce College and Atlanta University before he took over the leadership of the newly formed National Association for the Advancement of Colored People (NAACP). His approach was much more aggressive than Washington's, and he advocated

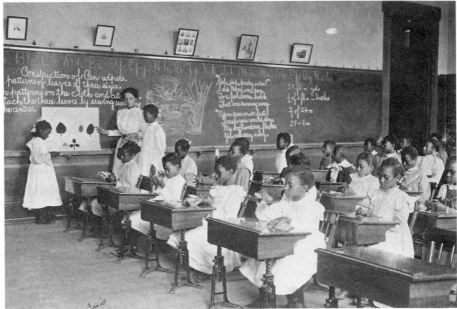

The country's attitudes toward racial and ethnic differences required many cultural and ethnic groups to establish their own schools. School segregation continued until after the Civil Rights movements of the 1950s and 1960s.

equal rights for African Americans in the United States. Du Bois viewed himself as an activist who fought for the rights of black Americans (Perkinson, 1991).

As late as 1860, Asian Americans were also prohibited from attending public school. As did African Americans, Asian Americans began to establish segregated schools for their children. The first schools that taught in Chinese were in San Francisco in the 1870s. Even after a law was enacted to end Chinese immigration, the education of Chinese children continued. The Japanese did not begin to immigrate until the second half of the century, and their schools were established mainly in Honolulu. These Asian Americans predated and established the importance of education for the more recent immigrants from Vietnam, Laos, Cambodia, and Thailand.

Native Americans were not treated fairly in the emerging educational system. The American settlers were intent on controlling the process for Native Americans children and ignored family and tribal culture. President Monroe provided money to Protestant missionaries so they could establish schools for Native Americans. They were to be educated so that they could understand Christianity. The missionaries tended to develop lessons and curriculum that attempted to teach Native Americans to be subservient, to abandon their tribal ways, and to adopt the white culture. For the most part, Native Americans ignored these attempts to educate them in the way of the colonists and conveyed the message that their own learnings and way of doing things met their needs (Button & Provenzo, 1989). Native Americans recognized that the white man's education would cause them to surrender their own culture and lifestyle. They resisted the attempt to educate them in the white man's ways and in some cases ridiculed the process. Territorial schools for Native Americans were closed during the Civil War and were replaced with boarding schools. The boarding schools removed children from their homes and families and did not provide parents input in the educational process of their children. Some schools focused on training Native Americans for manual labor associated with the agricultural economy.

The Mexican War of 1854 brought the first Hispanics into the U.S. educational system in the Southwest. Language instruction was one of the first concerns, and, almost immediately, laws were passed that recognized English as the language of instruction. In many states, legislation was designed to eliminate the Spanish language entirely. The discussions of language framed a bias against Mexican American students on the part of school officials. Many Mexican American parents avoided issues of language and cultural bias by sending their children to private Catholic schools.

While elementary and secondary schools were establishing policies dealing with race and culture that would remain for years, the higher education system was continuing to evolve with the help of the federal government. The Land Grant College Act of 1862 was the first federal aid to education and offered states a means to establish public colleges. States were given land that they were to sell to finance the building and establishment of new colleges. However, states did not always use the money as intended, and much of the money acquired by selling the property was used to build canals and bridges (Button & Provenzo, 1989). Normal schools were established to prepare elementary teachers, and universities developed programs to train secondary teachers. Two-year normal programs were open to students who were sixteen and wished to be teachers. Future teachers studied early forms of psychology and theories of teaching.

The 1800s marked many advances in the U.S. educational system. Early educational processes established precedents, beliefs, and attitudes that can be seen in our current educational processes. At the end of the 1800s, schools felt the impact of social and political changes in the nation (McMannon, 1995). Economic depression, political turmoil, and racial relations affected schooling in the country. Jobs became important resources, and schools were seen as one way to gain economic advantage. The most significant movements at the end of the century were free schooling, establishment of educational systems that began with schooling young children and continued through a university system, and establishment of policies and governance systems to oversee the educational system.

The 1900s and the Progressive Era

As the new century began, the education system was reviewed and found guilty of providing ineffective educational experiences for children. Educators criticized the traditional curriculum, textbooks, and materials used in the schools during the 1800s (Button & Provenzo, 1989). Philosophies and purposes of education were questioned, and new ideas and theories began to emerge. Progress in government was connected to school reform. Progressives—those who identified the importance of linking progress and education—encouraged adoption of a variety of educational strategies, some newly developed, others transported from abroad, and still others reconstituted from the past.

The Progressive movement encouraged the schools to develop the new role as liberator, helping children realize their talents and potential so that they could make contributions to political life, enriching the quality of democracy (Perkinson, 1991). Progressive educators began to shift curriculum from subject-centered schools to child-centered schools, where students' interests were considered when planning educational experiences. Two American theorist-philosophers, Francis Parker (1837–1902) and John Dewey (1859–1952), criticized traditional education that was developed in the 1800s and became affiliated with new ways of thinking about education. Among other things, Parker advocated doing away with the old books and curriculum and bringing in current magazines, newspapers, and student accounts of their experiences.

Dewey developed a comprehensive American educational philosophy that was known as pragmatism. He based his theory on discovery in an environment that encouraged learning. He believed a human's interaction with the environment was the basis for intellectual development (Tanner, 1997). Although often grouped with progressive educators such as Pestalozzi, Dewey resisted being

World Wide Web Site

You can learn more about John Dewey at this Web site:
http://www.siu.edu/~deweyctr/index2.html

Becoming a Teacher in a Field-Based Setting

DONNA WISEMAN

In the early 1900s, one-room schoolhouses were still common in rural communities, and teachers needed only one or two years of college to teach children of various ages.

known as a progressive educator and developed what he called a pragmatic philosophy. He considered change in education to be inevitable and that curriculum must constantly be reformed. He based his curriculum on problem-solving activity and experiences in natural settings. He joined the faculty at the University of Chicago and established an on-campus experimental laboratory school where his teaching ideas could be practiced. The laboratory school is considered a forerunner to the recent school–university partnerships in which teachers and university professors collaborate.

The early 1900s were marked by the attempt to make an exact science of education, and research and testing techniques were developed (Button & Provenzo, 1989). Educational research would ultimately have a huge impact on schooling. One of the major changes came in preparing teachers. Increasing numbers of colleges were offering courses in pedagogy. Scholars and teachers began to build a community of educators who studied and practiced the best of teaching. Much of the first research developed around testing and measurements. The study of teaching and learning resulted in viewing curriculum construction as dependent on knowledge of subject specialties and child development.

Schools in the early twentieth century were sensitive to national and international events, and during the Great Depression, many schools, especially those in the South, became particularly impoverished. Teachers' salaries began to diminish, and many teachers were laid off. The Depression was followed by World War II, which changed the way Americans thought about schools. Economy, labor, and the needs of the workforce began to influence what happened in our schools. The end of the war was followed by the baby boom, a large increase in birthrate, the children of which began to fill schools in the 1950s.

The 1950s and Beyond

The middle of the twentieth century may have seemed calm on the surface, but there were foreshadowings of the changes that were to influence education and society by the end of the 1900s. Research and development began to have an impact on medicine, technology, and economics (Nichols & Good, 2000) and suggested changes for every aspect of American culture including educational processes. The ethnic and racial makeup of the country was beginning to shift, and civil rights issues were emerging as important and controversial problems throughout the country. The wealth of the nation was also in balance as the economy changed from an agricultural and industrial base to a more technologically centered base. The youth of the mid-1900s were portrayed as obedient, clean-cut family members who were home for dinner every evening. That picture was also about to change.

Probably no event characterizes the educational context as well during this time as the impact of the Russian launch of the satellite Sputnik in 1957. Americans were shaken out of their complacency when their arch competitors, the Russians, managed to blast off into space in the first rocket. This event was immediately followed by much fault finding and finger pointing as Americans looked for someone to take the blame and for ways to explain why our research and development efforts were overtaken by those of a communist country. Eventually the blame centered on schools and their so-called failure to educate children and youth to be the thinkers needed for the modern competitive world. Immediately after Sputnik, amid calls for education to be restructured to make our students more competitive, the space race began to gain momentum. The federal government provided large grants to schools and universities to develop curriculum that focused on math, science, and technology. New ways of teaching subjects and innovative practices in education were implemented. The entire nation felt a sense of urgency to prepare the nation's children for international competition.

One of the results of Sputnik was an educational focus on technology development. During the 1950s, televisions were just beginning to become fixtures in living rooms. But with the advancements that came about as a result of renewed efforts and resources directed toward space research, a new innovation known as computers soon followed. It wasn't long before computers were used in research endeavors by universities and businesses. The computers of the 1960s and 1970s, although not as impressive as the ones that sit on our desks in the 2000s, began to make a difference in the way we lived and educated our children (Button & Provenzo, 1989). Technology revolutionized communication, changed jobs, provided new ways to spend leisure time, and affected transportation and manufacturing.

Not everyone had access to the good life, particularly African Americans, and as the century progressed, equality and civil rights became major issues. An important court decision in the 1950s, *Brown v. Board of Education* (see Chapter 4), began a three-decade movement toward equal rights in education. During the late 1950s and early 1960s, schools were the site of confrontations between supporters of civil rights and segregationists. Newscasts on the television sets that were now appearing in everyone's living room showed scenes of African American students being accompanied by security guards and police as they entered schools against the objection of state governors and others. The quiet times of the 1950s were certainly giving way to a more activist time that would change the very nature of schools and our nation.

Of course, we cannot discuss this era without mentioning the Vietnam War and the particularly violent social activism that prevailed at this time. The war;

the assassinations of President John F. Kennedy and his brother Robert and civil rights leader Martin Luther King Jr.; and civil unrest, urban riots, and student protests began to fray the nerves of Americans. Media changed the way we learned about and assimilated the changes in our society. History was occurring right before our eyes, leaving schools and their teachers no other choice than to deal immediately with what was happening in their neighborhoods, the country, and the world. The quiet, sedate, picturesque view of American life in the 1950s gave way to a tumultuous, frightening, but exciting time in the 1960s, in which new technology, civil rights, and media-based instant information were poised to have an impact on educational settings. All of these changes have contributed to the current educational context, which is the subject of discussion in Chapter 3.

Philosophical Themes

Educational history offers descriptions and stories that exhibit change of venue, people, and contexts, but educational questions remain relatively constant. Educators have constantly struggled with philosophical questions related to education: the purpose of education, the nature of the learner, what constitutes knowledge, and what is worth knowing; the strategies associated with teaching; and the struggle between religion, basic education, and liberal approaches. Educational philosophies have evolved around these timeless struggles.

Contemporary philosophies, which to a large extent have evolved from historical philosophies, form the basis for understanding the purposes of education and help develop theories about what should be taught and how students learn. There are many ways to discuss the philosophies, but most philosophies can be traced to one of four major historical stances. Idealism and realism, two of the oldest philosophical positions, and pragmatism and existentialism, both newer philosophical systems, all have had an impact on educational thought (Myers & Myers, 1995). In most cases, philosophies do not reflect only one view but represent an evolution of thinking that has guided decisions and theory building.

Idealism

The intellectual roots of educational philosophy can be traced back to ancient Greece and Rome. Socrates (469–399 B.C.) made contributions to teaching and the value of knowledge by searching for basic meanings and truth and by bringing others together to do the same (Power, 1991). He attempted to educate social and political leaders by connecting knowledge and civic duty, and he used probing questions to explore the worth of human acts. Even in ancient times, those who questioned knowledge transmission and the existing power authorities were not popular. Socrates' questions disturbed the status quo and upset those who held and accepted common assumptions. His constant questions became unpopular because they were viewed as revolutionary and an affront to the authority of those in power. As a result, he was eventually tried for opposing those in power, found guilty, and forced to commit suicide by drinking poison. Socrates is best remembered for using a process of constant questioning, the Socratic method, in teaching. He was a master at creating a series of questions that helped his students develop an awareness of their own thought processes.

Socrates' philosophy and his teaching methodology are widely known to us through his student, friend, and constant companion, Plato (427–347 B.C.). Many feel that all educational philosophy originated with Plato's ideas. He developed and articulated a pattern of thought that suggests that societies and the character of societies are highly dependent on the humans who control the processes. He was convinced that good citizenship and intellectual accomplishment were closely connected and that strong social structures were dependent on the education of citizens, although he had a clear preference for educating only the elite to provide leadership (Power, 1991). Plato's philosophy establishes that the purpose of education is to develop students' abilities so they can serve society (increase their social capacities). Plato is the founder of idealism, a philosophy that focuses on the spiritual and intellectual development of the individual.

Idealism includes ideas that go beyond the physical or concrete world. Idealists attempt to describe ideas, mind, consciousness, form, thought, energy, and other nonmaterial concepts. Ideals reside in the mind, and reality is identified through the subconscious. Idealism reflects Plato's ideas and views education as necessary for an individual's freedom and limitless creative growth. Conservatism is valued in personal and social life.

Today's classrooms may reflect idealism in several different ways. Teachers are models in their own classrooms, and they encourage students to recognize and emulate the thoughts and actions of great people. Knowledge is unchanging, and students should hone their reasoning skills to better get at "truth." Questioning strategies by teachers are valued, and students are asked to learn for the sake of learning—regardless of the practical application of the knowledge.

Schools that reflect modern interpretations of idealism may focus on "back to basics," and the literature used in their classrooms reflect traditional classics. Translations of history and science focus on the Euro-American experience and offer limited interpretations or perspectives. Many proponents of Christian and other current religious education movements draw on idealist philosophies to provide a rationale for the goals and content of education. However, applications of idealist philosophies do not necessarily have a religious focus. Mortimer Adler's (1982) *Paideia Proposal* is an example of a curriculum that advocates a strong academic core, featuring study of the great books that provides a focus consistent with an idealist view of what constitutes important knowledge to be transmitted to youth in our schools.

Realism

Aristotle (384–322 B.C.) studied in Plato's academy for seventeen years and introduced a novel educational philosophy—scientific empiricism—which became the basis for the philosophy known as realism. Aristotle felt that dialogue and questioning were too emotional and personal and failed to make good use of data. He considered the question methodology of Socrates and Plato a waste of valuable learning time because it depended too much on personal experiences. Instead, he encouraged learning to occur by writing and used descriptive prose as a teaching technique. His philosophy introduced the importance of habit and instruction, which he viewed as the basis of happiness.

Realism, antithetical to idealism, holds that objects and happenings exist regardless of how we perceive them. There is no dependence on our minds for interpretation; everything comes from nature and is subject to natural law. Scientific method is honored, and each content area is precisely structured. Pestalozzi, Locke, Jefferson, and Mann were all realists. Learning and teaching are viewed as a science based on hard facts. Realists focus on skills of reasoning and believe the major purposes of education are to promote thinking and to understand subjects. The current drive for accountability is based on a philosophy of realism (Myers & Myers, 1995). Aristotle's emphasis on the virtues required and nurtured by the good life have strongly influenced contemporary advocates for character education (Noddings, 1997).

In today's classrooms, realism is often represented in science and environmental studies. Instruction reflecting a realist philosophy may focus on the environment and its influence on humans. There is a specific theory and truth applied to understanding the world. Teachers who maintain realism as a philosophy are usually subject-matter specialists who focus on reason and thinking. Because idealism and realism share the view that reality and truth are unchanging, they are often combined in their influence on educational practice. Teachers who maintain that there is a common core of knowledge and skills that should be taught to learners, even if they cannot agree on the nature of this core knowledge, would feel most comfortable with the philosophies of idealism and realism.

Pragmatism

Pragmatism is a theory that constantly questions what is viewed as truth. John Dewey was a pragmatist who established experimental education and influenced notions of educational research. Knowledge is obtained and developed through experiences and interactions with the environment (Tanner, 1997). Humans become increasingly complex as they gain experiences and interact with the universe. Therefore, students need opportunities to act on their environment and undergo the consequences of that action. This experimentation goes beyond mere trial and error or mindless activity; it involves reflection on the connections between the action and its consequences.

From this perspective, education is defined as the reconstruction or reorganization of experiences (Dewey, 1916). A teacher who is a pragmatist will help students understand that what is known is changeable, that there are a number of ways to interpret events, and that there is no absolute truth. As noted previously, Dewey often avoided identification with popular notions of Progressive education, but he identified certain common principles shared by Progressive schools. An example of how different pragmatist classrooms may appear when compared

John Dewey is recognized as one of the most distinguished philosophers and educational theorists of the twentieth century. His philosophy, formulated in the early 1900's, is the foundation for experienced-based education and continues to impact current educational practices.

with those operating from idealist or realist traditions can be seen in the change in teaching and learning history that occurred during the Progressive era. Previously, teachers stressed lecture, recitation of facts, and notetaking by students as appropriate history instruction. Dewey, through influence on the Committee on Social Studies of 1916, reconceptualized the study of history as embedded in a social studies curriculum that was more child-appropriate, relevant, and active than previous approaches (Brophy & VanSledright, 1997). The struggle between philosophically opposing conceptions of the substance and goals of history reemerged in 1994 when the *National Standards for History* was published (National Center for History in the Schools, 1996) amid considerable controversy over what the history curriculum should look like (Brophy & VanSledright, 1997). (See Chapter 3 for more discussion on this topic.) At the heart of the issue was whether history consists of an unchanging set of facts to be learned or whether these "facts" are relative to time, place, and people.

Discovery learning and child-centered learning are themes associated with the pragmatist philosophy. A pragmatist philosophy promotes inquiry and uses reflective thinking to solve problems. Classrooms reflecting the pragmatic philosophy may be child-centered, discovery-based, cooperative, and motivated by student interests. Tasks are more likely to be "authentic" in that they reflect the world outside the classroom and can be directly applied to situations that students might encounter outside of school. Problem-based learning, project approaches, and community-based learning all would be consistent with a pragmatic philosophical approach.

Existentialism

Existentialism, a relatively recent philosophy emerging after World War I, focuses on the individual and interprets the world through feelings, anxiety, and choice. Existentialist thought establishes reality and humans as too complex and unpredictable to fit into a neatly predictable system. Truth is subjective. Based on the writings of some educational theorists influenced by the writings of Sartre, Nietzsche, Ortega, and Jaspers, existentialism has little to offer to educational philosophy and may even destroy education as it currently exists (Baker, 1974; Morris, 1963). However, Martin Buber (1957) has explicitly connected his general philosophy with an existentialist philosophy of education. From his perspective, teachers are in a position to impose their views of reality and truth on their students but choose instead to merely present their perspectives and allow students to develop their own views. Developing a capacity to love, appreciate, and respond emotionally are important elements of this philosophical stance. Values,

Field-Based Activity 2.3

With your classmates, list as many past and present educational issues or controversies currently being debated as you can think of. Can you and your classmates identify educational disagreements that are clashes of basic philosophies? Ask teachers or administrators in your school to join the class discussion and review some of the major educational issues currently under discussion. What philosophies do you recognize during the discussion? Write a summary paragraph of the ideas you recognized during the discussion.

arts, and multiple perceptions are used to explain events and to interpret concepts. Self-actualization and self-realization are themes often associated with this view of existentialism.

A classroom of today that reflects an existentialist philosophy focuses on individuals and their perceptions of events. Students are encouraged to build meaning from their own experiences. A classroom interpretation of existentialism encourages students to accept responsibility for their actions and focuses on respecting one's own ideas as well as the ideas of others. Perhaps the best-known example of existentialist applications in education was the experiment at Summerhill, which emphasized student choice and was based on the conviction that students will make good choices about their own learning (Neill, 1960). Schools that follow the Summerhill model tend to forgo any set curriculum and feature activities and experiences that revolve around student interests and questions. Curriculum is personalized, and teachers emphasize personal interaction among teachers and students above facts and ideas. Given the emphasis on educator accountability related to student testing in today's schools (see Chapter 3), existentialist approaches to education are not as prevalent in public schools today as they were in the 1960s.

Current educational systems have been influenced by the philosophers and educational philosophies previously described, but many contemporary philosophies display a unique outlook, or focus. Nevertheless, there is a link between past and present philosophies. Philosophers from the past inform contemporary philosophies that influence today's schools directly. As a result, many contemporary philosophies are outgrowths of the four basic categories of philosophy.

Recently, a more critical stance has played a role in educational philosophy. Critical philosophers focus on how and why society and schools oppress some people and not others and on how political issues are influenced by oppression. Racism, sexism, religion, and economics form the basis of their critical analysis of

Field-Based Activity 2.4

Divide into small groups. Each group should choose one of the four philosophical approaches described in this section and prepare a vignette or concrete description of an activity in a classroom that exemplifies that particular approach. Have a representative from your group read your vignette to the rest of the class, and ask them if they can identify the philosophical approach.

curriculum, instructional strategies, and attitudes in the schools (Piner, 1998). They encourage teachers to question their classroom actions and to understand how teachers contribute to the success and failure of minority groups, women, and poverty groups in today's classrooms.

Over time, despite the influences of formal philosophy, most teachers develop their own versions of educational philosophy and theory, which are deeply rooted in their own beliefs about the nature of knowledge and the learner as well as their experiences with learning and with what works in their classrooms. Teachers' educational philosophy will determine how comfortable they feel with innovations (see Chapter 3) and how willing they are to change what they do in the classroom. For example, teachers who feel more comfortable with idealist and realist notions of the enduring quality of knowledge and reality will be less likely to adopt constructivist approaches to education (described in Chapter 6).

Portfolio Reflections and Exhibits

Prepare an exhibit that illustrates what you learned as you read and discussed the concepts in this chapter. Your responses to the activities and to these suggestions will provide you with some ideas that might contribute to a professional portfolio.

Suggested Exhibit 2: Philosophy of a Preservice Teacher and Plans for Providing Appropriate Experiences

1. Review your response to Activity 2.1. Use the response as the first step to identify your own philosophy of teaching. Prepare a demonstration of your philosophy. Write a poem, develop a collage, picture, essay, or identify a life story that helps you illustrate your perspective on education. Make reference to the established history and philosophy presented in this text and other readings.

2. Share your philosophy and evaluation of your experiences with your college professor and classroom teacher mentor. Allow them to provide you with feedback.

Self-Reflection

WHAT IS YOUR EDUCATIONAL PHILOSOPHY?

Review and consider how strongly you agree or disagree with the following statements. Use this scale to indicate your level of agreement with each item: 5 = Strongly agree, 4 = Agree, 3 = Neutral, 2 = Disagree, 1 = Disagree strongly.

_____ 1. The most important role of a teacher is to be a model for intellectual and moral excellence in the classroom.

_____ 2. By studying humans in their natural settings, we can discover universal moral laws.

_____ 3. Although truth is changeable, we can discover it by using the scientific method.

_____ 4. The main question teachers should ask students is "What does this idea or content mean to you?"

_____ 5. Although vocational studies have their place, most students should be required to have a strong liberal arts education.

_____ 6. The most important task for a teacher is to promote reasoning within a particular content area.

_____ 7. The role of the teacher is to engage students in active problem solving applied to social and personal problems.

_____ 8. Truth is subjective and based on personal experiences and beliefs.

_____ 9. There are enduring and unchanging truths and values in all subject areas that students need to understand.

_____ 10. To learn facts and truth in a content area, teachers may need to use considerable drill and practice.

_____ 11. Use of the scientific method is a major goal of education.

_____ 12. The teacher's primary role is to enable students to create their own values.

_____ 13. Students learn best when they study the ideas and the works of great people.

_____ 14. There are enduring truths in all subject areas that students can discover by careful reasoning.

_____ 15. When deciding what curriculum should be emphasized for students, decisions should be based on real-life usefulness of the content.

_____ 16. If forced to choose between covering the content and exploring personal perspectives, a teacher should choose personal exploration.

_____ 17. Time-tested great literary works should be required reading for all students even at the expense of more popular readings.

Continued on next page

Continued from previous page

_____ 18. The curriculum should be based on "the basics" and rely on drill and memorization as learning strategies.

_____ 19. The most important role of the teacher is to facilitate reflection and use the scientific method to solve problems.

_____ 20. The most important concepts to explore with students in the classroom revolve around love, freedom, responsibility, death, and values.

Transfer your scores to this chart and add each column.

A	B	C	D
1. _____	2. _____	3. _____	4. _____
5. _____	6. _____	7. _____	8. _____
9. _____	10. _____	11. _____	12. _____
13. _____	14. _____	15. _____	16. _____
17. _____	18. _____	19. _____	20. _____

Total Scores

_____   _____   _____   _____

How much did you agree or disagree with the educational philosophies discussed in this chapter? Each column represents one of the philosophies of learning: A = idealism, B = realism, C = pragmatism, and D = existentialism. The more points you have in each column, the more your own philosophy matches with established philosophies. The highest possible score in any column is 25, and the lowest score is 5. A score of 20 or above in any column indicates strong agreement, whereas a score of less than 10 indicates little agreement. Where are your highest scores, and where are your lowest? Is your own philosophy highly representative of the classical ways of thinking about education, or do you have a tendency to embrace more than one philosophical stance?

Teachers who feel more comfortable with existentialist views of student choice, responsibility, and freedom will feel frustrated by externally imposed accountability systems. Understanding and reflecting on learning theories, teaching methodology, classroom management, and curriculum helps teachers understand their own philosophy of education. Teachers can learn about their philosophy through their own teaching experiences and by comparing their beliefs and actions to principles embodied in established educational philosophies. Take time now to complete the Self-Reflection exercise and to think about what you have learned.

InfoTrac College Edition Extension

Log on to the InfoTrac College Edition Web site, and use it to find out more about the philosophies and programs exemplifying these philosophies that were introduced in this chapter. If you still need information to help you understand the philosophies, try the first suggestion. If you feel comfortable with your level of knowledge about each philosophy, try the second suggestion.

1. Using the subject guide search, type in the name of one of the philosophies (idealism, realism, pragmatism, or existentialism). On the next screen, choose "View Reference Book Excerpts." Choose one or two of the excerpts to deepen your philosophical understanding. Repeat the process with another philosophy.

2. Using the keyword search, type in the name Mortimer Adler. Choose an article that explains his great books program.

Related Readings

The following books will help you understand more about the topics discussed in this chapter:

Cuban, L. (1993). *How teachers taught: Constancy and change in American classrooms 1880–1990*. New York: Teachers College Press.
 This book looks at the past century of American teaching and presents an interesting account of how elementary and secondary classrooms are influenced by history, sociology, and education. Cuban uses classroom observations of teachers throughout the past one hundred years to provide "snapshots" into classrooms. It is through this process that he identifies a remarkable continuity as well as instances of classroom change.

Postman, N. (1997). *The end of education: Redefining the value of school*. New York: Alfred A. Knopf.
 Postman questions some of the assumptions and values on which current educational practices are built. He presents narratives and metaphors that help us consider different ways to think about schools.

Tanner, D. (1997). *Dewey's laboratory school: Lessons for today*. New York: Teachers College Press.

    Tanner explains how teachers developed and implemented curriculum in Dewey's laboratory school. She relates Dewey's teaching and learning philosophies to modern trends and issues. This book is a good introduction to Dewey and helps the reader make connections between Dewey and today's classrooms.

References

Adler, M. (1982). *The Paideia proposal*. New York: Macmillan.

Angus, D. L., & Mirel, J. E. (1995). *The failed promise of the American high school: 1890–1995*. New York: Teachers College Press.

Baker, B. F. (1974). Existential philosophers on education. In J. Park (Ed.), *Selected readings in the philosophy of education* (4th ed., pp. 128–138). New York: Macmillan.

Brophy, J., & VanSledright, B. (1997). *Teaching and learning history in elementary schools*. New York: Teachers College Press.

Buber, M. (1957). *Between man and man*. Boston: Beacon Press.

Button, H. W., & Provenzo, E. F. (1989). *History of education and culture in America*. Englewood Cliffs, NJ: Prentice-Hall.

Dewey, J. (1916). *Democracy and education*. New York: Macmillan.

Frankena, W. K. (1974). Model for analyzing a philosophy of education. In J. Park (Ed.), *Selected readings in the philosophy of education* (4th ed., pp. 139–144). New York: Macmillan.

McMannon, T. J. (1995). *Morality, efficiency, and reform: An interpretation of history of American education*. Work in Progress Series, No. 5. Seattle: Institute for Educational Inquiry.

Morris, V. C. (1963). *Selected readings in the philosophy of education* (2nd ed., pp. 551–552). New York: Macmillan.

Myers, C. B., & Myers, L. K. (1995). *The professional educator: A new introduction to teaching and schools*. Belmont, CA: Wadsworth.

National Center for History in the Schools. (1996). *National standards for history: Basic edition*. Los Angeles: UCLA.

Neill, A. (1960). *Summerhill: A radical approach to child rearing*. New York: Hart.

Nichols, S. L., & Good, T. L. (2000). Education and society, 1900–2000: Selected snapshots of then and now. In T. L. Good (Ed.), *American education: Yesterday, today, and tomorrow, ninety-ninth yearbook of the National Society for the Study of Education, Part II* (pp. 1–53). Chicago: University of Chicago Press.

Noddings, N. (1997). Character education and community. In A. Molner (Ed.), *The constructions of children's character* (pp. 1–16). Chicago: NSSE and University of Chicago Press.

Perkinson, H. J. (1991). *The imperfect panacea: American faith in education 1865–1990*. New York: McGraw-Hill.

Piner, W. E. (Ed.). (1998). *Curriculum: Toward new identities*. New York: Garland.

Power, E. J. (1991). *A legacy of learning: A history of western education*. Albany: State University of New York Press.

Smith, S. (1979). *Ideas of the great educators*. New York: Barnes & Noble.

Tanner, D. (1997). *Dewey's laboratory school: Lessons for today*. New York: Teachers College Press.

Timm, J. T. (1996). *Four perspectives in multicultural education*. Belmont, CA: Wadsworth.

CHAPTER 3

Understanding the Current Educational Context

 *y several general measures, American secondary education, just like Tillson High School, has changed little since 1981. As a result of political pressure on school authorities, students are taking moderately different patterns of courses from earlier ones, concentrating more on the established basic subjects (mathematics, English, science, and social studies) and less on electives with titles such as "Life Skills." . . .*

The past decades' hue and cry over the need for high school reform makes sense. The existing system doesn't work. What is far less clear and what there should be substantial argument about—is what should replace the schools we have today. . . .

The prospect of fundamental changes in how education is institutionally delivered is as troublesome as it is inevitable. . . . School reform at the end of this century is cast against a backdrop of extraordinary new influences, both philosophical and practical. Those responsible for the schools cannot pretend that these influences do not exist or are too paltry to deserve attention. On the contrary, they

threaten to swamp the public school system as we know it, altering our assumptions about learning and

teaching, about what a school in fact is and who has the right to control it. The danger that the educa-

tional system may continue to ignore these opportunities depresses Horace. The prospect of facing up to

them, of seizing them in the service of substantial reform, however, gives Horace hope.

Getting people to change their minds about what school should be, even in a limited way, is a slow

business, one requiring small but persistent steps. . . .

—Theodore Sizer, *Horace's Hope**

Educators and the public seem to be preoccupied with making schools better. Educators, parents, corporate and other community members, banking and business people, and politicians are continuously engaged in discussions about improving education. Different groups of individuals have various educational agendas. Educators "reinvent" and develop new strategies for teaching and learning. Business, industry, social organizations, and educational institutions are developing new ways to work and need a workforce capable of adapting to new practices. New technologies require that we use different instructional tools. Organized groups often object to particular teaching approaches or new strategies. There are constant mandates, suggestions, and discussions that require educators to respond, consider, and change teaching and learning strategies. Schools and the teaching that goes on within the schools have been "scrutinized, criticized, eulogized, and 'reformed'" (Myers & Myers, 1995, p. 25). The calls for reform have been intense during the past twenty years, and teachers who begin their careers during the twenty-first century are likely to experience continuing change. In this chapter, we will answer these questions:

- What are some recurring themes related to teaching and learning?
- What are some current successful programs addressing changes in teaching and learning?

---

*From *Horace's Hope: What Works for the American High School*, by Theodore Sizer (pp. 16, 125, 127). New York: Houghton Mifflin, 1996.

- What effects do you think reform movements will have on your teaching?
- What are some of the reasons people resist educational change?

Most would agree that the more complex requirements of our society—the rapid influx of technology, the diversity of our population, and the increase of children in poverty—require that schools change to meet new demands, but no one can be assured what direction changes and restructuring should take. An overview of some of the issues, challenges, and successes of educational reform provide a context for understanding the nature of modern schooling and the places where new teachers will begin their careers.

Twenty Years of Educational Reform, 1980–2000

During the past twenty years, school reform has taken several forms (Myers & Myers, 1995). In the early 1980s, several national reports warned that U.S. schools were in trouble. One report that alarmed the nation about the status of schooling was *A Nation at Risk*, released in 1983 by the National Commission on Excellence in Education. This report contributed to a national attitude of concern for our schools that continues to have an impact on education even in 2001. The report cited an alarming weakening and mediocrity of teaching and learning, suggested that the state of our schools would put the entire country at risk, and issued dire predictions about the future of our country. The report provided indicators such as lower standardized test scores, lower SAT scores, higher illiteracy rates, lower graduation requirements, and more students in remedial college courses as examples that our educational system was not working. This document proved to be a major critique of education in our country, framing many citizens' concerns and focusing issues in a condensed set of statements. The report recommended (1) an increased amount of content taught at schools, (2) higher standards and expectations for students, (3) increased time for learning, (4) higher standards for teachers, and (5) increased leadership and fiscal support from elected officials.

These public concerns about the status of education prompted politicians to establish goals designed to build a national commitment to education. Formulation of these goals began with the Republican administration of President Reagan and continued into the Democratic administration of President Clinton. The original effort was outlined by the governors, who worked to develop six national goals designed to guide educational reform. These goals (outlined in Table 3.1) are known as "Goals 2000: Educate America" and were passed by

World Wide Web Site

For more information regarding the National Educational Goals, contact this Web site or write to the address listed here:

Web site: **http://www.ed.gov/legislation/ESEA/Guidance/app-c.html**

Address: **Department of Defense Education Activity (DoDEA)**
4040 North Fairfax Street
Arlington, VA 22203-1635

Congress in 1994. (See Chapter 8 for additional discussion of issues related to Goals 2000.)

Even before the first calls for reform settled, a second wave of change was initiated, primarily at the state level. Teaching processes became the focus of attention, with teacher and student testing as measures of accountability for student learning the major outcome. Recommendations from the second round of educational reports, occurring in the mid-to-late 1980s, included a more subject-centered curriculum, a back-to-basics approach, a greater focus on mathematics and science instruction, and a strong connection between testing, promotion, and graduation. The reports also called for alternative and flexible ways to educate

Table 3.1 America's Educational Goals for the Year 2000

1. All children in America will start school ready to learn.

2. The high school graduation rate will increase to at least 90 percent.

3. American students will leave grades four, eight, and twelve having demonstrated competency in challenging subject matter including English, mathematics, science, history, and geography; and every school in America will ensure that all students learn to use their minds well, so they may be prepared for responsible citizenship, further learning, and productive employment in our modern economy.

4. U.S. students will be first in the world in science and mathematics achievement.

5. Every adult American will be literate and will possess the knowledge and skills necessary to compete in a global economy and exercise the rights and responsibilities of citizenship.

6. Every school in America will be free of drugs and violence and will offer a disciplined environment conducive to learning.

teachers and included plans for merit pay, increased workloads, and longer school days. Salaries of teachers were increased, leadership skills of principals and teachers were honed, and competencies for students and teachers were specified.

The reform efforts of the 1980s were confusing and rather disjointed. There was an effort to control what teachers taught, while at the same time, recommendations suggested that decision-making processes should be decentralized and based in the school settings (Apple, 1996). A series of isolated innovations, including attempts to structure the teaching process into isolated behaviors and leadership training encouraging site-based decision making, came and went with regularity. In spite of the 1980 reform efforts, problems and concerns associated with educational change were not eradicated, but simply worsened. In reality, the reforms did little to change the content of instruction, failed to directly involve teachers in the reform process, and were unsuccessful in altering the practices related to teaching and learning that might bring about lasting change (Smith & O'Day, 1991). This period was extremely stressful for teachers who felt that they were neither involved in the change processes nor recognized for their efforts on students' behalf.

Toward the end of the 1980s and the beginning of the 1990s, reform movements began to take on a different tone from earlier calls for change. Innovations became more comprehensive, and themes related to basic values and recognition of family began to emerge (Hlebowitsh & Tellez, 1997). The development of standards for student achievement and teacher preparation became the focus of many reform movements. Change efforts attempted to connect requirements for student learning with teacher preparation and professional development of experienced teachers. There were also efforts to provide more educational choices to students and their parents, and schools worked to be more flexible.

The state educational agencies played an important role in facilitating educational change. One of the most comprehensive overall state change efforts was implemented by Kentucky. In 1990, the Kentucky Education Reform Act facilitated a complete rebuilding of the school systems (Holland, 1997). The new school system was developed around three major areas: administration, curriculum, and finance. The changes included "establishing elected councils of educators and parents to run local schools, reorganizing the lower elementary grades into primary school classrooms that included children of different ages and abilities, and setting up a high-stakes accountability system that rewarded or sanctioned teachers and principals according to students' test scores" (Holland, 1997, p. 265). State officials reported that as a result of the law more than 92 percent of the state's 1,400 schools improved student achievement between 1992 and 1996 (Rothman, 1997). But the law mandating the complicated changes is still hotly contested, and most agree that it is not yet possible to determine whether improved student learning can be maintained.

During the second half of the 1990s, school reform activity was widespread and extremely varied (Shields & Knapp, 1997). Even though there was evidence that students were taking more difficult courses and that the school dropout rate had stabilized, the SAT scores had not increased substantially, college professors were still complaining that students were not ready for university curriculum, and employers still believed high school graduates were unprepared for the workplace (Jennings, 1995). After nearly twenty years of intense change effort, it is clear that attention to school reform is no guarantee of improved learning opportunities for children and young people. Calls for American education to reinvent itself are still heard.

In the early 2000s, reform efforts are focusing on increasing the flexibility and variety of educational opportunities. Educators are focusing on localized changes and encouraging collaboration among parents, policymakers, state and national agencies, and communities (see Chapter 10). Changes in educational funding allow the states to take control of the resources, and some state governments have encouraged local districts to allow students choice in where they attend schools. The most recent reforms attempt to link change efforts and, in doing so, become more comprehensive. The latest round of reforms also focuses on students who were overlooked by past reforms; there is general agreement that special steps are needed to address the needs of poor and culturally diverse populations (Jackson, 2000).

Many believe that high educational expectations and accomplishments will be attainable only with the help of all concerned with the well-being of children. The recognition that educators alone cannot change the educational process has resulted in a clamor for collaboration among schools, universities, businesses, and social service agencies. Schools will have a better chance at succeeding when society values and supports children. As Goodlad (1992) stated, "Healthy nations have healthy schools, not the other way around" (p. 237). He goes on to explain that a large number of agencies and institutions must work together to develop an educational ecology that promotes improved lives for people in all segments of our society.

There have been some changes in the way teachers teach, how children's learning is assessed, and how teachers, administrators, and others are held accountable for meeting the goals set forth by particular reform movements. But many believe we must change the basic structures of our schools before we can make real differences. One fact has remained constant throughout the flurry of activity directed at improving our schools—the answers to questions relating to

Field-Based Activity 3.1

Pay attention to radio, television, and newspaper reports about education and note the nature of the topics discussed. Are they primarily critical of education? Are they calls for change? Criticism of current practice? Reports of what is or is not working in education? Relate current issues to concerns and practices in your school setting. Share these with your classmates.

teaching, learning, and our schools are not easy. There is no secret formula, no panacea.

Current Educational Themes

When all the dust settled from the public's discussions about education from the 1980s through 2001, a wide range of topics emerged, ranging from reforms in school funding to students' rights reforms. Some recurring themes include issues related to accountability, standards for students and teachers, school choice, professionalization of teaching, and equitable education for all students.

Accountability and Testing

Declining test scores, rising rates of illiteracy, and demands for greater accountability from schools have contributed to public interest in testing. The public feels that it is the schools' responsibility to provide an education to students and wants some evidence that schools and teachers are effective. Criticism of what graduates know and are able to do have prompted many U.S. citizens and leaders to demand that students pass a series of standardized tests. The emphasis on testing as a way to hold schools accountable reflects the perspective that good teaching is measured by students' achievement (Clark, 1995). As a result of this emphasis, many states have developed curriculum requirements and companion standardized tests that are administered at predetermined intervals during primary and secondary schooling.

The major tool for holding educators responsible for student learning is testing. During the last few years, it has played a major role in what is being taught in the classroom. Testing of students' learning is a major influence on the teaching

TONY FREEMAN/PHOTOEDIT, INC.

Demands for greater accountability in schools has lead to a widespread acceptance of testing as a way to measure school and teacher effectiveness. Educators agree that testing is necessary, but many are concerned about the over emphasis of testing and the negative teaching and learning processes that may result from over-reliance on the results.

processes in modern classrooms because test results are used to measure the effectiveness of teaching. Every school uses standardized achievement tests to document students' achievement and growth over time. Tests are used for comparative, administrative, and political reasons, but few teachers accept the idea of measuring their students' growth and achievement with only one test score. Tests are a sampling of students' abilities and may not represent the full range of knowledge, skills, and abilities of students in classrooms.

The testing movement suggests that there is general agreement among education professionals about just what should be taught to each and every student in our schools. However, the ideas associated with testing and the accountability movement are highly debatable. How success should be measured can be viewed in very different ways. Some would argue that the definition of educational excellence is rather static and has been the same for many years. Others suggest that different learners may need different content and presented in different ways depending on their needs and their past experiences (Piner, 1992). For example, some people would include the infusion of African and African American knowledge (that is, history and literature) in the school curriculum. Others disagree and say that the curriculum basics should come from traditional topics and approaches.

Despite some disagreement over the content and form of testing, few would argue the merits of evaluation in general. Teachers must assess what students know to plan for instruction. Testing helps teachers discover what concepts children understand and what experiences they need to continue effective learning. When teachers know their students, they are able to plan more effective, motivating activities and interactions. Continuous and long-range assessment identifies growth patterns and results from experiences. However, it is not entirely clear whether the tests associated with the accountability trends provide educators with needed information.

There are undesirable effects related to the reliance on standardized tests (Falk, 2000). Due to perceived pressures from administrators and parents, teachers may "teach to the test." Some teachers are so concerned about their students' performance on the tests that they look to tests to guide curricular and instructional decisions. Another danger of the tests is the role they may play in developing students' perceptions about their ability to learn. Teachers may expect less from students who do not perform well on a test.

Standardized tests are not in themselves a deterrent to learning if they are used with caution. Testing, or any other single effort, cannot constitute an accountability and evaluation system. A school creates effective evaluation and assessment policies and procedures by using various tools that inform, contribute to decision making, and correct problems (Hlebowitsh & Tellez, 1997). When teachers know their students and use multiple methods to assess and evaluate learning, interpretation of school achievement will be more effective and improve instruction for all children. Regardless of how tests are used in the classroom, the results of testing are often a stated catalyst for change and reform in education. We must understand the contributions and potential dangers of standardized testing to truly understand reform and change movements in our schools.

Standards for Teaching and Learning

One of the benchmarks of recent educational change is the development and implementation of standards. Standards are frameworks that focus on academic behaviors and assessments, and their purpose is to encourage high academic performance (Cohen, 1995). Goals 2000, the education goals that have guided three presidents, encourages the development of national standards. Similarly, state-based frameworks reflect the expectations for what teachers teach and students learn.

The Illinois Learning Standards (Illinois State Board of Education, 1997) are similar to other state standards that are developed to help design state assessment programs, guide school curriculum development, assess student progress, focus school improvement plans, and communicate the purpose and results of schooling to the community. The standards were developed with the input of teachers, administrators, parents, employers, community leaders, and representatives of higher education. Standards were developed in English language arts, mathematics, science, social science, physical development and health, fine arts, and foreign languages for early elementary, late elementary, middle/junior high school, early high school, and late high school. As you can see from the excerpt of the English language arts standards in Table 3.2, the first state goal is that all students "read with understanding and fluency." The framework then presents learning standards and the benchmarks that would indicate that appropriate student learning has occurred. Statewide achievement tests were developed to assess the learning standards.

World Wide Web Site

You can learn more about the Illinois Standards at this Web site:
http://www.isbe.state.il.us/ils/

In addition to state efforts, many of the subject areas have developed or reevaluated existing standards. Standards for specific content areas are emerging at national and state levels. Sometimes standards are developed though collaborative efforts, linking the state and national efforts together, but more often they are developed separately without articulation between the two. During the 1990s, professional organizations such as the National Council of Teachers of English, National Council of Teachers of Mathematics, and the National Science Foundation conducted a series of meetings, discussions, and studies that provided a basis for determining what should be taught to children of different ages. Specific goals and standards related to content areas taught in school have evolved from these national discussions.

The content area standards developed by some professional organizations generated concerns and disagreements from parents and other interested groups. As outlined in Chapter 2, the subject of social studies was particularly contentious and widely debated. Social studies educators interpreted standards from a broad perspective and accepted the history and culture of multiple perspectives as valid and desired. They presented an interpretation of social studies that recognized

Table 3.2 Illinois Learning Standards/English Language Arts

State Goal 1: Read with understanding and fluency.

As a result of their schooling, students will be able to:

LEARNING STANDARD	EARLY ELEMENTARY	LATE ELEMENTARY
A. Apply word analysis and vocabulary skills to comprehend selections.	**1.A.1a** Apply word analysis skills (e.g., phonics, word patterns) to recognize new words. **1.A.1b** Comprehend unfamiliar words using context clues and prior knowledge; verify meanings with resource materials.	**1.A.2a** Read and comprehend unfamiliar words using root words, synonyms, antonyms, word origins and derivations. **1.A.2b** Clarify word meaning using context clues and a variety of resources including glossaries, dictionaries and thesauruses.
B. Apply reading strategies to improve understanding and fluency.	**1.B.1a** Establish purposes for reading, make predictions, connect important ideas, and link text to previous experiences and knowledge. **1.B.1b** Identify genres (forms and purposes) of fiction, nonfiction, poetry and electronic literary forms. **1.B.1c** Continuously check and clarify for understanding (e.g., reread, read ahead, use visual and context clues, ask questions, retell, use meaningful substitutions). **1.B.1d** Read age-appropriate material aloud with fluency and accuracy.	**1.B.2a** Establish purposes for reading; survey materials; ask questions; make predictions; connect, clarify and extend ideas. **1.B.2b** Identify structure (e.g., description, compare/contrast, cause and effect, sequence) of nonfiction texts to improve comprehension. **1.B.2c** Continuously check and clarify for understanding (e.g., *in addition to previous skills*, clarify terminology, seek additional information). **1.B.2d** Read age-appropriate material aloud with fluency and accuracy.

Note: Examples are designated by "e.g." and enclosed in parentheses. They are meant to guide the teacher as to the general intent of the standards and benchmarks, not to identify all possible items.

Becoming a Teacher in a Field-Based Setting

WHY THIS GOAL IS IMPORTANT: Reading is essential. It is the process by which people gain information and ideas from books, newspapers, manuals, letters, contracts, advertisements and a host of other materials. Using strategies for constructing meaning before, during and after reading will help students connect what they read now with what they have learned in the past. Students who read well and widely build a strong foundation for learning in all areas of life.

JUNIOR HIGH SCHOOL	EARLY HIGH SCHOOL	LATE HIGH SCHOOL
1.A.3a Apply knowledge of word origins and derivations to comprehend words used in specific content areas (e.g., scientific, political, literary, mathematical).	**1.A.4a** Expand knowledge of word origins and derivations and use idioms, analogies, metaphors and similes to extend vocabulary development.	**1.A.5a** Identify and analyze new terminology applying knowledge of word origins and derivations in a variety of practical settings.
1.A.3b Analyze the meaning of words and phrases in their context.	**1.A.4b** Compare the meaning of words and phrases and use analogies to explain the relationships among them.	**1.A.5b** Analyze the meaning of abstract concepts and the effects of particular word and phrase choices.
1.B.3a Preview reading materials, make predictions and relate reading to information from other sources.	**1.B.4a** Preview reading materials, clarify meaning, analyze overall themes and coherence, and relate reading with information from other sources.	**1.B.5a** Relate reading to prior knowledge and experience and make connections to related information.
1.B.3b Identify text structure and create a visual representation (e.g., graphic organizer, outline, drawing) to use while reading.	**1.B.4b** Analyze, interpret and compare a variety of texts for purpose, structure, content, detail and effect.	**1.B.5b** Analyze the defining characteristics and structures of a variety of complex literary genres and describe how genre affects the meaning and function of texts.
1.B.3c Continuously check and clarify for understanding (e.g., *in addition to previous skills*, draw comparisons to other readings).	**1.B.4c** Read age-appropriate material with fluency and accuracy.	**1.B.5c** Evaluate a variety of compositions for purpose, structure, content and details for use in school or at work.
1.B.3d Read age-appropriate material with fluency and accuracy.		**1.B.5d** Read age-appropriate material with fluency and accuracy.

Continued on next page

Table 3.2   Illinois Learning Standards/English Language Arts *(continued)*

State Goal 1: Read with understanding and fluency.

As a result of their schooling, students will be able to:

LEARNING STANDARD	EARLY ELEMENTARY	LATE ELEMENTARY
C. Comprehend a broad range of reading materials.	**1.C.1a** Use information to form questions and verify predictions. **1.C.1b** Identify important themes and topics. **1.C.1c** Mark comparisons across reading selections. **1.C.1d** Summarize content of reading material using text organization (e.g., story, sequence). **1.C.1e** Identify how authors and illustrators express their ideas in text and graphics (e.g., dialogue, conflict, shape, color, characters). **1.C.1f** Use information presented in simple tables, maps and charts to form an interpretation.	**1.C.2a** Use information to form and refine questions and predictions. **1.C.2b** Make and support inferences and form interpretations about main themes and topics. **1.C.2c** Compare and contrast the organization of selections. **1.C.2d** Summarize and make generalizations from content and relate to purpose of material. **1.C.2e** Explain how authors and illustrators use text and art to express their ideas (e.g., points of view, design, hues, metaphor). **1.C.2f** Connect information presented in tables, maps and charts to printed or electronic text.

Becoming a Teacher in a Field-Based Setting

JUNIOR HIGH SCHOOL	EARLY HIGH SCHOOL	LATE HIGH SCHOOL
1.C.3a Use information to form, explain and support questions and predictions.	**1.C.4a** Use questions and predictions to guide reading.	**1.C.5a** Use questions and predictions to guide reading across complex materials.
1.C.3b Interpret and analyze entire narrative text using story elements, point of view and theme.	**1.C.4b** Explain and justify an interpretation of a text.	**1.C.5b** Analyze and defend an interpretation of text.
1.C.3c Compare, contrast and evaluate ideas and information from various sources and genres.	**1.C.4c** Interpret, evaluate and apply information from a variety of sources to other situations (e.g., academic, vocational, technical, personal).	**1.C.5c** Critically evaluate information from multiple sources.
1.C.3d Summarize and make generalizations from content and relate them to the purpose of the material.	**1.C.4d** Summarize and make generalizations from content and relate them to the purpose of the material.	**1.C.5d** Summarize and make generalizations from content and relate them to the purpose of the material.
1.C.3e Compare how authors and illustrators use text and art across materials to express their ideas (e.g., foreshadowing, flashbacks, color, strong verbs, language that inspires).	**1.C.4e** Analyze how authors and illustrators use text and art to express and emphasize their ideas (e.g., imagery, multiple points of view).	**1.C.5e** Evaluate how authors and illustrators use text and art across materials to express their ideas (e.g., complex dialogue, persuasive techniques).
1.C.3f Interpret tables that display textual information and data in visual formats.	**1.C.4f** Interpret tables, graphs and maps in conjunction with related text.	**1.C.5f** Use tables, graphs and maps to challenge arguments, defend conclusions and persuade others.

Source: Illinois State Board of Education (1997). *Illinois Learning Standards*. Springfield: Illinois State Board of Education.

different perspectives based on gender, race, culture, and religion. For example, the history of the western United States settlements included the role of women in the wagon trains. Including diverse views of events from differing perspectives changes the stories and narratives associated with important events. The new standards emphasized the importance of including roles of minorities in history and including minority literature. Some educators and parents believe their schools should be focusing on traditional aspects of history and geography. In many cases, parental beliefs regarding the content and subject matter taught reflect their own cultural and language experiences. The resulting disagreements were reported on the national news and delayed the approval of the new standards in many settings.

World Wide Web Site

You may access professional organizations and learn more about their subject area standards at these Web sites:

National Council for Teachers of English: http://www.ncte.org

National Council for Social Studies: http://www.ncss.org

National Council of Teachers of Mathematics: http://www.nctm.org

International Reading Association: http://www.reading.org

Professionalization of Teaching

Several of the reform movements suggest that one of the problems in education is the lack of professionalism among teachers. Professionalism refers to teachers' ability to regulate their profession, the provision of a qualified educational workforce, and effective professional development for all educators. However, professionalism of teaching as addressed in the reform movements usually focuses on how to hold teachers accountable for what they do in the classroom. One answer to this concern is to develop learning standards and to require student testing to make sure teachers are meeting established standards. The standards movement has had an impact on teachers in two ways: Teachers are held accountable for helping their students meet standards established by local districts or individual states. Students take the tests each year, and the reports are used to evaluate the quality of teaching.

Professionalism and standards also are connected in a second way. New standards or requirements for teaching may be adopted and result in the requirement of additional initial training and expanded requirements for maintaining certification. In many cases, teachers must pass statewide tests that reflect teaching standards before they are certified or licensed. Currently, state governments have a great deal of control over the regulations that define who will teach and who will be licensed. State certification is usually guided by state standards of competence and establishes the labels and descriptions of professionalism accepted by the educational community in the state.

The focus on establishing national standards to recognize and encourage excellence in experienced teachers has led to establishment of the National Board for Professional Teacher Standards (NBPTS). Teachers who receive certification from NBPTS must demonstrate their competence in five different areas: commitment to students and learning, knowledge of subject matter, ability to manage and monitor student learning, willingness to engage in reflective practice, and the propensity to participate in learning communities. For experienced teachers to be recognized as NBPTS teachers, they must undergo an intensive one-year evaluation process that requires them to develop a portfolio, be observed while teaching, take part in interviews, and pass a comprehensive subject area exam. It is an expensive process, but most teachers who complete the process feel that it increases their professionalism and acknowledges their efforts to improve their practice. A few states, such as Virginia, help teachers defray the cost of taking the test, and other states and districts may offer merit pay for teachers who complete the process. Most school districts have yet to recognize teachers who have completed the process by raising salaries when they become NBPTS certified. The impact of NBPTS is still being assessed in the profession, but the certification process for experienced teachers is one that future teachers will want to watch as they begin their career.

 World Wide Web Site

You can learn more about the National Board for Professional Teacher Standards (NBPTS) at this Web site: http://www.nbpts.org/

There is a similar process for beginning teachers. The Interstate New Teacher Assessment and Support Consortium (INTASC) establishes guidelines for preparing, licensing, and certifying educators. INTASC is set up around ten standards (Figure 3.1) and also requires a new teacher to establish a portfolio and take a test at the end of the preparation program. Some states may use INTASC assessment or similar processes to certify new teachers as they enter the profession. Check your state agency Web site or ask an advisor in your teacher education program about the requirements for new teachers in your state.

Figure 3.1 INTASC Draft Standards

Principle 1: The teacher understands the central concepts, tools of inquiry, and structures of the discipline(s) he or she teaches and can create learning experiences that make these aspects of subject matter meaningful for students.

Principle 2: The teacher understands how children learn and develop, and can provide learning opportunities that support their intellectual, social, and personal development.

Principle 3: The teacher understands how students differ in their approaches to learning and creates instructional opportunities that are adapted to diverse learners.

Principle 4: The teacher understands and uses a variety of instructional strategies to encourage students' development of critical thinking, problem solving, and performance skills.

Principle 5: The teacher uses an understanding of individual and group motivation and behavior to create a learning environment that encourages positive social interaction, active engagement in learning, and self-motivation.

Principle 6: The teacher uses knowledge of effective verbal, nonverbal, and media communication techniques to foster active inquiry, collaboration, and supportive interaction in the classroom.

Principle 7: The teacher plans instruction based upon knowledge of subject matter, students, the community, and curriculum goals.

Principle 8: The teacher understands and uses formal and informal assessment strategies to evaluate and ensure the continuous intellectual, social, and physical development of the learner.

Principle 9: The teacher is a reflective practitioner who continually evaluates the effects of his/her choices and actions on others (students, parents, and other professionals in the learning community) and who actively seeks out opportunities to grow professionally.

Principle 10: The teacher fosters relationships with school colleagues, parents, and agencies in the larger community to support students' learning and well-being.

Most people enter teaching to work with children and young people or because they enjoy and are excited about a certain subject area, but salaries are traditionally seen as an important issue in the teaching profession. Salaries are low in comparison to many other professions, but there has been a steady improvement in most regions of the nation. The average salary for teachers rose in the last decade to $38,500—a 20 percent increase since 1980 (Sadker & Sadker, 2000). Salaries are higher in larger school districts and in urban areas and tend to be lower in the southern states. Public school teachers are paid more than private

World Wide Web Site

You can learn more about the Interstate New Teacher Assessment and Support Consortium (INTASC) at this Web site: http://www.ccsso.org/ intasc.html

school teachers. Although salaries still tend to be a major issue related to the profession, most individuals who teach believe they will be able to live on existing salaries.

Another issue related to professionalism is set forth by those who feel teachers should have more freedom to make decisions and control their profession. Critics of the national standards movement feel that standards, assessment, and accountability—as set forward in the United States—actually reduce the professionalism of teachers by maintaining outside control of the profession through licensing and testing. Because teachers do not have a great deal of control over licensure and evaluation and testing, many argue that standards, testing, and accountability do not contribute to professionalism. Those who hold this view suggest that professionalism of teachers is dependent on the amount of control teachers have over the establishment and maintenance of standards and testing.

Although there are differences in opinion about national standards and the status of the profession of teaching, there is no doubt that teaching is moving toward a "higher, more complex demanding plane" (Myers & Myers, 1995, p. 616). The debates and consideration of teacher controls, standards establishment, and how teachers are held accountable are necessary before the profession is perceived as credible and fully functioning. Defining a profession is an evolutionary process influenced both by those in the profession and by external events. Those of you who are currently becoming teachers will make a major contribution in the struggle toward professionalism that is a constant theme in teaching.

School Choice

In an effort to recognize parental opinions and desires, several innovations increasing school choice are currently popular. Supporters of school choice believe that parents have the right to select the school they wish their children to attend and that they should not have to send their children to the school in their neighborhood or school district. One of the ideas behind the popularity of school choice is the belief that schools can compete for students and make changes so that they can attract students by providing the best educational experiences possible. Most school choice programs provide for redirection of funds based on parents' decisions about where to educate their children.

Vouchers are one way to increase the choices parents have in selecting schools. Instead of providing tax money to neighborhood schools, tuition vouchers are provided to parents so they can enroll their children in a school of their choice, whether it be public or private. Traditionally, students are required to attend schools in their districts and neighborhoods, and the schools receive monies based on school attendance. Private and parochial schools do not receive public educational funding. Vouchers expand the types of schools receiving tax money appropriated for education. Vouchers present a very different way of school funding, and there are differences of opinion about the value of voucher systems. Supporters argue that parents have the right to send their children to any school of their choice. Others argue that using vouchers would dramatically change the concept of public schooling, enabling private schools to compete with traditional public schools and greatly reducing funding to public schools.

The development of charter schools is another innovation evolving from the desire to expand school choice. Charter schools are newly created, state-funded public schools offering a unique educational concept or theme. Museums, communities, businesses, individuals, teachers, and even for-profit organizations may develop a charter for a school. Charter schools can be established when a local school board or the state department of education approves an educational plan. The charters describe the finances, curriculum, organizations, and other logistical considerations. The students who attend charter schools must meet state assessment expectations, but administrators and teachers in the school may facilitate the learning in nontraditional ways. The first charter school was established in Minnesota in 1991, and by 2000 there were 1,700 charter schools in thirty-two states and the District of Columbia, enrolling some 350,000 students (Manno, Finn, & Vanourek, 2000).

There are many different charter school themes and arrangements. Charter schools often target low achievers or at-risk students and attempt to raise achievement by innovative and creative teaching and learning environments. Existing charter schools have evolved around traditional basic skills, homeschooling, store-front programs, "distance learning," and computer-based learning (Oliva, 1997). They may encourage curriculum themes that focus on economics, bilingualism, or great books. Because the teachers and administrators are not held to state requirements and curriculums, charter schools are seen as a way to make changes in traditional methods of teaching and learning. This concept not only encourages innovation but is seen as a way to force traditional schools to change their approaches to compete for and maintain their student populations.

Supporters of school choice feel that increasing choices for the education of children will provide competition, which will ultimately improve teaching and learning processes. Many feel that parents and communities have a right to establish educational systems that meet the unique needs of their children and youth. Critics are concerned that the resources taken away from public schools will be particularly severe in communities where schools are already underfunded. There is some concern that charter schools will undermine the entire system of public schooling by restructuring the funding process. Still, charter schools are favored by a majority of parents, politicians, and businesspeople.

World Wide Web Site

You can learn more about charter schools at this Web site:
http://www.csr.syr.edu/index.html

One important choice available to both schools and parents is the option of privatized and for-profit schools. Many private-sector companies, such as Sylvan Learning Systems, are filling a niche as providers of specialized educational services such as tutoring. Disney Corporation is another example, supporting the Celebration School near Disney World in Florida. Large for-profit ventures also have targeted schooling during the past few years. One of the best known, the Edison Project, is attempting to establish a successful franchise assuring student success. Several large public schools have transferred resources to the Edison Project hoping that the for-profit organization can change their schools into places in which all children succeed. The Edison Project, and other large operations such as Tesseract, manage schedules, hire teachers, purchase equipment and supplies, maintain transportation, and make other important educational decisions. They assure improvement in student achievement and greater parental satisfaction. There is a great deal of criticism from educators, the National Education Association, and the American Federation of Teachers about making a profit from the education of children. The concern will probably be one that future teachers must consider during their careers.

Homeschooling has emerged as a choice that many parents make for educating their children, and the number of children who are taught in their homes by their parents, relatives, or close friends has grown to 1.5 million during the last decade (Sadker & Sadker, 2000). There are many reasons parents decide to play such an important role in their children's education. Usually parents who home-school feel that the public or private school system cannot provide the type of education they want for their children. The desire to include religion or a strong fundamentalist doctrine in a child's learning process is one of the most common reasons for homeschooling. Other parents may want to provide their children with art, music, or other experience-based educational approaches. Still other parents do not feel the schools in their community provide a safe environment nor effective education for their children. There is an entire industry developing around homeschooling. Parents can access curriculum provided by private groups, the Internet, or their churches. In many cases, parents homeschool for the early years of elementary school and then send their children to public school as they reach middle and high school years. The critics of homeschooling cite the uneven quality offered by untrained educators and the reduced opportunities for children to become socialized by being around other children as drawbacks to this approach. Nevertheless, many children who are homeschooled and receive individualized instruction in a supportive home-based environment do quite well. There are plenty of anecdotal success stories about children who are home-schooled and win admittance to highly competitive universities, become doctors, or do quite well in competitive endeavors when compared to public and private school graduates. Just recently homeschooled children won the national spelling bee two years in a row.

World Wide Web Site

Here is one example of the many Web sites devoted to homeschooling: http://www.teelfamily.com/education/

Whether or not school choice improves the overall educational process is still debated among educators, politicians, and community leaders. Studies looking at the effectiveness of school choice are inconclusive at best. Many parents support the idea of school choice, believing that if they can transfer educational resources paid by the government to any school of their choice then their children will be guaranteed the best education possible. But many critics feel that it simply assists those with adequate resources to improve their situation while working against families that have limited resources. For example, the neediest students may be left behind in schools that have reduced support and under-funded programs because parents with additional resources have chosen to leave neighborhood schools. Often it is a basic matter of not being able to transport

Field-Based Activity 3.2

Divide your class into four or five groups. Have each group choose a particular past decade, for example, the 1960s. Choose a journal like *Educational Leadership* or *Phi Delta Kappan*, which typically depicts educational issues and innovations, and have each group copy the table of contents for an issue from each year of the decade. Then summarize the issues and reform movements of the decade based on the titles and topics listed. Share group findings and discuss similarities and differences across decades. Relate your findings to current reform movements.

children that prevents lower income parents from making choices about where they send their children to school. Issues of school choice are bound to have an impact on teaching and teachers in the future.

Equitable Education for All Students

Student diversity and a wide range of economic stratification among the children in our country have forced the topic of educational equality into the forefront of educational issues. All students, including the poor, nonnative English speaking, and disabled, deserve a quality education. Teachers must consider how issues of diversity affect the way children respond to schooling, recognize that differences influence learning, and take those differences into account when planning instruction. This challenging task is necessary to provide equitable education for all students.

One way to view equity issues relates directly to how teachers perceive the potential achievement of their students. Differences such as culture, race, family status, and socioeconomic background have historically been related to success or failure in schools. Some students' learning difficulties arise from teachers' expectations. Teachers often believe, for example, that children who are poor or who speak English as a second language will not succeed in school. Life situations do affect children's achievement, but it does not mean that these children are doomed to failure. One of the first steps teachers can take to eliminate learning difficulties is to accept all children and honor their differences. It is the very wise teacher who uses these differences to enrich schooling experiences for all students.

Equity issues are particularly glaring when school funding is considered. U.S. students who live in rich communities have schools that are better funded than schools in poor communities. The funding of schools, combined with the poverty

Schools are required by law to modify teaching approaches and change the structure of school buildings so that all students, regardless of their physical differences, are able to experience equal access to learning.

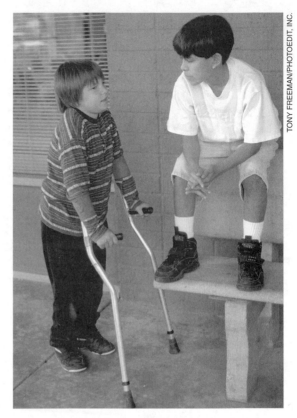

of some children, handicaps a large number of children and young people in our schools. The differences in school funding generate large disparities in student achievement (Payne & Biddle, 1999). The level of funding should be equalized throughout our nation before there is true educational equity: "Until this is done, it is useless to talk about public education providing a 'level playing field' and absurd to think that we can compete with other industrialized nations where equal funding for schools is already the law of the land" (Payne & Biddle, 1999, p. 12). A broader discussion of educational equity and equality is presented in Chapter 5.

Success in Times of Change

With each wave of reform, the general public becomes a bit more cynical about true change in our schools. Many believe that schools have changed little in the past hundred years (Cuban, 1984) and hold the view that they will continue as they have in the past, despite change efforts. Schools often appear to be resistant to change, and when change occurs it is very difficult, stressful, expensive, and time-consuming for all involved. Despite these challenges, educational reform has made a difference for many children and youth. Several successful programs for comprehensive school reform implemented by innovative educational leaders have led to improved conditions and provide us with models of success for all children. The programs outlined in the following sections have had their successes documented by extensive research.

Theodore Sizer: Essential Schools

Theodore Sizer takes on the mountain of issues and problems associated with secondary schools and has established a network of high school–university partnerships across the country to improve secondary school teaching and learning. Changes in high schools are made based on nine common principles that help the schools set clear and simple goals about intellectual skills and knowledge for their students. Schools that adopt his model establish a vision of integrated, comfortable, trusting environments that focus on collaboration (Sizer, 1992, 1996).

Schools following Sizer's model focus on helping all adolescents to master skills and use their minds as opposed to merely memorizing content. Teachers involve students in hard work and become the coaches as their students work to learn. There is no strict age grading, but students are judged successful on the basis of exhibitions or demonstrations of their learning. Sizer's Essential Schools movement utilizes larger blocks of time for instruction than are traditionally scheduled and puts students in smaller, more manageable working groups so that instruction can be more personalized.

 World Wide Web Site

You can learn more about the Coalition of Essential Schools at this Web site: http://essentialschools.org/

Robert Slavin: Success for All

Robert Slavin determined that many of the instructional interventions designed to improve the attitudes and achievement of hard-to-teach students (for example, pullout programs, special education, reduced class size) actually have had a detrimental effect on school achievement and attitudes (Slavin & Madden, 2000). As a result, he and his colleague developed an intervention model that focuses on helping students before they drop behind. His model focuses on instructional procedures and goals that are self-paced and utilize cooperative learning techniques (see Chapter 7). Tutors, schoolwide curriculum, family support teams, and facilitators who work with teachers are important components of the schoolwide Success for All program. His first efforts focused on instructional methods in reading, writing, and language arts from kindergarten to grade six. Recently, he has added Roots and Wings, a mathematics, social studies, and science curriculum (Slavin, Madden, & Wasik, 1996). There are also several Spanish bilingual adaptations of the program.

Teachers who work in schools that adopt the Success for All model believe they contribute to students' success and that it is their responsibility to prevent students from falling behind. His model is responsive to individual needs of students and involves students in their own learning. Slavin and Madden (2000) have conducted a great deal of research that shows that his program results in consistent, substantial success for all groups of students.

World Wide Web Site

You can learn more about Success for All and Roots and Wings at this Web site: http://successforall.net

---

James Comer: School Power

Convinced that educational systems have failed black children, James Comer developed a model for inner-city children that recognizes and addresses cultural heritage and diverse socioeconomic situations (Haynes & Comer, 1990). Comer's model emphasizes nurturing students who are identified as hard-to-teach. He acknowledges the importance of adults in children's lives, and his programs require a great deal of adult involvement. He believes school governance teams are the most important structural component of a school and proposes new methods of school leadership. His schools are governed by teams of ten to fifteen representatives from all the adults who work with students in the school, including teachers, counselors, principals, parents, and social workers. The team focuses on building strong relationships among the children and adults. His model is characterized by a particularly strong parental involvement program that involves parents and families in everything from school governance to curriculum planning. Instructional activities tend to focus on dual development of academics and social skills. His model consistently results in improved achievement scores and improved attitudes and behaviors for children who were not succeeding in traditional school organizations (Comer, 1994). He is currently expanding his model to include middle and high school.

World Wide Web Site

You can learn more about James Comer at this Web site:
http://info.med.yale.edu/comer/

Characteristics of Successful Programs

Effective and successful school programs produced evidence that schools can make a difference and provide positive programs for all children. Schools that succeed usually have a staff of enthusiastic and caring teachers who are knowledgeable in subject matter and pedagogy; a cohesive teaching and learning plan that is integrated across all subjects in the curriculum; recognition of diversity in students' backgrounds, cultures, and talents; a high level of teacher and student engagement; and strong parental involvement (Smith & O'Day, 1991). Crucial to each of the three programs briefly described here is the involvement of caring, trained educators who hold the belief that all children can learn if expectations are high and meaningful.

Characteristics of successful programs can easily be transferred to most educational systems and offer some ideas about the ideal results of school reform. Most successful schools are small organizations with fewer students than the average enrollment expected in today's schools. Teachers work together to plan for teaching and learning. The vision, goals, and means of achieving the goals are clearly articulated and developed through continuous discussion and reflection. Teachers have professional development and planning time and are encouraged to collaborate and plan integrated approaches that consider language and cultural diversity. Caring for students is an important component of successful school reform. This is particularly true in Comer's model, for example, in which the importance of developing a supportive, caring relationship with the adults in the school is explicit (Rossi & Stringfield, 1995). Innovative learning strategies are incorporated to engage students in motivating and relevant activities. Most successful programs present a "parent and family friendly" school where many

Parents and families should feel welcome in classrooms and successful schools encourage them to contribute to their children's school experiences in a variety of ways.

different individuals are welcomed as a caring community (Minicucci et al., 1995). Successful schools are good for children and for teachers, and the common characteristics of successful programs suggests what new teachers should look for in schools when they begin their careers. Take time now to complete the Self-Reflection exercise and to think about what you have learned about school reform.

The Case against Change

Not everyone agrees that change is needed, and some believe that change efforts are expensive, time-consuming, and take away from the educational process. Some even suggest that the call for reform is bogus and politically motivated. One major report from the Sandia National Laboratory concludes that the nation's educational system does not need an overhaul (Carson, Huelskamp, & Woodall, 1993; Tanner, 1993). This report suggests that the data used in support of reform has been skewed to justify the need for change. They believe that the call for change is economically motivated and generated by businesses that see testing and for-profit schools as a money-making endeavor. Others do not want

Self-Reflection

RECOGNIZING REFORM

In this list of successful school programs, check off those you are familiar with and place a question mark in the second column if you are unfamiliar with the program.

	Familiar	Unfamiliar	Of Interest
School Development Program http://info.med.yale.edu/comer/	_____	_____	_____
Roots and Wings http://www.successforall.net/curriculum/ rwprogdescr.htm	_____	_____	_____
Edison Project http://www.edisonschools.com/	_____	_____	_____
Core Knowledge http://www.coreknowledge.org/	_____	_____	_____
Accelerated Schools http://www.acceleratedschools.net	_____	_____	_____
Talent Development High School http://scov.csos.jhu.edu/Talent/high.htm	_____	_____	_____
Atlas Communities http://www.edc.org/ATLAS/	_____	_____	_____
Modern Red Schoolhouse http://www.mrsh.org/	_____	_____	_____
High Schools that Work http://test.sreb.org/programs/hstw/ hstwindex.asp	_____	_____	_____
Expeditionary Learning Outward Bound http://www.elob.org/	_____	_____	_____

Now count the number of check marks. If you score less than six out of ten, visit the Web sites for these programs. After visiting the Web site, put a check mark in column three for those that really look interesting to you. If you want to know even more about a particular reform program, search InfoTrac College Edition for more in-depth articles.

new, innovative educational techniques implemented but instead call for a return to the way they remember schools. They want to return to the "basics" of reading, writing, and arithmetic taught in a traditional manner. The objections to changes in schools during the last few years have gone beyond the typical past disagreements about philosophy and use of successful strategies. They now carry a great deal of political weight and can be heard in the rhetoric of presidential speeches, new laws, federal budget debates, and church pulpits.

A great deal of the recent criticism of schools has originated from business, industry, and government. The criticism by and increased involvement of businesses and government in education produces two schools of thought. On one side, business and industry claim that test scores are terribly low, that U.S. students are not performing well in international assessments, and that work habits of young people have deteriorated. The involvement of business is encouraged, and school is viewed as a way to train future employees. On the other side, Berliner and Biddle (1996) and Bracey (2000), make the case that many of these beliefs are myths that have damaged public schools. They claim that test results in the United States are holding steady in international assessments and that "school bashing" has been a popular sport for years. This controversy is rooted in the belief by some that big business and government are too involved in schools and are involved for the wrong reasons. As Berliner and Biddle (1996) themselves admit, this argument is based on a fundamental difference in values and beliefs of what education is about.

World Wide Web Site

You can learn more about the Berliner and Biddle study at this Web site: http://epaa.asu.edu/

Many of the arguments against change are centered on a return to basics and encompass the restoration of traditional values of family, religion, and assimilation of immigrants through education. In President Reagan's 1984 State of the Union address, he urged Americans to return to traditional values in education. "Excellence must begin in our homes and neighborhood schools, where it's the responsibility of every parent and teacher and the right of every child . . . restore discipline to schools . . . encourage the teaching of new basics . . . and put our parents back in charge" (McGraw, 1984, p. 39). In 1989, strategists for the Christian Coalition established the "Contract with the American Family," which supported school vouchers, discouraged teaching history from a multicultural perspective, and advocated the elimination of the Department of Education, reducing the arts in schools, and denying or withholding benefits for young unmarried mothers. The 2000 presidential campaign also focused on education and reiterated the call for reform and excellence in education.

One particularly powerful group that opposes school change is known as the New Right. When the New Right discusses parental involvement in education, it means strong control and implementation of parental beliefs (Fege, 1993). A network of national, state, and local agencies was formed in the 1990s to promote the causes of the New Right and to attempt to influence a more conservative approach to education. On the local level, school board elections have provided the New Right with easy entry into the school policy arena.

Calls for change are often confusing and frustrating for teachers. Most teachers want to focus on their own classrooms and the children and young people who are there to learn. Some of the calls for change do make a difference in the classroom, and teachers need to be informed about calls for change and who may have an impact on their work.

There will always be calls to make changes in teaching and learning, and these calls will be surrounded by controversy and blame. The different calls for change come from a wide range of groups including parents, community members, politicians, religious groups, and business. Many changes related to education result from differing philosophical stances (see Chapter 2), others result from new information and technologies, and still others from the needs of students. But the key factor in the reform movement is the classroom teacher (Hord, 1992). Teachers who are educated in ways that encourage them to support all students' learning will attempt changes in their classrooms that support their students' successes and achievement.

Portfolio Reflections and Exhibits

Throughout this chapter you completed a series of field-based activities. The activities may serve as the basis for a portfolio representation, or you may develop your own portfolio representation or complete these suggested portfolio activities:

Suggested Exhibit 3: Educational Reforms

A portfolio representation for this chapter might include these items:

1. Review your responses to the field-based activities in this chapter. Itemize factors that cause change in most educational settings.

2. Develop a "change" chart that illustrates the origin of reform or change movements. Indicate whether the changes are the result of differences within the educational community, diverse ideas about the purpose of education, demands from society, changes in technology, or something else. The chart should illustrate the origin of the reform and include a statement about the impact of outside influences on the teaching profession.

InfoTrac College Edition Extension

Log on to the InfoTrac College Edition Web site, and use it to find out more about current testing issues in today's schools. Using the subject guide, type in "high stakes testing." Choose an article about testing for either students or teachers. What are the arguments for and against testing of this type?

Related Readings

The following books will provide you with more information about the topics discussed in this chapter:

Cunningham, P. M., & Allington, R. L. (1999). *Classrooms that work: They can all read and write* (2nd ed.). New York: Longman.

Cunningham and Allington describe what works for classroom teachers who care about the literacy development of the children they teach. This book presents a positive view of one of the most contentious topics in elementary school teaching—teaching reading and writing. The authors also explain that change does not happen overnight. If we want to see real differences in the classroom, we must be patient and give it some time.

Sizer, T. (1989). *Horace's compromise: The dilemma of the American high school.* Boston: Houghton Mifflin.

Sizer, T. (1992). *Horace's school: Redesigning the American high school.* Boston: Houghton Mifflin.

Sizer, T. (1996). *Horace's hope: What works for the American high school.* Boston: Houghton Mifflin.

Horace Smith, a fictional teacher, and other characters make Sizer's arguments and suggestions for changing American high schools informative, inspiring, and positive. These three books demonstrate successful educational changes.

Wasley, P. A. (1994). *Stirring the chalkdust.* New York: Teachers College Press.

In this book you can read about teachers who are involved in the changes that come about when Sizer's Coalition of Essential Schools processes are put in place. Secondary teachers who are working to change the way they teach write about the rewards and challenges of change. The book also presents a description of the most common changes teachers are making.

References

Apple, M. W. (1996). *Cultural politics and education.* New York: Teachers College Press.

Berliner, D. C., & Biddle, B. J. (1996). *The manufactured crisis: Myths, fraud, and the attack on America's public schools.* New York: Addison-Wesley.

Bracey, G. W. (2000). The 10th Bracey report on the condition of public education. *Phi Delta Kappan, 82*(2), 133–144.

Carson, C. C., Huelskamp, R. M., & Woodall, T. D. (1993). Perspectives on education in America. *Journal of Educational Research, 86*(5), 259–310.

Clark, C. (1995). *Thoughtful teaching.* New York: Teachers College Press.

Cohen, D. (1995). What standards for national standards? *Phi Delta Kappan, 76*(10), 751–757.

Comer, J. (1994). Home, school and academic learning. In J. I. Goodlad & P. Keating (Eds.), *Access to knowledge* (pp. 23–42). New York: College Board.

Cuban, L. (1984). *How teachers taught.* New York: Teachers College Press.

Falk, B. (2000). *The heart of the matter: Using standards and assessment to learn.* Portsmouth, NH: Heinemann.

Fege, A. F. (1993). A tug of war over tolerance. *Educational Leadership, 51*(4), 22–23.

Goodlad, J. I. (1992). On taking school reform seriously. *Phi Delta Kappan, 74*(3), 232–238.

Haynes, N., & Comer, J. (1990). Helping black children succeed: The significance of some social factors. In K. Lomotey (Ed.), *Going to school: The African American experience* (pp. 103–113). Albany: State University of New York Press.

Hlebowitsh, P., & Tellez, K. (1997). *American education: Purpose and promise.* Belmont, CA: Wadsworth.

Holland, H. (1997). KERA: A tale of one teacher. *Phi Delta Kappan, 79*(4), 264–271.

Hord, S. M. (1992). *Facilitative leadership: The imperative for change.* Austin, TX: Southwest Educational Development Laboratory.

Illinois State Board of Education (1997). *Illinois Learning Standards.* Springfield: Author.

Jackson, J. F. (2000). What are the real risk factors for African-American children? *Phi Delta Kappan, 81*(4), 308–312.

Jennings, J. (1995). School reform based on what is taught and learned. *Phi Delta Kappan, 76*(10), 765–769.

Manno, B. V., Finn, C. E., & Vanourek, G. (2000). Beyond the schoolhouse door: How charter schools are transforming U.S. public education. *Phi Delta Kappan, 81*(10), 736–744.

McGraw, O. (1984). Reclaiming traditional values in education: The implications for educational research. *Educational Leadership, 38*(1), 30–42.

Minicucci, C., Berman, P., McLaughlin, B., McLeod, B., Nelson, B., & Woodworth, K. (1995). School reform and student diversity. *Phi Delta Kappan, 77*(1), 77–80.

Myers, C. B., & Myers, L. K. (1995). *The professional educator: A new introduction to teaching and schools.* Belmont, CA: Wadsworth.

National Commission on Excellence in Education. (1983). *A nation at risk: The imperative for educational reform.* Washington, DC: U.S. Department of Education.

Oliva, P. F. (1997). *Developing the curriculum* (4th ed.). New York: Longman.

Payne, K. J., & Biddle, B. J. (1999). Poor school funding, child poverty, and mathematics achievement. *Educational Researcher, 28*(6), 4–13.

Piner, W. F. (1992). The curriculum. In J. L. Kincheloe & S. R. Steinberg (Eds.), *Thirteen questions: Reframing education's conversation* (pp. 31–38). New York: Peter Lang.

Rossi, R. J., & Stringfield, S. (1995). What we must do for students placed at risk. *Phi Delta Kappan, 77*(1), 73–77.

Rothman, R. (1997). KERA: A tale of one school. *Phi Delta Kappan, 79*(4), 272–275.

Sadker, M. P., & Sadker, D. M. (2000). *Teachers, schools, society* (5th ed.). Boston: McGraw-Hill.

Shields, P. M., & Knapp, M. S. (1997). The promise and limits of school-based reform: A national snapshot. *Phi Delta Kappan, 79*(4), 288–294.

Sizer, T. (1992). *Horace's school: Redesigning the American school.* Boston: Houghton Mifflin.

Sizer, T. (1996). *Horace's hope: What works for the American high school.* Boston: Houghton Mifflin.

Slavin, R. E., & Madden, N. A. (2000). Research on achievement outcomes of success for all: A summary and response to critics. *Phi Delta Kappan, 82*(1), 38–67.

Slavin, R. E., Madden, N. A., & Wasik, B. (1996). *Success for all: A summary of research.* Baltimore: Johns Hopkins University.

Smith, M. S., & O'Day, J. (1991). Systemic school reform. In S. Fuhrman & B. Malen (Eds.), *The politics of curriculum and testing* (pp. 116–133). Philadelphia: Falmer Press.

Tanner, D. (1993). A nation truly at risk. *Phi Delta Kappan, 75*(4), 288–297.

CHAPTER 4

Considering Legal and Ethical Issues

IN THIS CHAPTER

- **Governmental Authority**
- **The Laws that Change Educational Contexts**
- **Students Rights and Responsibilities**
- **Ethical Issues for Teachers**

*T*hat I can be a forceful, productive member of the board is clear. It was I who made public this sad story regarding a boy who was removed from class merely because of his desire to express his patriotism. Even though I am not yet a member of the board, I was able to meet with Superintendent Seymour—who has, I assure you, my deepest respect—and discuss in a calm, rational fashion what might be done. When it became clear that the problem was not with school policy itself, but the misguided judgement of a particular teacher—a teacher out of touch with Harrison values—a solution was worked out that is equitable to all—and preserves the good name of our community. The boy is back in class, where he belongs and wants to be. The teacher in question will get a needed refresher course in our values and return to her duties next year better able to teach.

—Avi, *Nothing But the Truth**

---

*From *Nothing But the Truth: A Documentary Novel*, by Avi (p. 198). New York: Avon Flare, 1993.

This fictional example from the young adult novel *Nothing But the Truth* illustrates a struggle between a teacher's actions, a high schooler's rights, and the school board's authority. Although the story is fictional, the events leading up to this speech by the prospective board member are certainly believable. Legal decisions are often required to solve problems in our schools, and ethical dilemmas are even more difficult to deal with because we rarely have the benefit of a law or previous case to guide our decision making. The legal and ethical issues emerging in school settings are almost always complex and difficult.

Teachers and their students have rights embedded in the Constitution of the United States. The laws, and less directly the ethics of our society and profession, govern all individuals in the schools, but interpretation of these laws is often more difficult when children and young people are involved.

At one time, contracts with the schools where teachers taught tightly regulated their lives. Their duties were specifically outlined down to the clothes they were required to wear. Men had to wear a jacket and tie, and women had to wear dresses and skirts. Personal lives were also regulated. A female teacher's career was terminated if she married, and teachers were not allowed to drink or engage in any behavior that would not set a good example for their students. All teachers were expected to live up to strict ethical and community guidelines—guidelines not required of most other professionals.

This attitude was maintained throughout the early 1900s, but changes in other aspects of our society from that time forward also had an impact on how teaching and other professions were governed. The 1960s civil rights movement began to change many of the strict regulations on teachers. Although teachers' personal actions and behaviors are no longer as constrained as they once were, teachers are not free to act irresponsibly. Legal and ethical considerations guide teachers' decisions, behaviors, and words. It is crucial that teachers have a basic understanding of the legal and ethical issues relevant to their profession. This chapter introduces and answers some basic questions about legal and ethical relationships to education:

- What constitutional rights and responsibilities support education?

- What laws govern the teaching profession?

- What are the rights of teachers and students?

- What are the important ethical issues related to teaching, and what dilemmas do they present to teachers?

Becoming a Teacher in a Field-Based Setting

Governmental Authority

The laws that contribute to educational governance are legislated at the federal, state, and local level. Each level of government has a very different role and responsibility when it comes to school policy.

Federal Authority

Schools are not considered a responsibility of the federal government, and federal laws tend to be indirect when dealing with education. Although education is not addressed specifically in the Constitution, several of its provisions are important for education. Through constitutional interpretation by federal courts and the Supreme Court, the federal government has had a great impact on education (Myers & Myers, 1995). The three constitutional amendments the courts have considered with regard to what happens in schools are the First Amendment, which guarantees freedom of speech, the Tenth Amendment, which delineates education as a function of state governments, and the Fourteenth Amendment, which assures citizens freedom from unreasonable search and seizure (Figure 4.1).

Figure 4.1 Constitutional Amendments That Have an Impact on Educational Settings

Amendment I [1791]

Congress shall make no law respecting an establishment of religion, or prohibiting the free exercise thereof; or abridging the freedom of speech or of the press; or the right of the people peaceably to assemble, and to petition the Government for a redress of grievances.

Amendment X [1791]

The powers not delegated to the United States by the Constitution, nor prohibited by it to the States, are reserved to the States respectively, or to the people.

Amendment XIV [1868]

Section 1. All persons born or naturalized in the United States, and subject to the jurisdiction thereof, are citizens of the United States and of the State wherein they reside. No State shall make or enforce any law which shall abridge the privileges or immunities of citizens of the United States; nor shall any State deprive any person of life, liberty, or property, without due process of law; nor deny to any person within its jurisdiction the equal protection of the laws.

None of these three amendments establish schools, but they each have an impact on education in various ways. When cases about education come before the courts, for example, interpretation of one of these amendments is usually at the core of the case. The First Amendment assures freedom of speech in any place that people assemble. Freedom of speech is often the basis of debates over what should be read or discussed at school, school prayer, and even if topics such as evolution should be taught. The Tenth Amendment assigns the process of establishing schools as a state responsibility by acknowledging that any activity not established in the Constitution will reside in the states. Finally, the Fourteenth Amendment makes it clear that citizens of the United States have a right to all privileges. One of the privileges of our country is education. Educational policies related to civil rights have been greatly influenced by the Fourteenth Amendment.

The limited power of the federal government established by the Constitution in establishing schools does not prevent Congress, the president, and the U.S. Department of Education from formulating national policies and guidelines, providing funds to schools, and encouraging school improvement (Myers & Myers, 1995). In the last few presidential elections, education has been a major issue in the political debates, and the public looks toward the federal government to help maintain schools.

State Authority

The Tenth Amendment places the responsibility for education with the individual states. There is wide variability in how state laws support educational issues, but there is remarkable conformity across the country in how schools are governed and regulated. For example, each state has compulsory attendance. State legislatures, the governor, state departments of education, and state boards of education are responsible for representing citizens' views in making educational decisions (Myers & Myers, 1995).

The role of the state in supporting educational initiatives is wide ranging. The state establishes and interprets educational laws and policies and makes sure schools comply with these rules and regulations. State agencies levy taxes and distribute funds to the schools. School funding, teacher certification, and curriculum are all decided at the state level. State agencies also administer tests, keep records, and provide goals and objectives for students.

Many decisions about education are made by the courts and legislative mandates. Decisions about highly debated issues such as school prayer and integration have been argued and ultimately decided in the Supreme Court.

Local Authority

Elected officials, mayors, county executives, city councils, township supervisors, and local judges implement laws that govern public and private schools. Many of their decisions influence the types of schools that are established and how they are run. Local school boards and the school superintendents they hire are responsible for the day-to-day operation of schools. They employ teachers, appoint principals, set tax rates, approve budgets, build and maintain school buildings, buy equipment, set school calendars, and negotiate salaries. Even though state and national regulations and policies dictate their responsibilities, the actions of local school boards have the most direct impact on teachers, students, and learning. These local policies and actions reflect the community and the ways citizens of the community want their schools to operate. Many decisions are made at local school board meetings that are open to the public.

The Laws that Change Educational Contexts

Several court cases have had a tremendous impact on schooling in the United States. Federal and district courts commonly make rulings that affect teachers and students, and their decisions are often controversial. Some of the issues and the accompanying court rulings are presented here to demonstrate the impact of court cases on the teaching profession.

Equity

Supreme Court decisions concerning access and equity come from the Fourteenth Amendment, which specifies that "no State shall . . . deny to any person within its jurisdiction the equal protection of the laws." The courts have addressed segregation and integration over the years, and the courts have occasionally reversed long-standing beliefs and practices. Such cases include racial segregation, services for students with special needs, instruction for non-native speaking students, and school finance equity. Several important court cases illustrate the impact the Supreme Court has had on equity.

In 1896 the courts established the "separate but equal" rule in *Plessy v. Ferguson*, which established segregation (Timm, 1996). The country supported and encouraged building segregated educational systems until the 1954 case of *Brown v. Board of Education*. An elementary student named Linda Brown in a Topeka, Kansas school sued the board of education, alleging that the racially separate school she was attending had a negative effect on the learning of black students. The state courts ruled against her, stating that separate but equal facilities assured similar educational opportunities. The Supreme Court rejected that argument and by doing so issued one of the broadest rulings related to education—that is, that segregated public schools were unconstitutional. The case challenged the "separate but equal" laws and established that segregation has a detrimental effect on children's educational opportunities.

Nevertheless, the Supreme Court ruling alone was not enough to make significant changes in our society, and it wasn't until Congress passed the Civil Rights Act of 1964, which outlawed segregation in our schools, that the interactions between minorities and majorities changed markedly. Most likely, court tests of the Fourteenth Amendment will continue despite increased societal change. The problems and contexts of the cases may change, but the courts will continue to make sure that there is equal protection and opportunity in our public schools.

English as a Second Language

As early as 1964, the landmark case of *Lau v. Nichols* established transitional bilingual education for schoolchildren who do not speak English (Fischer, Schimmel, & Kelly, 1998). More recently, a group of Chinese American students and their parents claimed that their rights were being violated when they were taught in a language they could not understand. They made a case that they were excluded from participating in a program that received federal support. The Supreme Court agreed that when children cannot understand what is being taught and no effort is made to help them learn the language their rights are violated. Since that time, several states have legislated mandates that provide transitional programs and other opportunities for students to maintain and improve their native speaking skills. Nevertheless, there is no agreement on the best way to prepare second language learners in English, and debate about what should be done continues.

The Supreme Court has reviewed important cases dealing with language instruction and has been asked to deal with situations in which a state has proclaimed that English is the major language. Students' entitlement to instruction in their first language during the time that they are learning English is often at the center of the controversy. Those who support teaching in English believe that everyone needs to speak English to bind our country together; others feel that it is their right to receive instruction in their native tongue, thereby honoring different languages. The debate is ongoing and will most likely continue to be discussed as our society grows even more diverse.

New Arrivals

Related to the language debates are issues of public education for immigrant children. States and the federal government are in constant debate about using tax money to educate children who are in our country illegally. Texas and California have been at the center of cases related to this issue. In 1980, after hearing several other related cases, the District Court of Southern Texas ruled that illegal immigrant children's needs were no different from the needs of any other children and that they were entitled to an education. In these cases, courts tend to view children as innocent bystanders who should not be punished because their parents are in this country illegally (Timm, 1996). Issues of language differences and immigration are likely to be part of educational discussions for years to come. Teachers will need to stay abreast of the changing laws and policies related to these issues.

Religious Freedom

Controversy about the role of religion in schools has gone on since the earliest days of public schooling in the United States. Because religion is so important in the lives of many people, powerful emotions are associated with this issue.

All students can attend schools no matter what their religious preferences, but they are not free to act out their religious beliefs in the classroom nor to impose their actions or beliefs on others. This seems like a simple distinction, but religious ideas and perspectives are related to education in many ways. Many disagreements about religious freedom in schools originate from differences in attitudes toward the separation of church and state. The courts are often expected to help determine when religious behavior infringes on individual rights.

Most often the debate between church and state is characterized by discussions about the role of school prayer and Bible reading during school. The courts have ruled that prayers or Bible reading must be excluded from public schools based on First Amendment rights. It is legitimate to study about religion at school, but religious exercise, rituals, and celebrations are against the law. Activities or discussions that approach religious issues and practices from a secular or nonreligious stance are lawful. When the activity or discussion serves a religious purpose, however, it is not in keeping with the legal separation of church and state. Any school-based activity that is established to further religion will not be supported by the Constitution.

The courts regulated prayer and Bible reading at school nearly forty years ago, but occasionally there are violations. The 2000 decision in *School District of Santa Fe v. Doe* is a recent example of the repeatedly contested Supreme Court ruling on the separation of church and state. Using freedom of speech as its basis, the Santa Fe, Texas school district persisted in conducting student-led prayers before football games despite a court ruling that prayer before school events violated separation of church and state laws. The Supreme Court agreed to hear the case to determine if student votes indicating widespread student support of prayer would change the long-established law. Once again, the Supreme Court ruled that officially sponsored prayers cannot be part of public school programs where a captive audience of students must listen—whether they care to or not.

Special Needs Students

Case law and legislative mandates have made it illegal to exclude children with disabilities from school or to place them improperly in separate educational programs. The most powerful law that protects special needs students is Public Law

Field-Based Activity 4.1

Identify a recent court case that focused on an educational issue. The *Santa Fe v. Doe* case is one example. Research the background of the case on the Internet. You will find newspaper articles, court documents, and arguments supporting multiple viewpoints. Read about the origin of the case, how long it has been working its way through the courts, and the final outcome. What impact does the case have on education? How could the ruling of the court case you researched affect you when you are teaching?

No. 94-142. It assures free and appropriate education and forbids discrimination against students no matter what their situation. Schools must comply with federal law and meet the needs of all their students or risk losing federal and state funds. Compliance centers around provision of individual education plans (IEPs) for identified students, assessment, reevaluations, and parental rights. This law has been rigorously enforced to provide equal opportunities for all students no matter their status.

Teachers' Legal Rights and Responsibilities

Teachers have the same rights as other citizens, and the "right to privacy" protects much of their personal lives. There can be no job discrimination based on age, weight, or ethnic origin. Citizenship, however, can be considered in hiring teachers. Teachers' personal or lifestyle preferences are often upheld legally, but it is rare for teachers to be protected against immoral behavior if they involve students. If a teacher becomes sexually involved with a student or promotes any sexual behavior, the teacher would typically lose the right to teach. If teachers knowingly permit or participate in a student's sexual involvement with others or encourage activities involving alcohol or drugs, they are held accountable. Other rights and responsibilities are not as clear-cut, and courts often must make decisions about the rights of teachers.

When courts must rule on teachers' actions, a major consideration is the likelihood that the conduct negatively affected students or school programs (Strike, 1990). Community standards may also play a role in court decisions. When members of a community believe that certain conduct is immoral, the court ruling may reflect that sentiment. In all cases, court rulings must balance the rights of the teacher against the interests of the schools' academic programs.

Academic Freedom and Freedom of Speech

There was a time when teachers were unable to voice their opinions about what happened in schools. In 1969, a Supreme Court ruling proclaimed that teachers had the right to express their views about the schools where they work. If teachers make false and misleading statements or accusations, however, their freedom of speech is not protected (Fischer et al., 1998).

Teachers do not have total freedom to teach whatever they want, and their manner of presentation is also controlled. The school can regulate both the content and the methodology of what is taught. That does not mean, however, that teachers do not have the right to discuss ideas, even if they are unpopular. They can also criticize values and practices.

Teachers' rights to teach what they want—their academic freedom—is usually measured against public values. Local school boards do have the right to prohibit the use of certain texts and to control the content of classes. Teachers cannot refuse to use required texts or to present the established curriculum (Fischer et al., 1998). If there is a disagreement between a teacher and a school board, the school board has the final word (Fischer et al., 1998). However, the courts usually protect teachers if they use controversial materials that are relevant to instructional goals and nondisruptive. Recently, judges have been articulating a narrower view of academic freedom, supporting school restrictions on teachers' methods and materials.

Child Abuse

Teachers are often the first responsible individuals to realize that children are being harmed or neglected by other adults. The National Child Abuse Prevention and Treatment Act requires teachers to report any known or suspected instance of child abuse. Teachers who fail to report a case of child abuse are legally liable. Any responsible adult who fails to report a suspected case of abuse can be sued. The same law assumes that a teacher will report in good faith and protects teachers from lawsuits if there is no abuse where it was reported. If a teacher has reason to believe that a child is being abused and reports a concern, the teacher cannot be sued even if the report is unsubstantiated. A teacher who suspects that a child is abused or neglected should report the situation to the principal or superintendent who then reports it to authorities—either the police or social workers.

Unions and Negotiations

In some states, professional associations such as the National Education Association and the American Federation of Teachers help teachers negotiate employment contracts with school boards. A union representative engages in collective bargaining and negotiates with the school board to set salaries and establish certain working conditions for all the teachers in a school district. If negotiations are unsuccessful and teachers are not happy with some aspect of their contracts, they may strike in states where it is legal to do so. Teachers may put pressure on the local school board to meet the demands for a new contract by refusing to report to work, leaving students without teachers in classrooms. States may outlaw strikes, and the courts often order teachers back into the classrooms. Supporters of unions point to increased teachers' salaries and improved working conditions as results of collective bargaining. Critics of unions highlight reduced professionalism and the possible harmful effects to student learning as a result of union-sponsored strikes.

World Wide Web Site

You can learn more about these professional organizations at these Web sites:

National Education Association: http://www.nea.org/

American Federation of Teachers: http://www.aft.org/

Students Rights and Responsibilities

Just as teachers are guaranteed certain rights by law and have certain responsibilities that are legally prescribed, students also have certain rights and responsibilities. Most important, all children must receive an education and are guaranteed that right by the Constitution and state laws.

In Loco Parentis and Family Rights

When parents place their children in schools, they delegate their supervision and safety to teachers. Teachers have a responsibility and in fact the power to protect and supervise students in their classrooms. The doctrine that authorizes the supervision of students by schools is known as *in loco parentis*, which means "in

Issues related to drugs and violence have required schools to supervise and restrict students' behaviors at school. Students' rights while at school must be balanced with concerns related to safety of the entire student body.

place of parents." This doctrine provides the state with the right to exercise custodial control over students while they are at school. Recently, the doctrine has been weakened by court rulings (Fischer et al., 1998). Nevertheless, the responsibility still exists, and schools can be held liable for failing to protect students from school environments where danger is created or enhanced. Schools are also liable if they have been deliberately indifferent in failing to protect children from danger. Generally, schools are held liable if they deliberately ignore or fail to act when possible harm can come to children. As students get older, however, the law holds students increasingly more responsible for their own actions.

Searches and Seizures

Many cases related to students' rights are based on the right to be protected against unreasonable searches and seizures (Myers & Myers, 1995). Students' rights are guarded by the Fourth Amendment, "the right of the people to be secure in their persons, houses, papers, and effects, against unreasonable searches and seizures." Well-publicized cases of gun violence in schools and the long-time efforts directed at reducing drugs in schools have resulted in many schools taking a stand on the rights of school officials to search lockers and backpacks. Metal detectors, X-ray machines, and alcohol breath tests—all considered ways to search students—are commonplace in some schools. Courts regularly weigh students' rights against safety issues and balance these conflicting issues when making rulings.

Freedom of Expression

Legal questions regarding freedom of speech for students often emerge out of the struggle between students' First Amendment rights of freedom of expression and the school district's obligation to provide an orderly environment in which to learn. Students do not lose their freedom of speech when they are in a classroom, but there are some limitations. Schools can impose limits to free speech when there are legitimate pedagogical concerns. This discretion is increased or limited based on the age of the students, community standards, and other relevant factors.

Another issue of student freedom involves dress and appearance. A great deal of national prominence has been given to the issue of student dress codes at school. Often schools regulate dress with the idea that there will be improvements in school climate and student self-esteem. At one time, school boards and educators went unchallenged when exercising control over student dress, but recent court decisions have supported students' rights to wear certain clothing unless the presence of the clothing would disrupt or interfere with the teaching–learning environment.

The emergence of the Internet as a teaching tool will, no doubt, spawn new court rulings related to students' rights involving free speech and search and seizure. On one hand, students should have free access to the information available on the Internet. On the other hand, some form of screening from exposure to inappropriate materials is necessary (Gorski, 2001). Educators must protect their students from pornographic materials, and effective screening software is one way to block access to objectionable sites. There are many resources to help teachers with this new technology, and educational Web sites such as 50 Great Sites for Kids provide guidance. Also, the American Library Association provides guidance concerning Internet safety for students.

Observe or take part in a state or local school meeting that focuses on policies established by state or local laws. One of the following activities would allow you to see laws in action and the impact of certain policies on the teaching profession.

- Attend a campaign event, such as a speech or debate, held to provide the public with an opportunity to understand the views of a local political candidate. Listen to what the person says about education. What role does education play in the candidacy? What educational laws and policies does the candidate suggest should be enacted?

- Visit a school board meeting in your local community. Some may televise their meetings on local channels. Who attends the meetings? What decisions do they make? Identify discussions that relate to laws and policies established by state authority or local control.

- Attend an NEA or AFT meeting. Do they discuss laws and policies related to the teaching profession? If there is a strike in the district where you teach, attend any open meetings that may help you to understand why teachers disagree with the local school board.

- If there are no meetings convenient for you to attend, listen to public radio or local television commentaries. What laws and policies are making news? How does public opinion influence interpretations of laws and policies affecting teachers?

Ethical Issues for Teachers

Legal responsibilities define the rights and requirements of teachers, but ethical codes also influence the decisions teachers make about students, teaching, and their own behavior. Ethics are the principles of conduct that govern either an individual or a group. They include standards of behavior as well as moral principles and values. Legal and ethical decisions may at times be related, but laws do not typically specify ethical standards for teaching.

Teaching is considered by many to be primarily a moral endeavor necessitating considerable teacher reflection on ethical and moral issues related to education (Goodlad, Soder, & Sirotnik, 1990). Teachers, by definition, are in a position of power and responsibility over students in their classrooms, and the exercise of this power and responsibility involves ethical and moral decision making (Fenstermacher, 1990). Each time a teacher assigns a grade, deliberates on a punishment, or intervenes to resolve a student dispute, questions of ethics arise. In

The community may scrutinize teachers' actions, personal values, and goals since their behavior serves as models for their students.

addition, teachers are often seen as models of moral and ethical behavior for their students. All teachers lecture students on the importance of fairness and honesty, but what teachers do in or outside the classroom when faced with opportunities to exercise either fairness or honesty is more often remembered by students than what they say. For this reason, although recent incidents of alteration of test answers by educators in states that have high-stakes testing may have legal ramifications, the ethical issues they raise and the messages they give to students are even more serious. Reflecting on moral values and ethical issues—what is fair or right or good related to students and teaching—is important for teachers at all stages of their careers.

At times, tensions may exist between a teacher's personal values and goals and those of the community. As a beginning teacher, you may feel that both you and your actions are being scrutinized, particularly in the context of the typical probationary status of new hires in most districts. This is further confounded because "right" and "legal" are not necessarily synonymous, and making on-the-spot decisions does not allow a great deal of time for consultation of law experts

Field-Based Activity 4.3

As you observe in your classroom, identify the day-to-day ethical dilemmas a teacher faces. Many of the issues involve interactions with students. What struggles do teachers face with grading and evaluating student work, dealing with plagiarism—particularly from the Internet—fairness in punishment, and equity in resources, time, and teacher attention. Share your observations during a small-group discussion among your peers.

or books—nor would doing so necessarily resolve every issue. Nevertheless, teachers are governed by ethical and moral mandates as well as legal ones.

It would be difficult to list all the situations teachers may encounter that require ethical decision making during their careers, but some common issues that arise can be described. The choices teachers make about what content will be emphasized, how students will receive or experience information, and how students will be judged to have been successful in these experiences go beyond technical questions of instructional decision making. For example, most educators agree that using information or information delivery in a manipulative, coercive, or rote manner to indoctrinate students is unethical (Strike, 1990). Instead, as educators we value enabling students to learn to think and reason using content and to consider opposing arguments. Likewise, grading and evaluation practices that are unfair, inaccurate, or lacking information about how and why the grades or scores were given are generally considered unethical. Teachers ethically are bound to have reasons for the assignment of grades, to do their best to minimize bias during the grading process, and to apply a defensible, consistent standard to determine grades. Other ethical concepts that are central to teachers include intellectual freedom and honesty, respect or tolerance for diversity, due process for students in matters of discipline and grading, fairness in punishment, and equity in the allocation of resources such as teacher time and attention (Strike, 1990). Take time now to complete the Self-Reflection exercise and to think about what you have learned.

The National Education Association (1975) established a Code of Ethics of the Education Profession that provides standards by which to judge educators' conduct. The code includes a preamble and two principles. The preamble describes protection of the freedoms of learning and teaching and the guarantee of educational opportunity. The two principles feature guidelines for commitment to the student and to the teaching profession. According to the NEA, ethical behavior related to student learning suggests, among other things, that teachers will not keep students from the pursuit of learning and will not deny access to

Becoming a Teacher in a Field-Based Setting

Self-Reflection

LEGAL AND ETHICAL DILEMMAS

Consider each of these situations and decide whether it is more aptly described as a legal or ethical issue. In some cases, you may check both columns.

	Legal	Ethical
1. A teacher likes to drop by high school parties on the weekend.	_____	_____
2. A girl in your class shows up with bruises on her legs and arms that she tries to hide.	_____	_____
3. You smell alcohol on Johnny's breath when he comes to school.	_____	_____
4. Janie misses school often to take care of her younger siblings.	_____	_____
5. You notice that the lower level English classes have an overrepresentation of minority students.	_____	_____
6. A group of your students came to you and asked you to start each class with a prayer.	_____	_____
7. You plan on having students read *Huckleberry Finn* and an African American parent objects.	_____	_____
8. Suzy is supposed to be mainstreamed into your class, but the door is not wide enough for her wheelchair.	_____	_____
9. The Tranh's have just moved into your school district, and no one at the school speaks Cambodian.	_____	_____
10. Your school does not believe in teaching evolution.	_____	_____
11. You ignore the fact that one of your students and his or her family are residing in the United States illegally.	_____	_____
12. You think one of the teachers on your team tampered with his students' answers on the state-mandated tests.	_____	_____
13. You notice that the math teacher only calls on boys during math class.	_____	_____
14. A student turns in a paper that he took from the Internet as his own.	_____	_____

Continued on next page

Continued from previous page

Items 2, 4, 6, 7, 8, 9, 10, 11, and 12 have laws that guide a teachers' responses, although they may also be unethical. If you missed any of these, review the discussion on laws in this chapter. The remaining items are ethical in nature and will need to be considered in the context of personal, school, and community values. If you had difficulty identifying legal and ethical issues, you may want to discuss this activity with your classmates.

different points of view. Ethical behaviors related to others in the profession are described as not making false statements and not assisting a noneducator in the unauthorized practice of teaching. Each principle lists specific behaviors that further illustrate what constitutes ethical behavior for educators.

World Wide Web Site

The National Education Association code can be found in its entirety on this Web site: http://www.nea.org/aboutnea/code.html

Despite the existence of a code of ethics, teachers may still find it difficult to distinguish between ethical and unethical behavior in some situations. The code is very general and vague, whereas concrete situations are often complex. Consider this statement in the code: "The educator shall not disclose information about students obtained in the course of professional service, unless disclosure serves a compelling professional purpose or is compelled by law." In the case of child abuse, you have a legal responsibility to report this information to the appropriate authorities. But suppose a student confides to you that he is worried that his girlfriend may be using drugs. What is your ethical obligation in this case? On one hand, you have a commitment to confidentiality; on the other, you have a commitment to the health and well-being of your students. To further complicate matters, the story is hearsay and may not be legitimate. Your first task would be to try to determine the facts as best you can prior to making any decision about informing others. Then, if you determine that the risk of silence on your part is too great to your students, either physically or psychologically, you may have to report the information to a school counselor, nurse, or principal, risking the loss of trust and further communication. Unless you have specific education in this area, you probably should not handle this alone. As a beginning

Portfolio Reflections and Exhibits

Throughout this chapter you have completed a series of field-based activities. They may serve as the basis for a portfolio representation, you may develop your own portfolio representation, or you may complete the suggested portfolio activities listed here.

Suggested Exhibit 4: Ethics and Legal Concerns

1. Identify one law or policy that has the potential to have an impact on you during your teaching. Some specific examples include rulings regarding special or bilingual education or those that deal with school prayer or Bible reading in the classroom. Find the origin of the law or policy. Use the Internet to research your law or topic. Produce a flow chart, diagram, drawing, or written summary that illustrates the political and legal steps that occurred before it affected individual educators. Then indicate on the diagram the possible impact of the law on your own actions in the classroom.

2. Begin to consider a rationale for your classroom grading or discipline policies. Review the student or teacher handbook from your school that describes these policies. Which aspects of the policies do you feel comfortable enforcing? Which ones would be more difficult for you? Consider any extenuating circumstances that might come up and cause you to question the policy. What does this tell you about your own ethics related to grading? Write a rationale that will serve as a guide when you grade or discipline students. Be sure to consider how your views might be different from those of a teacher from another culture who has had different experiences or education.

teacher, seek the advice of a more experienced educator who is familiar with your setting—perhaps a mentor teacher or an administrator.

In *The Ethics of Teaching*, Strike and Soltis (1998) define ethical issues related to punishment, intellectual freedom, and equal treatment of students. They provide a series of case studies designed to elicit reflection and discussion about underlying ethical issues and possible approaches depending on the philosophy and values of those involved. Strike (1990) suggests that consideration of cases involving ethical issues may be the best way to prepare teachers for the difficult ethical decisions they may later need to make. Despite legal and technical prescriptions for classroom behaviors, teaching is at heart an ethical and moral activity. In the words of Chris Clark (1990):

> *At its core, teaching is a matter of human relationships. Human relationships, whatever else they may be, are moral in character and consequence. After that between parent and child, the most profoundly moral relationship our children experience is that between the teacher and the taught.*

There are few guidelines for ethical conduct, and those that exist are typically brief and vague. Few school districts have explicit ethical codes of conduct. Students of teaching can prepare for the difficult decision making related to legal and ethical issues by being aware of laws affecting education, analyzing their own values and those of the community in which they teach, and reflecting on decisions—their own and others—related to the ethical concepts central to teaching.

InfoTrac College Edition Extension

Log on to the InfoTrac College Edition Web site, and use it to find out more about issues related to students' and teachers' use of technology, particularly the Internet. Using a keyword search, type in the term "cyber ethics." What are some of the issues? How will you handle them in your classroom?

Related Readings

The following books will provide more information about some of the topics and ideas in this chapter:

Fischer, L., Schimmel, D., & Kelly, C. (1998). *Teachers and the law* (5th ed.) New York: Longman.
>   *This is a relatively easy-to-read book in a question-and-answer format that provides a comprehensive view of the laws that may have an impact on the classroom teacher. Many examples are provided, and court cases are described in ways that help the reader understand the legal process and its effect on the rights of teachers and students.*

Kinchloe, J. L., & Steinberg, S. R. (Eds.). (1992). *Thirteen questions: Reframing education's conversations.* New York: Peter Lang.
>   *This is a series of philosophical and ethical essays that introduce important issues from differing perspectives. The voices in this book are often critical of existing practices and set out new solutions to some old problems. The chapter authors present information that is often omitted from traditional discussions of educational ethics.*

References

Clark, C. M. (1990). The teacher and the taught: Moral transactions in the classroom. In J. I. Goodlad, R. Soder, & K. A. Sirotnik (Eds.), *The moral dimensions of teaching* (pp. 251–265). San Francisco: Jossey-Bass.

Becoming a Teacher in a Field-Based Setting

Fenstermacher, G. D. (1990). Some moral considerations on teaching as a profession. In J. I. Goodlad, R. Soder, & K. A. Sirotnik (Eds.), *The moral dimensions of teaching* (pp. 130–154). San Francisco: Jossey-Bass.

Fischer, L., Schimmel, D., & Kelly, C. (1998). *Teachers and the law* (5th ed.). New York: Longman.

Goodlad, J. I., Soder, R., & Sirotnik, K. A. (Eds.) (1990). *The moral dimensions of teaching*. San Francisco: Jossey-Bass.

Gorski, P. C. (2001). *Multicultural education and the Internet: Intersections and integrations*. New York: McGraw-Hill.

Myers, C. B., & Myers, L. K. (1995). *The professional educator: A new introduction to teaching and the schools*. Belmont CA: Wadsworth.

National Education Association. (1975). *Code of ethics of the education profession*. Washington, DC: Author. [Available Online: http://www.nea.org/aboutnea/code.html]

Strike, K. A. (1990). The legal and moral responsibility of teachers. In J. I. Goodlad, R. Soder, & K. A. Sirotnik (Eds.), *The moral dimensions of teaching* (pp. 188–223). San Francisco: Jossey-Bass.

Strike, K. A., & Soltis, J. F. (1998). *The ethics of teaching*. Thinking about education series. New York: Teachers College Press.

Timm, J. T. (1996). *Four perspectives in multicultural education*. Belmont, CA: Wadsworth.

CHAPTER 5

Describing the Status of Contemporary Children

*M*y own teachers encouraged me and demanded nothing less than excellence. They made me feel smart and I responded. But there was still something wrong with my education. There were lots of smart kids in my elementary school, but they weren't all as economically stable as I was—I came from a working-class family with a father who was a laborer and a mother who was a clerk. I remember one girl in particular; her name was Portia. She was the smartest person I had ever met. She could sum a column of numbers with lightning speed. She could reason beyond her years. But she almost never came to school with her hair combed. Her teeth had not seen a toothbrush in years and she often smelled of urine. I liked her because she was smart and had a great sense of humor. It did not bother me that her house was dark, smelled funny, and had furniture that looked like the kind of stuff people set out curbside to be collected with the trash. I lost track of

Portia after elementary school. She did not attend the junior high school where I went to school across town. The last time I saw her was in eleventh grade. Portia was pregnant and had dropped out of school. As smart as I believed I was, I knew I was not as smart as Portia. So why wasn't she on the fast track to college? Why had she been passed over in the academic shuffle?

—Gloria Ladson-Billings, *The Dreamkeepers**

Good teachers relate to their students and place a high priority on maintaining an environment where children can succeed academically and socially. To accomplish this difficult task, a teacher must not only understand children and accept their differences but also be willing to accept a wide range of ways of looking at the world. Successful teachers understand the impact of family and community experiences, cultural and language diversity, and the changing nature of society. Understanding children and their differences is one important factor in providing an environment in which all children can have success in their school experiences.

Effective teachers must have a good understanding of what it is like to be a child or young adult in contemporary society and use that knowledge to react, interact, and respond to their students. Gaining an understanding of students is a complex process that will require an examination of personal beliefs and biases as well as cultural and societal issues. To enhance your understanding of students in today's classrooms, this chapter will focus on these questions:

- How are family structures different than they were a decade ago?
- What impact do culture and language have on classroom contexts?
- What are some of the major social issues affecting children's lives?
- What can future teachers learn from children and young people who have backgrounds different from their own?

---

*From *The Dreamkeepers*, by Gloria Ladson-Billings (pp. 76–77). San Francisco: Jossey-Bass, 1997.

Families and Communities

The structure of families has changed over the past thirty-five years. In 1965, more than 60 percent of Americans lived in a family unit with a working father and a stay-at-home mother who provided childcare and managed the house. Today, only 10 percent of families in the United States reflect this traditional structure, and the Internal Revenue Service recognizes thirteen different variations of the family—including dual-career families, single-parent families, and step-families. Although many family issues have remained constant, today's society has some unique characteristics that have an impact on children's educational experiences. Divorce, working parents, and differing lifestyles all contribute to family organizations that may or may not resemble what a teacher is expecting or has experienced.

Divorced and Single Parents

Many children and young people experience divorce and separation from important family members. Four out of ten children in the United States live with one parent, and most live with their mothers. The stress related to divorce affects children's reactions and responses at school and often results in less successful school experiences. Some statistics suggest that children of single-parent families have higher dropout rates, lower grades, and poorer attendance than do children who come from two-parent families (Bennett, 1995). However, with support from teachers and parents, children of divorce are certainly not doomed. Most children demonstrate an amazing resiliency that enables them to rebound from changes in their family structure due to divorce.

Different Family Lifestyles

Divorce is only one factor leading to a myriad of family structures. Children may need to make other adjustments when and if their parents remarry. Almost 20 percent of U.S. families are reconstituted or step-families, which are formed when parents remarry and combine children and families (Sadker & Sadker, 2000). Most children and young people who live in step-families have a diverse array of step-parents, siblings, grandparents, and other relatives.

Other differences in families occur when individuals from different cultures and races marry. Interracial marriages, once rare, are becoming more and more common in today's diverse society. Cultures also are mixed within a family

The number of children who spend time in childcare has increased due to single family parenting and the economic changes which require both parents to work.

through adoptions. Although the numbers are relatively small, many families today do not reflect a single cultural description.

Alternative family structures are also becoming more prevalent, including relatives or friends who serve as custodians of children, same-sex couples who are raising children, and nonmarried couples living together and raising children. Society is more and more accepting of a wide range of family structures, but the curriculum at school may still reflect the 1965 view of family life. Teachers can play an important part in helping all children and young people feel comfortable about their own family structures.

Working Parents

In more and more families, both mothers and fathers have joined the workforce. In 1970, only 32 percent of mothers of preschoolers worked outside the home, but by 1990, 58 percent were in the workforce. Today, three of four mothers with school-age children are employed, and most of them work full time. In households with two working parents, adequate supervision of children, level of family income, and support for school activities are some of the concerns that may affect learning.

Working parents are usually away during the day, and work schedules often do not match school hours. Between the time school lets out and the time parents return from work, children may attend day care or spend time with a baby-sitter. Teachers, particularly ones of young children, need to consider that caretakers may be involved in the early afternoon activities of their students and accept that homework or other school-related activities may be supervised by someone other than parents.

Many children of working parents are left at home alone, unsupervised by any responsible adult, for several hours. In the United States, 42 percent of all children between the ages of five and nine are home alone often or at least occasionally, and up to 10 million children are "latchkey" children, spending most afternoons alone (Wilwerth, 1993). Schools have tried to help parents care for children after school, implementing after-school programs that provide tutoring, snacks, and supervised activities for children of working parents. Even older children need attention after school. Adolescents who are left unsupervised are more likely to engage in substance abuse, experiment with sex, or have run-ins with the law.

When parents arrive home in the evenings, children must compete with hectic schedules for parental attention. One study of a thousand adolescents found that they spend only about five minutes a day exclusively with their fathers and about twenty minutes a day with their mothers (Csikszentmihalyi & Larson, 1984). Working parents' busy schedules are reflected in school involvement, and their participation in school-related events is greatly reduced. Unless the workplace supports parental involvement in school activities, it is difficult for working parents to volunteer at school or to attend school functions.

Communities that once felt a collective responsibility for the children may not offer the support they once did. Modern mobility and the reshuffling of neighborhoods provide less stability than was once available in neighborhoods. However, many churches and other community organizations still play an important role in children's and young people's lives. The importance of the community in raising children should not be overlooked.

Homelessness

One very jarring factor affecting many families is loss of a home or lack of affordable housing. The number of homeless families with children has increased over

Field-Based Activity 5.1

Learn about the neighborhood where the students in your classrooms live. These activities will help you understand more about your students' lives:

- Describe your cultural background and that of your family. Include a description of the community where you grew up.

- Take a walk or drive through your students' neighborhoods. If possible, have a student or parent give you a tour of the neighborhood.

- Attend church or a local festival in the area.

- Try to find out where your students spend their weekends, what stores and neighborhood spots they regularly visit, and the heroes and leaders important to their families and neighbors.

- Find out where your students go after school. Who cares for them? What do they do after they leave the school grounds? If they go to an organized activity such as boys' or girls' clubs, church day care, or after-school programs, spend a few afternoons with them.

Compare and contrast the community where you grew up with the one where your students live. Identify cultural and community factors that should be considered by teachers.

the past decade (National Coalition for the Homeless, 1999). Forty percent of the nation's homeless are families (Shinn & Weitzman, 1996), leaving anywhere from 225,000 to 500,000 of America's children without a home (Kelly, 1993). Homelessness was once considered primarily to be an urban problem, but there are many without homes in rural settings too. Homeless children have poorer health, more learning problems, and may exhibit more behavior problems (Shinn & Weitzman, 1996). Our country has not responded well to providing shelter for homeless families. Many children are shuttled from shelter to shelter, remain hungry and tired, and may not be able to provide birth certificates or other records necessary for school attendance. As a result, teachers are recognizing an increased need to address not only the academic needs of their students but also their social needs.

Even with all the problems confronting America's children, schools can make a difference. Many schools are beginning to work with communities and parents to provide a safe, nurturing environment for all children. Effective schools are reaching out into the community to become a center of learning for all members.

Parent and community involvement and support in schools contributes to students' successful school achievement. When parents are involved, their children earn higher grades and test scores and stay in school longer. The performance of all children in the school tends to improve when parents are involved in a variety of ways at school. The more the relationship between families and school approaches a comprehensive, well-planned partnership, the higher the student achievement (Berla & Henderson, 1994). Strong community support and involvement is necessary for schools to begin to address the variety of problems and needs facing the children they serve. A comprehensive discussion of parent and family involvement can be found in Chapter 10.

Diversity in Our Schools

Our schools have not seen so many immigrants enter their doors since the beginning of the twentieth century. Today, one in five children comes from an immigrant family. With the faces in our nation's schools changing dramatically,

The children in today's classrooms represent a wide range of cultural, ethnic, and religious diversity. Elementary children's representations of their own faces illustrate the diversity that today's teachers will find in their classrooms.

Becoming a Teacher in a Field-Based Setting

cultural diversity is having a profound impact on educational needs. Currently, 35 percent of U.S. students are members of a minority group, and by 2040 more than 50 percent of our children will be from minority groups (Olson, 2000). Hispanics are the largest minority group, and by 2025 nearly one in four students will be of Hispanic origin. More than 150 languages are spoken in schools across our country, and the number of children identified as having limited fluency in English doubled between 1993 and 2000.

Immigrant minorities come to the United States for economic gain, more personal or political freedom, and an overall better lifestyle. Historically, Germany, Italy, Ireland, the United Kingdom, the Soviet Union, Canada, and Sweden sent the most immigrants to the United States, but the growing number of immigrants from other regions of the world is changing our makeup. We are no longer a nation of Europeans. Immigrants now also arrive from Mexico, the Philippines, Korea, China, Taiwan, India, Cuba, and the Middle East. These regions bring to the United States a wide variety of languages, foods, and religions that are far different from the European culture that formerly dominated our society and schools. Many of these immigrants maintain their own cultural identity, enriching the American mosaic.

Cultural and Language Diversity of Students

The changes in culture and language representation make the learning needs of today's students varied and complex. To best meet the needs of all the students in the classroom, teachers must understand how instruction and learning are influenced by culture and language differences (Pang, 2001). Without this vital knowledge, teachers may unknowingly limit the potential achievement for students by prejudicial or ethnocentric practices in the classroom.

Our country is undergoing a dramatic language diversity shift. The number of children who speak English as their second language has doubled since 1980 (Arends, 2000). In the past, the first language of many was one of European origin such as German, Italian, or French. Spanish is now the dominant first language of immigrant children, with Arabic, Vietnamese, Russian, and Tagolog among the many languages represented in our classrooms. The number of children speaking European languages such as Italian, Hungarian, and Polish is decreasing

Children from different countries bring a great deal of diversity to classrooms. In addition to language differences, these children know and understand different geography, clothing, holidays, foods, family interactions, religion, and gender roles. Even their manner of thinking and problem solving may differ from that of their classmates and teachers.

One classroom may include Native Americans, African Americans, Hispanics, Asian Americans, and others, and within these broad categories there are children from many diverse cultural groups. For example, not all Hispanic children represent the same culture. Some may come from Mexico, others from Puerto Rico, and still others from Cuba. Asian American children may represent Chinese, Japanese, Vietnamese, or Indochinese cultures. Each child in the classroom may represent not only a different cultural background but also a different level of assimilation in mainstream U.S. culture. Some of these children may be very much like children who have spent their entire life in this country, whereas others may dress, celebrate, and worship in ways that represent their native cultures.

The differences between the school curriculum and practices and diverse families and communities can cause difficulties for some students. "There is a mismatch between what these children know and can do and what is expected of them by schools that are organized to accommodate and reinforce white, middle-class values, beliefs, and behavior. The social world of the school operates by different rules from the ones these children and their families know and use" (Bowman, 1994, p. 219).

The wide range of cultural differences in the classroom can be used to help all students develop more positive attitudes toward different religions, languages, and ethnic groups. Because of the changing nature of our society, it is important for all Americans to view events and issues from diverse cultural perspectives. Culturally diverse classrooms can serve as a place for everyone to learn about the richness of a multicultural society and the resulting vibrant democracy that can emerge from common understandings and acceptance.

Challenges for Teachers

One of the barriers to success that minority students face is the lack of opportunity to interact with teachers of color. Even though one-third of the classroom population is composed of children from minority groups, little representation of their background and culture will be seen in the teaching staffs of the schools. In the United States, only 13 percent of teachers come from an ethnic or racial minority group. The increasing gap between the cultural backgrounds of teachers and students is critical and may have an impact on children's classroom experiences. With little or no diversity in the teaching profession, the white culture continues to form the basis for most teaching decisions—even though the educational needs of the growing number of students from different cultural backgrounds are not being met through traditional methods. This problem is further

Field-Based Activity 5.2

This exercise can help you identify the range of cultural differences represented in your classroom and compare it with your own experiences. Take a class photo of your students. Locate, or reflect on, a class photo from a classroom you attended when you were a student at approximately the same age. What similarities do you see? What differences? What experiences have you had in your past that might help you relate to today's students?

complicated as students see fewer and fewer role models in the teaching profession that might inspire them to enter the profession in the future.

Teachers, no matter what their ethnicity, are critical to the success of students. Teacher expectations constantly influence classroom interactions and student achievement. Everything in the classroom is filtered through the teacher. Teachers implement the curriculum and select learning strategies for the classroom, drawing on their own background and experiences. Teachers, therefore, must constantly reflect on their teaching habits to discern any prejudicial barriers keeping their students from succeeding. In spite of the fact that many teachers lack a frame of reference in dealing with culturally and linguistically different students, it is possible for them to recognize and accept the differences in the classroom.

Certain classroom practices are particularly relevant in dealing with a wide range of diversity in classrooms. Sensitivity to differences can be represented in something as simple as learning to pronounce names. It may take extra effort to learn the correct pronunciation of names such as Miguel, Chu, Xiou, or Hide, but learning how to say a student's name shows cultural and personal respect. Classroom environments can be enhanced by reflecting the past experiences of all students through literature and examples that are familiar to children from different cultures. Teachers may also need to provide classroom learning opportunities that are responsive to different learning styles. Some students may learn best by working alone, others in cooperative groups, and still others may need more structure. Finally, teachers should also make an attempt to give attention to all students in the classroom. White, middle-class students already receive more attention in curricular materials, so a teacher may need to make an extra effort to provide cultural and linguistic referents that represent a wide range of student backgrounds. Many of the suggestions for working with students of diversity are sound instructional guidelines that are good for all students. Teachers may not completely understand the culture of every child in their classroom, but they can provide a classroom environment built on the foundational belief that all children can learn. In this environment, all children in that classroom will have the chance to succeed.

Societal Changes and Challenges

Children come to school with overwhelming concerns about the world in which they live. They may be unable to concentrate or to see the connection between their world and the world of school. When children leave school at the end of the day, they go home to many different communities with unique challenges and benefits. Some children may go to bed hearing the sounds of gunshots in their neighborhood. Others may spend most of the time away from school in front of a television set. Still others may have many opportunities to interact with people of all ages. Recognizing that children may be dealing with problems or concerns that go beyond the classroom can help teachers meet their educational needs. Teachers who understand the concerns of today's children and young people will be more apt to build classroom contexts that result in student success and empowerment. Poverty, violence, and health care are all important challenges in today's society. Take time now to complete the Self-Reflection exercises and to think about your beliefs.

Self-Reflection

RECOGNIZING YOUR BELIEFS ABOUT POVERTY

Before you read the section on poverty, consider your beliefs about poor families.

Do you believe that . . .	Yes	No	Not sure
individuals in poor families do not have jobs?	_____	_____	_____
not many poor families are white?	_____	_____	_____
poverty is mainly an urban problem?	_____	_____	_____
poor children come from single-parent homes?	_____	_____	_____
poor parents do not provide adequate care for their children?	_____	_____	_____

Becoming a Teacher in a Field-Based Setting

Poverty

Even though the number of children living in poverty has decreased since the high in 1993, the current number is still higher than twenty years ago (Olson, 2000). More children than any other group of people in our country live in poverty. Research has shown that children who live in poverty are much more likely to do poorly in academic areas (Olson, 2000). In fact, a poor child is about twice as likely to be a low-achieving student in the classroom. Poverty is a strong indicator of how well a child will do in school or even how well a school with a high number of poor students will perform (McLaren, 1994). Children—even those who are not poor—who attend schools that have a high percentage of students living in poverty are much more likely to be low achievers in school. In fact, a student who is not poor but who attends a poor school is even more likely to be a low achiever than a poor student in the same school (Olson, 2000).

Teachers in today's classrooms confront poverty in the faces of their students every day, yet most teachers come from a middle-class background with few life experiences to prepare them for the reality of true poverty. Their belief system can be clouded with many myths and misconceptions about children living in poverty. Let's examine some of these myths.

• *Myth #1: Poor families are unemployed and on public assistance.* Two-thirds of poor children under age six live in families where one or both parents work (Olson, 2000), and almost one-third of these families include an adult with a full-time job who still cannot earn enough money to raise the family's income above the poverty line. In reality, most poor families earn more money than they receive from welfare (Sherman, 1994). Many family incomes remain below the poverty line, and the number of "working poor" families who earn less than $16,000 a year is growing.

• *Myth #2: Poverty only exists among minority children.* Poverty is colorblind. There is evidence of child poverty in every race and ethnicity, but the rate of poverty is higher in minorities. African American and Latino children are far more likely to live in poverty than whites. The percentage of poor African American and Latino children is growing, from 47 percent in 1990 to a projected 60 percent by 2015 (Olson, 2000).

• *Myth #3: Poor children live in big cities.* Poverty is usually associated with urban life, but nearly 60 percent of poor preschool children live in suburban and rural areas. The percentage of children living in poverty is growing much faster in the suburbs than it is in urban or rural locations (Olson, 2000). But, poor families and children living in rural areas often also face isolation and other barriers that keep them from getting health care and human support services that are more readily available in the cities.

- *Myth #4: Poor children come mostly from single-parent homes.* Statistics may show that many poor children live in single-parent homes, but almost half of America's poor children and young people live in homes with both parents. If children live in single-parent homes headed by women, there is a 50 percent chance they will live in poverty. Those numbers are even higher with minority children living in single-parent homes headed by women of color (Reed & Sautter, 1990). The average annual income for single-parent homes headed by women is just over $11,000, whereas the average annual income for married couples with children is above $36,000 (Hodgkinson, 1993).

- *Myth # 5: Poor children do not have strong family support systems.* Just because children are poor does not mean that they do not have people who care about them, and many children from single-parent homes have strong family support systems. Parents and caretakers of poor children want their children to be treated fairly, to succeed in school, and to gain skills that will help them work and play successfully. Many of these parents and caretakers see school as particularly important because it is a way out of poverty, and they support their children's academic growth in any way possible.

Teachers' attitudes about children who live in poverty may be influenced by long-held beliefs, many of which may indeed be myths. Crucial differences in teacher expectations and the provision of equal access to learning can be greatly influenced by questioning long-standing beliefs about children and young people's circumstances. Value judgments about children and young people are often based on the teachers' own experiences, which may vary greatly from their students' experiences and values.

Many children overcome great obstacles to succeed in spite of their income level. Teachers who enter classrooms with preconceived ideas about children's abilities based on income will present an even larger obstacle to poor students. Teachers' beliefs that children from low socioeconomic levels cannot learn as well as their classmates can be translated by the teacher, often unknowingly, into everyday classroom practices. Grouping procedures, questioning strategies, and even curriculum choices are all based on teachers' beliefs about students' capabilities for learning. Teachers who believe students from low socioeconomic groups are not able to excel in school may use expectant voice prompting, less interaction, and differential activities and questions. Students internalize these lower expectations into their own self-assessment, and the teacher's beliefs become the students' beliefs as well. Take time now to complete the Self-Reflection exercise and to think about what you have learned.

World Wide Web Site

You may learn more about the impact of poverty on children at:
http://www.childrensdefense.org

Violence

Neighborhoods and communities are no longer as safe for children as they once were. Even though murder rates have fallen in the past several years, far too many children are killed by gunfire, and hundreds are wounded or experience violent crime in some way. Almost one in six students report that they have experienced crime-related incidents on school grounds, and one out of ten high school students admits carrying a gun to school (NEA, 1996). Several recent high-profile incidents have caused the public to consider school violence as a grave concern (Sadker & Sadker, 2000), but, in fact, school violence is on the decline. Children

Gang membership in most towns and cities is declining, but the potential involvement of students is a concern for parents and teachers. Students join gangs to meet a need to belong to a group.

are safer at school than they are in their neighborhoods, and school homicide is uncommon (U.S. Department of Education, 1998).

What may be more important, however, is that students are more fearful of school violence than they were in the past. Schools have responded to public and student concern by establishing very strong policies designed to protect teachers and children. Schools have implemented zero-tolerance rules against students carrying any type of weapon to school, established collaborative programs with communities, and developed school safety plans. Together schools and communities evaluate the problem of violence in their neighborhoods, design interventions, and implement plans that create safer schools. Conflict resolution and peer mediation programs have been implemented by some schools and districts to prevent unavoidable conflict from turning into violence.

Not only are children the victims of violent crimes, but they are also responsible for committing crimes. Juvenile arrests make children the fastest growing criminal population in the United States. Seventy percent of juvenile offenders are released from the justice system only to commit crimes again (Bennett, 1995). Some children live in neighborhoods that are full of crime, and gangs and drug

Becoming a Teacher in a Field-Based Setting

dealers may threaten their safety. All of this affects their state of mind in the class-room, leaving children preoccupied during the day and struggling to remain motivated to learn. Two other forms of violence—gang activity and child abuse—also may have a profound effect on children's success in school and in life.

Gang Activity　People of all ages have a strong need to belong, and gangs are organizations that meet a young person's need to belong to a group. Unlike the benefits associated with some other social organizations, gang life can also lead to crime, drugs, and violence. Gangs, like schools, are in the business of teaching children. Gangs teach students' role relationships and communication styles, and young people learn the rules of the gang quickly in order to be accepted by their peers. Youth gangs can also meet needs for safety, status, and a sense of belonging (National Crime Prevention Council, 1990). Schools, churches, and family can offer positive alternatives, deterring many children from joining destructive groups.

Most experts agree that gang activity among youth is cyclical. During the early 1990s, gang activity was at a high level, but a decrease in crime in general is also reflected in decreased gang activity. Still, gang violence should always be a concern at school, and efforts to care for and attend to disenfranchised youth who are potential gang members should be a focus of school settings. Early intervention with services designed to strengthen family connections is one of the most effective ways to prevent gang violence.

Child Abuse　Another form of violence that can have a profound affect on children is the sad reality of child abuse. Classroom teachers are often the first adults

World Wide Web Site

You may learn more about violence in schools at:

National Alliance for Safe Schools: http://www.safeschools.org/

National School Safety Center: http://nssc1.org/

National Center for Education Statistics: http://nces.ed.gov/pubsearch/

Eric Clearing House on Urban Education: http://eric-web.tc.columbia.edu/

**Michigan State University Libraries, Criminal Justice Resources:
http:// www.lib.msu.edu/harris23/crimjust/gangs.htm/**

to recognize and report abuse, which can be physical, psychological, or sexual. It can be an isolated incident or occur repeatedly over long periods of time. Teachers are in a position to take action, and this responsibility weighs heavily on them. Many incidents of child abuse are reported in the media, but thousands more are reported only by a classroom teacher. Reporting suspected child abuse is a necessary, although difficult, responsibility in the classroom (Fischer, Schimmel, & Kelly, 1999). Teachers worry about the child's safety when reporting the abuse and are often discouraged by the lack of easy solutions to a complex problem. Teachers must also continue to teach these victims, in spite of the circumstances, and help them succeed in the classroom (see Chapter 4).

Health Care

Many children in the United States do not have access to proper health care. According to the most recent census numbers (Newacheck, Brindis, Cart, Marchi, & Irwin, 2000), 10.8 million children eighteen years of age and under lacked health coverage in 1999, and many of these children were from low-income families (incomes less than $26,580 for a family of three in 1999). Although 1.1 million fewer children are uninsured than in 1995, many poor families are still unable to provide private health insurance. Compared with insured children, uninsured children are far less likely to receive medical and dental care and may go without prescription medication or eyeglasses.

One-fourth of all the babies born in the United States receive inadequate prenatal care, and our infant mortality rates are higher than those in twenty-one other developed nations. Nearly 40,000 babies die in the United States each year before reaching their first birthday. In 1992, almost half of all two-year-olds had not been fully immunized against preventable childhood diseases (Children's Defense Fund, 1994), and in a 1991 survey, 21 percent of children in the United States had not seen a doctor in the past year (Plante, 1993). Health conditions, just like economic and family situations, strongly influence a child's readiness to learn. Schools can help by providing connections with health professionals that guide children and families to affordable health care. Three health care concerns that affect the educational achievements of our children are teenage pregnancies, which often cause young mothers to drop out of school entirely, and nutritional deficits and drug abuse, which inhibit classroom learning.

Teenage Pregnancy At an all-time high in the late 1980s, teen pregnancies have continued to decline during the last decade. Even so, the number of births by U.S. teenagers remains high. Approximately 1 million teenagers become pregnant every year (Henshaw, 1997); three-fourths of teenage parents are unmarried and nearly 200,000 are under age eighteen (Ventura, Peters, Martin, & Maurer, 1996). Many young parents, usually females, face multiple challenges as they enter adulthood and strive for self-sufficiency. Research shows that the children of teenage parents are poor and more likely than other children to have illnesses during childhood, experience more and greater developmental delays, and generally be less successful in school (Stephens, Wolf, & Batten, 1999). However, many school programs now offer support to young mothers as they complete their education and go through training to support their children.

World Wide Web Site

An excellent fact sheet, suggestions for ways to prevent teen pregnancy, and help available for teenage mothers can be found at the following Web site: http://www.womenshealthchannel.com/teenpregnancy/index.shtml

Nutritional Deficits   Poor nutrition during any period of childhood can have harmful effects on the cognitive development of children (Tufts University School of Nutrition Policy, 1993). Nutritional deficits have an impact on the behavior of children, their school performance, and their overall learning development. Even relatively short-term deficiencies can affect a child's behavior. A shortage of iron in a child's diet, for example, can have a direct impact on the child's attention span and memory, and yet an estimated one-fourth of all low-income children in the United States currently suffer from anemia. Poor children who attend school hungry are often tired and uninterested in school and perform significantly lower on standardized tests than do children who are not hungry. Poor nutrition, in addition to environmental factors associated with poverty, can permanently inhibit physical growth, brain development, and cognitive functioning. The longer a child's nutritional needs go unmet, the greater the chance for overall learning deficits. Free breakfast and lunch programs are now available at many schools for children whose families may not be able to afford balanced meals.

Drug Abuse   Although substance abuse occurs within all groups and social classes, there is a higher rate of abuse among low-income populations. Despite this trend, few substance abuse programs are available to poor families. Most programs and treatment centers target middle- and upper-class insured substance abusers (Orland, 1994).

The behavior of an addicted parent can have serious long-term consequences for children and youth. Pregnant women who abuse alcohol and other drugs put their unborn children at risk. Children may be born developmentally impaired or addicted to substances such as crack and heroin. Adult drug abuse can affect children in different ways. By the time children reach early adolescence, many have made alcohol and other drugs a part of their life, and this pattern of substance abuse is increasing. In one study, approximately 15 percent of eighth-graders, 25 percent of tenth-graders, and 33 percent of twelfth-graders reported having five or more alcoholic drinks in the past two weeks (Winters, 1999).

Teachers can help identify children from alcoholic or substance abuse homes by watching for behavioral problems in the classroom that may indicate abuse at home (Edwards & Zander, 1985). Children from an alcoholic or substance abuse home can change drastically in personal appearance and health from day to day and exhibit poor attendance and tardiness. They may also exhibit wide ranges of academic performance—one day performing well on academic tasks and the next unable to complete even the simplest assignment. These children may be overly concerned with pleasing adults and are often afraid of parent–teacher interactions. Today many professionals are available to assist teachers when their students are involved with substance abuse. Teachers may help children become aware of the dangers of drug abuse by openly discussing these issues and by offering ways to learn more about the problem.

Gender

Many of today's schools have different expectations for boys and girls (Kohl & Witty, 1996). These differing expectations lead to different school experiences that ultimately guide career choices and perpetuate economic differences between men and women. Girls will often choose to take fewer science and mathematics classes in school, usually completing only the minimum required for graduation. Girls are also more likely to be found in introductory or lower level courses than in advanced courses (Pipher, 1994; Tavris, 1992).

Gender issues continue to confront women in adulthood. Even though women now earn half of the bachelor's and master's degrees awarded in the United States, they remain drastically underrepresented in fields with strong mathematics and technical requirements, opting instead for majors in traditionally female-dominated careers with lower status and less pay (Tavris, 1992). This

Field-Based Activity 5.3

Watch the local television news and collect articles that have to do with the community where your students live. Note politics, conflicts, education, fine arts, sports, and other cultural affairs. How many of these events have an impact on your students' lives? Develop a map that illustrates where in the community events occur. Does this provide you with any additional information about your students' environments?

discrepancy is also seen in the workplace with women currently representing less than 5 percent of the engineers and scientists in the United States.

Females make up the only group of students who enter school ahead—with higher achievement scores than males in all academic subjects—and lose ground throughout their school years. How do schools perpetuate unequal opportunities for boys and girls? And what can teachers do to equalize the educational setting for boys and girls? School structure and teacher–student interactions are two important factors that relate to differences in achievement between boys and girls.

The average female student in the classroom is simply ignored—not scolded, not praised—and high-achieving females receive the least attention of all students (Sadker & Sadker, 2000). Even though girls traditionally learn verbal and math skills and develop small motor skills quicker and much earlier than their male classmates, schools are structured around the development of male students. The introduction of material, such as when students learn to write in cursive or read books or learn long division, is traditionally based on the readiness of the boys in the classroom. Girls, waiting to be challenged, can become bored. Girls also learn to hold back their answers and wait quietly for boys to reach their level of understanding (Pipher, 1994; Tavris, 1992).

Sadker and Sadker (1986, 1993) found that boys received significantly more responses from teachers than did girls—especially responses intended to help correct a student, such as praise and criticism. Boys were also able to gain the

World Wide Web Site

You may learn more about gender issues from the American Association of University Women at: http://www.aauw.org

teacher's attention by calling out responses. In fact, boys in elementary and secondary schools were eight times as likely as girls to call out responses in class, demanding the teacher's attention and response. In comparison, when girls called out responses, teachers corrected the response with a behavioral comment to remind the girls to raise their hand and wait to be called on, relegating girls to a role of passive observers of the academic interactions in the classroom.

Teaching approaches can offset girls' and boys' reactions to classroom instruction. "The most valuable resource in a classroom is the teacher's attention. If the teacher is giving more of that valuable resource to one group, it should come as no surprise if that group shows greater educational gains. The only real surprise is that it has taken us so long to see the problem" (Sadker & Sadker, 1986, p. 514).

Learning Disabilities

Children with handicapping conditions and learning impairments are entitled to the same educational opportunities as other children. "Special education" is individualized instruction designed to meet the needs of students with disabilities (Blackhurst & Burdine, 1993). Public Law 94-142 and the Americans with Disabilities Act (ADA) of 1990 state that people with disabilities should be educated in the least restrictive environment and allowed to live, work, and attend school in settings that provide the greatest possible amount of freedom and contact with people who do not have disabilities. With the support of this legislation, special needs students are no longer being separated from regular students but are included in regular classroom settings and in all the activities of the school. This trend toward inclusion has emphasized the growing need for schools to create educational programs that meet individual needs. "Students who have special education needs are only some of the many students who require carefully designed interventions and support to enhance their learning and life situation" (York & Reynolds, 1996, p. 821).

Regular classroom placement of a student with disabilities can have a great impact on the classroom and the teacher. Administrative and family support are important to the successful placement of such students (Villa & Thousand, 1990). Learning specialists can also help ease the transition and provide needed support for the classroom teacher (Margolis & McCabe, 1989). Teachers must be trained in practices and methods that support learning for special education students and must often learn to work together with special education personnel to team-teach classes with special needs students.

Resiliency of Children

Children, no matter what their background, will have challenges to overcome and adjustments to make. Some children must adjust to extremely disruptive events such as divorce or acts of violence. Other children may have to deal with their own or family illnesses. Even children who have a rather stable home life will have some life crises that cause stress in their lives. They may clash with a family member, lose a pet, experience racism, or move from their home.

Children are known to possess qualities that can help them adapt and transform any risk or adversity into a positive experience. When children overcome difficulties and adjust to stress, they are displaying characteristics of resiliency (Bernard, 1995). All children have a capacity for resilience that is activated when certain stressful events occur in their lives. Children who exhibit characteristics of resiliency are able to interact and gain support from others and plan strategies that help them deal with problems. Usually they are self-confident and believe that they can improve their lives. They are hopeful, optimistic, and connected to others (Bernard, 1995).

PHOTODISC

Most children grow up happy. They show a great propensity to overcome hardships and demonstrate resiliency as they adapt to adversity and transform risks.

Several characteristics that can be established in schools, homes, churches, and the community can foster child resiliency (Heath & McLaughlin, 1993; Weis & Fine, 1993). The first is that there is at least one person who cares for the child. Positive role models should never be underestimated, and a favorite person can be a confidant and serve as an example for personal identification. A teacher can fill this role in the everyday processes of teaching and learning. Student support systems also provide support to children under stress. The teacher who works to create a caring classroom community will provide children with many options for caring support.

High expectations also contribute to resiliency among children (Heath & McLaughlin, 1993; Weis & Fine, 1993). Children and young people develop resiliency if they believe they are worthwhile, and high expectations contribute to their belief in themselves. Schools and teachers are able to communicate high expectations through curriculum that is challenging and meaningful. The learners understand why they are learning and why it is important. A curriculum built on the diversity of learning styles enables each student to depend on his or her strengths and is an important way to foster child resiliency. Flexible learning opportunities enable students to meet expectations and perform well in school.

Finally, opportunities for participation in activities and involvement with others contribute to resilience in children (Heath & McLaughlin, 1993; Weis & Fine, 1993). Children and young people feel respect and care when they work with others. Being a member of a group and finding ways for all children to contribute to ongoing activities foster traits of resilience. Schools and teachers can help children and young people develop the skills that are needed for them to cope with stress in their lives.

Providing Equal Educational Access to Learning

One of the fundamental goals of the U.S. education system is to educate all children. Despite all our attention toward this goal, disparities in measured opportunities to learn are many times greater in our country than in some other countries (Darling-Hammond & Ancess, 1995). The United States has attempted to educate a wide range of students in public schools for a very long time. Our schools have traditionally provided good experiences and opportunities for some, but they have delivered greatly different experiences to others. Providing vastly different experiences for children results in a group of people in our country who consistently have fewer opportunities than others. Many factors contribute to the social dilemma of educational inequity. Differences in school funding, the number of children who live in poverty in a given school district, different levels of excellence in teacher training and teaching, and troubled schools and families make the inequities in education of children and youth major issues in today's society. To provide access to social and technical knowledge, educators must strive to provide equity. Equity is not the same as equality. Equality means that all children are treated the same, regardless of the starting point. Equity means that resources are supplied based on need. To meet the goal of educating all children, those children who have more needs will require more resources.

Although some issues related to equity, such as resource equalization, are beyond teachers' influence, classrooms can provide the flexibility, respect, responsiveness, and rigor that encourage students to achieve (Darling-Hammond & Ancess, 1995). Structures that focus on individuals and make the best of their talents, interests, and past experiences can help educators ensure equity for all students.

Teachers in U.S. schools have never before faced classrooms of learners so varied in abilities, language, social class, and race. Many classrooms include a wide variety of cultures and languages, making the classrooms of today far more diverse than most societies in the world. Yet the expectation of our society remains the same: Teach all children. Teaching all children—with all their differences—requires teachers to develop an equitable classroom climate where all are valued and all are respected.

Successful teachers who are effective with a wide range of differences in students are self-reflective about their own attitudes, beliefs, and actions. They constantly work to recognize and eliminate teacher expectations based on race, class, or gender. Effective teachers provide diversity in instructional activities and classroom environment.

Many children come to our classrooms each day with all the indicators associated with failure, with overwhelming problems that threaten to distract them from learning, and yet they succeed and even excel in an academic setting. Many children from a wide variety of backgrounds and cultures experience few problems with learning within the school context. Within the walls of your classroom, you will meet examples of all of these young people—students with problems to overcome and students who learn easily and quickly. But the mission will be the same: Teach all children. "Suffice it to say that all children must be prepared for responsible participation as citizens and for critical dialogue in the human conversation, and that the pedagogy and stewardship of teachers must embrace all children and young people and the whole of the schools' moral functioning in a social and political democracy" (Goodlad, 1990, p. 186).

Portfolio Reflections and Exhibits

Throughout this chapter you completed a series of field-based activities. They may serve as the basis for a portfolio representation, you may develop your own portfolio representation, or you may complete these suggested portfolio activities.

Suggested Exhibit 5: Determining the Status of the Children You Teach

1. Develop a representation (collage, Venn diagram, computer graphic, picture collection, or written description) contrasting your background with the background of the children in your classroom. Show what is similar and what is different. Illustrate similarities and contrasts between cultures, family structures, neighborhoods, and recreational experiences. Summarize by writing or illustrating how your attitudes have been affected by your past and present experiences. Be sure to include how this knowledge will affect your approach to teaching.

2. Interview one of your student's parents, caretakers, or family members. Ask them about their work, what they like to do in their free time, their own experiences at school, and where their extended families reside. Summarize what you learned from your talk and explain why it is important for teachers to know their students' families.

InfoTrac College Edition Extension

Log on to the InfoTrac College Edition Web site, and use it to find out more about issues related to contemporary children. Choose from the following:

1. Using the keyword search, type in "teaching and cultural differences." Choose an article about cultural differences related to teaching or teacher education that looks interesting to you.

2. Using the subject guide search, type in "poverty." Then choose the View Subdivisions option and select one or more of the following subdivisions: psychological aspects, social aspects, health aspects. Look for articles about families, youth, or children. What do they tell you about the effects of poverty that might influence your teaching?

Related Readings

The following books will provide more information about some of the topics and ideas discussed in this chapter:

Ballenger, C. (1999). *Teaching other people's children: Literacy and learning in a bilingual classroom*. New York: Teachers College Press.

> *This book describes Ms. Ballenger's efforts to teach children who do not share her cultural background. She describes how she listened to and learned from children. She explains how even the time-honored teaching strategy of reading aloud to young children can be challenged in culturally diverse classrooms.*

Carger, K. L. (1996). *Of borders and dreams: A Mexican American experience of urban education*. New York: Teachers College Press.

> *This story of Alejandro, a Mexican American youth growing up in a West Side Chicago neighborhood, describes the struggles and frustrations of bilingual and bicultural children in urban schools. Ms. Carger works with the family to help improve Alejandro's chances in the public school system but finds that even those who understand the system can be frustrated by its bureaucracy.*

Kozol, J. (1991). *Savage inequalities: Children in American schools*. New York: HarperCollins.

Kozol, J. (1995). *Amazing grace*. New York: Crown.

> *Both of Kozol's books are sobering descriptions of poor children's lives. In Savage Inequalities he describes the results of limited resources on several inner-city school districts. Amazing Grace describes the day-to-day lives of some of the poorest children in our country. Neither of these books is particularly uplifting, but both present some realities that middle-class Americans need to understand.*

Michie, G. (1999). *Holler if you hear me: The education of a teacher and his students*. New York: Teachers College Press.

> *This compelling book tells the story of what it means to be an urban high school teacher. It is told with hope and humor and provides insights about students whose worlds are different from the teacher's world. Michie also helps us hear the voices of his Latino and African American students by having them tell what they learn as students in urban settings.*

References

Arends, R. (2000). *Learning to teach*. New York: McGraw-Hill.

Bennett, W. (1995). What to do about the children. *Commentary, 99*(3), 22–28.

Berla, N., & Henderson, A. T. (1994). *A new generation of evidence: The family is critical to student achievement*. Washington, DC: National Committee for Citizens in Education. (Distributed by the center for Law and Education, 1875 Connecticut Avenue, N.W., Suite 510, Washington, DC 20009.)

Bernard van Leer Foundation. (1995). *Promoting resilience in children*. (Annual Review 1995, no. 3). The Hague, Netherlands: Author. (ERIC Document Reproduction Service No. ED 399076)

Blackhurst, A., & Burdine, W. (Eds.). (1993). *An introduction to special education* (3rd ed.). New York: HarperCollins.

Bowman, B. (1994). The challenge of diversity. *Phi Delta Kappan, 76*(3), 218–225.

Children's Defense Fund. (1994). *CDF report*. Washington, DC: Author.

Csikszentmihalyi, M., & Larson, R. (1984). *Being adolescent: Conflict and growth in the teenage years*. New York: Basic Books.

Darling-Hammond, L., & Ancess, J. (1995). Democracy and access to education. In R. Soder (Ed.), *Democracy, education, and the schools* (pp. 151–181). San Francisco: Jossey-Bass.

Fischer, L., Schimmel, D., & Kelly, C. (1999). *Teachers and the law*. New York: Longman.

Edwards, D., & Zander, T. (1985, December). Children of alcoholics: Background and strategies for the counselor. *Elementary School Guidance and Counseling, 20*(2), 121–128.

Goodlad, J. (1990). *Teachers for our nation's schools*. San Francisco: Jossey-Bass.

Heath, S. B., & McLaughlin, M. W. (Eds.). (1993). *Identity and inner-city youth: Beyond ethnicity and gender*. New York: Teachers College Press.

Henshaw, S. K. (1997). Teenage abortion and pregnancy statistics by state, 1992. *Family Planning Perspectives, 29*(3), 115–122.

Hodgkinson, H. (1993). American education: The good, the bad, and the task. *Phi Delta Kappan, 74*(8), 619–623.

Kelly, D. (1993, March 9). A haven for homeless students. *USA Today*, 10.

Kohl, P. L., & Witty, E. P. (1996). Equity challenges. In J. Silula (Ed.), *Handbook of research on teacher education* (2nd ed., pp. 837–866). New York: Macmillan.

Margolis, H., & McCabe, P. (1989). Easing the adjustment to mainstreaming programs. *Educational Digest, 55*(4), 58–61.

McLaren, P. (1994). *Life in schools: An introduction to critical pedagogy in the foundations of education*. New York: Longman.

National Coalition for the Homeless. (1999). *Who is homeless?* [Fact Sheet #3]. Washington DC: Author.

National Crime Prevention Council. (1990). *Changing perspectives: Youth as resources*. Washington, DC: Author.

National Education Association. (1996). *Safe schools* [NEA action sheet]. Washington, DC: Author.

Newacheck, P. W., Brindis, C. D., Cart, C. U., Marchi, K., & Irwin, C. E. (2000). The unmet health needs of America's children. *Pediatrics, 105*(4), 989–997.

Olson, L. (2000, September 27). Children of change. *Education Week, XX*(4), 30–41.

Orland, M. E. (1994). Demographics of disadvantage: Intensity of childhood poverty and its relationship to educational achievement. In J. I. Goodlad & P. Keating (Eds.), *Access to knowledge: The continuing agenda for our nation's schools* (pp. 43–58). New York: The College Board.

Pang, V. O. (2001). *Multicultural education: A caring-centered, reflective approach.* Boston: McGraw-Hill.

Pipher, M. (1994). *Reviving Ophelia: Saving the selves of adolescent girls.* New York: Ballantine.

Plante, K. L. (1993, February). *The competitiveness and production of tomorrow's workforce: Compelling reasons for investing in healthy children* [Fact sheet prepared for participants in children as capital corporate health policy retreat]. Washington, DC: American Academy of Pediatrics & Washington Business Group on Health.

Reed, S., & Saulter, R. C. (1990). Children of poverty: The status of 12 million young Americans. *Phi Delta Kappan, 71*(10), K1–K12.

Sadker, D., & Sadker, M. (1993). *Failing at fairness.* New York: Scribner.

Sadker, M., & Sadker, D. (1986). Sexism in the classroom: From grade school to graduate school. *Phi Delta Kappan, 67*(7), 512–515.

Sadker, M., & Sadker, D. (2000). *Teachers, schools, & society.* New York: McGraw-Hill.

Sherman, A. (1994). *Wasting America's future: The Children's Defense Fund report on the costs of child poverty.* Boston: Beacon Press.

Shinn, M., & Weitzman, B. (1996). *Homelessness in America: Homeless families are different.* Washington, DC: National Coalition for the Homeless.

Stephens, S. A., Wolf, W. C., & Batten, S. T. (1999). *Improving outcomes for teen parents and their young children by strengthening school-based programs: Challenges, solutions, and policy implications.* Washington, DC: Center for Assessment and Policy Development.

Tavris, C. (1992). *Mismeasurement of women.* New York: Simon & Schuster.

Tufts University School of Nutrition Policy. (1993). *Statements on the link between nutrition and cognitive development in children.* Boston, MA: Author.

U.S. Department of Education. (1998). *Update: Indicators of school crime and safety, 1998.* Washington, DC: National Center for Educational Statistics.

Ventura, S. J., Peters, K. D., Martin, J. A., & Maurer, J. D. (1996). Births and deaths in the United States, 1996. *Monthly Vital Statistics Report, 46*(1), 2. Hyattsville, MD: National Center for Health Statistics.

Villa, R., & Thousand, J. (1990). Administrative supports to promote inclusive schooling. In W. Stainback & J. K. Stainback (Eds.), *Support networks for inclusive schooling: Independent, integrated education* (pp. 201–218). Baltimore: Paul H. Brookes.

Weis, L., & Fine, M. (Eds.). (1993). *Beyond silences voices: Class, race, and gender in United States schools.* New York: State University of New York Press.

Wilwerth, J. (1993, March 1). "Hello? I'm home alone . . ." *Time*, 46–47.

Winters, K. C. (1999). *Treatment of adolescents with substance use disorders: Treatment improvement protocol (TIP) series 32* (DHHS Publication No. [SMA] 99-3283). Rockville, MD: U.S. Department of Health and Human Services, Center for Substance Abuse Treatment.

York, J., & Reynolds, M. (1996). Special education and inclusion. In J. Sikula (Ed.), *Handbook of research on teacher education* (2nd ed., pp. 820–836). New York: Macmillan.

Becoming a Teacher in a Field-Based Setting

CHAPTER 6

Interpreting Classroom Learning Theory

IN THIS CHAPTER

- **Learning as Behavior**
- **Learning as Cognition**
- **Learning as Constructivism**
- **Putting It All Together: Using Behavioral, Cognitive, and Constructivist Theories**

*C*hris should have pointed her station wagon north, toward a greener town where children scored high on Basic Skills Tests in rough proportion to their parents' incomes and years of schooling. But on most of those spring mornings she was eager to get to her room. When she thought of this class now she saw that many were performing very well, better than ever. It was a good class, all in all. . . .*

She'd come hurrying across the parking lot at a quarter to eight always a few minutes behind, overballasted and listing slightly under her bookbag, eyes on the front door. The top math group discovered geometry—first of all, at her direction, in the many angles they'd noticed in the room during daydreamy times: the joints in the metal trim around chalkboards, the intersecting lines of their classmates' legs under desks. The low group had finally finished with division. She had administered a final review test to make sure and when she had gone over the last of the papers in the Teachers' Room, Chris had smiled and said, "I haven't changed Henrietta's attitude. I haven't changed Manny's. They're still going to be as obnoxious as the day is long. But they know long division."

Every child worked, even Robert. Some sat in circles of twos and threes, their voices mingling as they read each other their rough drafts. Others bent over their desks, writing assiduously. . . . Chris thought she saw signs of new progress in grammar, syntax, and consecutive thinking.

—Tracy Kidder, *Among Schoolchildren**

You have probably frequently heard statements such as "teachers are born, not made." The phrase is true to some extent, and it implies that teaching is an art rather than a science. Some teachers seem to have natural abilities and personality traits that cannot be taught—at least not during the relatively brief period of preservice teacher education. Thinking of teaching as solely an art implies that people must be born with the ability to reach and teach children and adolescents or they will not become good teachers. Does this mean you should abandon your desire to teach if you feel that you do not "instinctively" know what to do when you are working with children? The answer is "No."

Fortunately, we know that we can pass on to novice teachers the skills and knowledge that contribute to good teaching. These skills and knowledge form the scientific basis of the art of teaching and often differentiate merely good teachers from great ones (Gage, 1984). Expert teachers draw on this knowledge when planning, making decisions, and implementing instruction. Although we cannot directly teach some of the dispositions associated with our notion of good teachers, such as caring, enthusiasm, or empathy, we can provide experiences that may be more likely to help you develop them. Part of the value of your field-based program lies in the opportunity you have to interact with teachers who possess these qualities.

A large part of the science of teaching is knowledge about the ways humans learn: how we process information, what motivates us to learn, and how learning and motivation change over time and with experience. Understanding how learning takes place helps teachers plan instruction and experiences for students that match their particular needs. Knowledge about how factors such as the type of tasks students perform, interactions with other people, and how attitudes and feelings influence learning enables teachers to reflect about teaching successes and failures. Knowing how previous experiences and learning affect new learning

---

*From *Among Schoolchildren*, by Tracy Kidder (pp. 221, 222). New York: Avon.

Future teachers are often surprised about the long hours spent planning lessons and activities and by the effort it takes to provide feedback and evaluate students' responses.

enables us to tailor our instruction for individuals of different ability levels who may come from different cultures or conditions or speak different languages than we do. Although we teach groups in the classroom setting, individuals learn. Understanding how individual differences relate to human learning makes us better teachers.

As you continue through your program, you will need more and more knowledge about human learning to assist you in planning and implementing instruction, managing groups, and recognizing and addressing individual problems of learning. You may have already taken classes in educational psychology, learning theory, or child and adolescent theory, or you may be planning to study these as you continue in your program. The intent of this chapter is not to replace those courses but to challenge you to think about teaching decisions in relation to what we know about how students learn. Typically, experts in teaching and learning have operated in isolation from each other, resulting in difficulty in applying or even seeing the utility of psychological theory for teaching (Alexander & Knight, 1993). Aside from the educational psychology textbooks provided in courses and often seen by students as unrelated to the real world of classrooms, few teacher education texts draw explicitly on psychological learning theory as a basis for instructional decision making. We have chosen a very limited selection of content in this area to demonstrate how knowledge of learning processes might inform your teaching and to provide a basis for observing and analyzing the classes you see in your field-based program. However, you should not think of this as material you need to "memorize." Use the information to focus your observations and discussions with teachers and your peers. If you are familiar with the content, the application of it in classrooms should make it more personally meaningful. If much of the content of this chapter is new to you, you may want to consider it as a framework for helping you think about teaching and learning during this course and to familiarize yourself with the information you will study in more depth at a later time. The reference section at the end of the chapter lists a number of books and articles about learning and teaching that will be valuable to you as you increase your own scientific basis for the art of teaching.

Meanwhile, these questions will help you focus on the important information in the chapter as you read:

- What do I need to know about how humans learn in general to plan and implement effective instruction for my students?

- What do I need to know about how different conditions outside of the learner and characteristics and traits within the learner influence learning?

- What do the different theories of learning look like when they are used in a classroom?

- How can I combine the different definitions of learning in my teaching so that students learn in meaningful ways?

What we know about learning and its relationship to effective teaching cannot possibly be contained or even summarized in a single chapter in an introductory textbook for students in a field-based program. Many learning theory courses are taught in university classrooms with little contact with schools, students, or teachers. These theories often seem to contradict each other, and you may be left feeling more confused than enlightened. As you read the following sections about different approaches to how students learn, think about your own learning experiences. Do you learn some kinds of information best through more direct methods such as lecture or demonstration? Are there other kinds of learning that you have to experience rather than be told?

You have an opportunity through this course to make learning theories meaningful through observation and application. In this chapter we discuss learning from three perspectives that have been useful to educators as they design and implement instruction. No one theory can explain all types of learning in all kinds

Field-Based Activity 6.1

Think of a learning experience you have had that was particularly powerful. Be prepared to describe the event to one of your classmates. What did you learn? How did you learn it? What were the conditions (the presence or absence of other people, the amount of time it took)? What made it so effective? Now do the same thing for an experience that was not effective for you. What were you supposed to have learned? Describe the event. List the characteristics of successful and not so successful learning experiences. Share the list with your class. Keep these two experiences in mind as you continue to read.

of situations for every learner. The term "learning" has different meanings for different people and for different tasks. However, reflecting on the different theories of learning while planning or troubleshooting and determining when to apply a particular aspect of a theory becomes part of the art of teaching that you will refine with experience.

Learning as Behavior

At first, Javier was doing well in geometry class. Then he got confused and failed a test. Now Javier has difficulty even completing a quiz because his hands shake so badly he can't hold a pencil. His teacher has decided to give him his next test orally after school.

Students in Ms. Gordon's class receive a construction paper "happy face" every time they move quietly from their reading group into center activities. When they have ten or more happy faces, they can trade them for something in the class "store," such as a sticker or school supplies.

A group of four students completes one of Mrs. Smith's learning centers and carefully puts away all materials. As they are doing this, Mrs. Smith says aloud: "Joe, Amy, Juan, and Alicia all get a 'scratch 'n' sniff' sticker because they have returned their center materials to the proper places."

What do all these scenes have in common? They all contain examples of the application of different types of behavioral learning theory in elementary or secondary classes. Behavioral learning theory has exerted considerable influence on educational practices in the United States for almost half a century. You will recognize many of the applications from your own school experiences and will see others as you observe in classrooms.

Behaviorism is not a single theory. There are various types of behavioral learning theory and multiple theorists associated with the approach. Many of the distinctions among the different theorists, although important to other theorists and researchers, do not significantly affect the application of the approach in educational settings. For this reason, we will focus on elements that all behavioral theories share and how these common elements apply to the classroom. When differences in theory result in different implications for teaching, as in the differences between observational learning theory and operant conditioning, we highlight and discuss differences as well.

From a behavioral perspective, learning is a lasting change in observable behavior that occurs as a result of experience. Notice that the definition specifies "lasting change." Random or unintentional behaviors do not indicate that learning has taken place. For example, if a student completes a multiple-choice test using a predictable pattern of responses unrelated to the content of the questions (alternating a, b, c, or d for each answer, for example) and gets 25 percent of the answers correct, we cannot say that the student has learned 25 percent of the material.

All behavioral theories also share an emphasis on observable, measurable behavior. A student may know the answers to all the questions on a test but may not respond to the test. Because we have not observed the behaviors, we cannot say that learning has occurred. According to strict behaviorists, experience that results in learning comes from interactions with the external environment. Changes due to internal mechanisms, such as those attributed to development, would not constitute learning. From a behavioral perspective, learning occurs when the connection between a stimulus (something in the environment) and the response (a behavior) has been strengthened. Learning is conditioning (recognizing relationships or associations between stimuli) and is dependent on reinforcement (something that strengthens the connection) of the stimulus with the response. All behaviorists share these principles, but they sometimes differ on the type and role of reinforcement in conditioning and the stimuli and responses of interest.

Classical Conditioning

The example of Javier at the beginning of this section is illustrative of a type of behavioral theory known as classical conditioning. Pavlov was a brilliant physician who won a Nobel Prize based on his work on digestion. However, his observa-

Field-Based Activity 6.2

Modern advertisements are consistent with classical conditioning principles. For example, when we see an Olympic participant win a gold medal in an event, what kind of emotional response does it evoke in us? Respect? Pride? Awe? A general feeling of well-being? What happens when we repeatedly see that award-winning athlete's picture on a box of cereal? Collect other examples of advertisements that might affect school-age children and share them with your class.

tions on the salivation of dogs in the absence of food initiated research that changed the direction of psychology at the time. Pavlov noticed that caretakers of the dogs he used in experiments rang a bell just before they gave them their food. The dogs eventually began to salivate in anticipation of food even when caretakers rang the bell and did not provide food. Pavlov theorized that the food served as a stimulus that naturally prompted a physiological response, in this case salivation. With repeated presentations of the food (unconditioned stimulus) and the bell (conditioned stimulus) together (contiguity of stimuli), the dogs began to associate the ringing of the bell with presentation of food and reacted to the seemingly dissimilar stimulus in the same manner. The unconditioned response of salivation in reaction to food then occurred as the conditioned response of salivation in reaction to the bell. Furthermore, salivation also occurred for sounds that were similar to the ringing of a bell, such as the sound of a tone or buzzer (generalization). Further research revealed that dogs could be taught to differentiate between similar stimuli (a buzzer or bell) depending on their association with food (discrimination). Association of food with a stimulus strengthened the response, and removal of the food from the stimulus resulted in a gradual weakening of the reaction (extinction).

Although this theory focuses on reflexive behavior, usually emotional and physiological responses to stimuli, it does have some applications to our work with children in classrooms. Javier's uncontrollable shaking of his hands when confronted with his geometry test is related to this theory. Javier's intense anxiety in response to his first failure on a particular geometry quiz now occurs when he attempts any geometry test. The unconditioned stimulus—in this case, the failure—has become closely related to the conditioned stimulus, the testing situation. The emotional anxiety that failure elicits, seen in his shaking hands, now occurs in a test-taking situation. The teacher is attempting to help him succeed by associating test-taking with a less stressful reaction, so he will no longer associate the two occurrences.

Operant Conditioning

Although classical conditioning has only limited application in the classroom because it deals primarily with involuntary reactions, B. F. Skinner's concept of operant conditioning has widespread application. Operant conditioning provides the framework for many of the basic skill development models, classroom discipline approaches, special education interventions, and computer-assisted instruction models used in schools. Skinner was particularly interested in the application of his theory to education, and he became actively involved in translating his work into practice (see, e.g., Skinner, 1954, 1958, 1968).

Operant conditioning focuses on voluntary behavior used in operating on the environment. From this perspective, the stimulus is something in the environment, and the response is the behavioral reaction. Learning occurs when the connections between the environmental stimulus and the voluntary behavior become strengthened through reinforcement. Reinforcement, defined as any consequence of the voluntary behavior that strengthens, or increases, the behavioral response to the stimulus, is contingent on performance of the behavior. Whereas other behaviorists waited for animals to learn through exploration, using the theory passively to explain behavior (e.g., Thorndike, 1913), Skinner actively manipulated the environment to obtain specific kinds of learning. Through the basic mechanisms of positive reinforcement, negative reinforcement, extinction, and punishment, he experimented with increasing or decreasing behaviors (Skinner, 1963, 1969).

Positive reinforcement involves receiving something desired as a consequence of operating in some way on the environment. The behavior increases because the reinforcement is contingent on performance of the behavior. Skinner's research on cats and pigeons indicated that this mechanism is perhaps the most effective way of increasing desired behavior. The keys to effective positive reinforcement include consideration of the degree of desirability of the reinforcer, or its potency, as well as issues of satiation, or "too much of a good thing." Although primary reinforcers, such as food, water, shelter, physical comfort, and affection, are powerful motivators, they may not always have the desired outcome or may not be feasible in instructional settings. Food works best when people or animals are hungry, for example, but withholding food to increase the potency of the reinforcer may present ethical problems in a school setting. Similarly, chocolate may be a child's favorite food, but children may soon tire of a steady diet of chocolate, reducing its potency as a reinforcer.

Secondary reinforcers are objects, gestures, or events that acquire the status of a primary reinforcer through association with that reinforcer. In classrooms, teachers use some primary reinforcements (candy, snacks, hugs), but they most often use secondary reinforcers such as praise or grades. To make sure that a reinforcer is desirable to students and to guard against satiation, teachers also may use systems that enable students to choose their own rewards. Teachers reward students for desired behavior with objects, or tokens, that appear to have little or no value but that can be "traded" by the student for a variety of desirable objects or experiences. The example at the beginning of this section of Ms. Gordon and the construction paper "happy faces" is representative of this type of token system using positive reinforcers.

Negative reinforcement, another mechanism to increase behaviors, involves removing something undesired. The removal of something unpleasant or unwanted, such as electric shock, is contingent on performance of desired behaviors, such as pushing a lever. An animal subjected to electric shock will push a lever as frequently as needed to avoid the shock. Likewise, an American history teacher might promise a class that if students do their homework all week they won't have any homework over the weekend. Students who view weekend homework as something to be avoided will do homework during the week. As with positive reinforcement, student perceptions of the degree of unpleasantness of objects or experiences determine the effectiveness of the negative reinforcer. Students who enjoy doing homework or students who never do homework anyway will not respond as desired. Another difficulty with this approach lies in reinforcing the notion that something like homework, which research indicates results in increased learning for students (Wang, Haertel, & Walberg, 1993), is something students should avoid. Teachers should carefully consider the unintended consequences of negative reinforcement.

A variation of negative reinforcement called the Premack principle (Premack, 1965) has been particularly useful in classrooms. In this approach, students agree to do a less desired behavior so that they will also be able to do a more desired one. For example, a band instructor may tell students that if they do a good job playing one of the classical tunes they are learning they can also play a modern one of their choice. Although playing the classical tune may not be entirely undesirable, playing the modern tune may certainly be more popular with students.

Positive and negative reinforcement increase behaviors, but Skinner determined that other mechanisms decrease behavior. Extinction, or reinforcement removal, eventually extinguishes behavior. For example, students who shout out answers to questions rather than raising their hand eventually should stop shouting out if the teacher does not acknowledge the contributions. However, the classroom is more complex than the laboratories where many of these experiments occurred. Students may continue to shout out if classmates provide

Field-Based Activity 6.3

What kinds of reinforcers do you see teachers in your building using? Ask your teacher how she or he uses reinforcement in the classroom. How do students respond? Share in your discussions what you are seeing, and compare the different methods of positive or negative reinforcement used in your school.

reinforcement by acknowledging the answers or by noticing the aggressive behavior. Although the teacher has removed reinforcement, other students provide reinforcement. Ignoring the inappropriate behavior, enlisting the cooperation of the class in also doing so, and providing positive reinforcement when students raise their hand may all be needed to solve this problem.

Punishment, in the form of painful or undesirable consequences, also decreases behavior. Punishment can be of two types: presentation punishment, which involves receiving something not desired, or removal punishment, which consists of removing something desired. Teachers or administrators who administer corporal punishment are engaging in presentation punishment. A secondary teacher who refuses to allow a student to attend a sixth-period pep rally because the student arrived late for class three days in a row is using removal punishment. An elementary teacher might place a misbehaving student in time-out, removing the student from participation with the rest of the class, as removal punishment. The premise for time-out is that the student sees participation in class as a desirable event and will decrease the incidents that result in the time-out.

Negative reinforcement may be confused with punishment; the important difference lies in the consequences of the particular action. Both negative reinforcement and presentation punishment involve an undesirable object or event. However, the intent of negative reinforcement is to encourage students to perform in a certain way to remove or avoid something undesirable. Reinforcement depends on performance of certain behaviors. Conversely, the intent of presentation punishment is to discourage certain behavior of students by providing a negative consequence or taking away a pleasant one. If the student behaves in a certain way, something unpleasant happens as a result.

Removal punishment differs from both negative reinforcement and presentation punishment because it involves loss of a desirable object or experience. However, teachers may have difficulty determining or controlling something that is desirable to students. One particular kind of removal punishment, response cost, works in conjunction with a positive reinforcement system to remove previously awarded reinforcers when behavior is inappropriate. As adults, we might recognize this approach in fines imposed for traffic violations or library book late returns. Using the example of Ms. Gordon given at the beginning of the section, students in her class might have to forfeit a "happy face" each time they fail to properly return materials.

Some of the examples of types of reinforcement may seem difficult to classify. For example, time-out could be considered negative reinforcement if the teacher makes removal of time-out contingent on some behavior (e.g., student calms down, stops crying or muttering angrily). The intent of this section is not for you to be able to label examples but to consider the examples in relation to teaching. The label merely provides a cue to help you reflect on the purposes and consequences of your actions and those of your students. With that proviso, can you figure out whether the following example is negative reinforcement, removal punishment, or presentation punishment?

Each third-grade student in Ms. Gordon's class starts the day with three Popsicle sticks. Each time a student misbehaves, she takes one of the Popsicle sticks away. If a student loses all three Popsicle sticks in one day, the student has to remain after school with Ms. Gordon.

Will Ms. Gordon's actions increase or decrease the misbehavior of students? Are the Popsicle sticks representative of something desired or undesired? What is the consequence of misbehavior? Is it pleasant or unpleasant? How would this be different if Ms. Gordon did not use the Popsicle sticks and just had students remain with her after school when they misbehaved? Would one approach be better than the other? Ms. Gordon's actions will affect student behavior, but the outcomes are complex.

Although some kinds of punishment can be very effective in decreasing undesirable behaviors, the side effects of punishment often make it less than effective for teachers. Punishment does not deal with the reasons or desires associated with misbehavior and may only suppress the behavior for as long as the punishment is in place. Students may expend more effort in "not getting caught" than in behaving appropriately and may continue to engage in negative behaviors when the teacher is "not looking." Even if students want to engage in appropriate behavior, punishment rarely provides any indication of what students should do or why the behavior is inappropriate, and it may cause resentment, particularly when physical punishment is used, which leads to further problems. The form of punishment used also may have unintended consequences. Giving extra schoolwork as punishment conveys that schoolwork is undesirable. This may reduce certain kinds of negative behavior, but it will not increase the kinds of positive behavior encouraged in most classes.

Certain patterns or schedules of reinforcement are more effective for some purposes than for others. Reinforcement schedules can be either continuous, which means that a desired response receives reinforcement every time it occurs, or intermittent, which involves reinforcement of desired responses periodically. Continuous-reinforcement schedules are most effective for encouraging development of new skills or knowledge. For example, an algebra teacher may demonstrate the steps involved in solving simultaneous equations and have students work with her. After each step, the teacher praises students liberally for correctly executing the step with her. This serves to give students feedback about their performance and strengthens correct performance at an early stage of skill learning. The opportunity for strengthening incorrect performance is less likely because the task has been broken down into small parts and students receive feedback about performance on each part before continuing to the next part.

When students have advanced somewhat in their skill development, however, an intermittent schedule becomes more effective. Two types of intermittent schedules exist: ratio and interval. Ratio-intermittent schedules depend on the number of times a response occurs and can be either fixed or variable. Fixed-ratio schedules provide reinforcement after a certain number of desired responses. For example, our algebra teacher might announce to the class that as soon as students have correctly done five problems in a row they can start on their homework assignment, with the possibility of finishing it by the end of class. A variable-ratio reinforcement schedule also relies on a certain number of correct responses prior to reinforcement, but that number varies in a way that is difficult for students to predict. In this schedule, students might have to finish only two problems on some days prior to beginning homework, five on others, or the entire set on others. The intent of the teacher would be to keep them working steadily because they never know how many problems they will have to have completed before they can start their homework.

Intermittent-interval schedules are time, rather than number, dependent and can also be either fixed or interval. That same algebra teacher might announce that all worksheets will be taken up on Friday each week for a grade, setting a fixed interval for reinforcement. The danger inherent in this schedule is that students will wait until just prior to the time for reinforcement to do their work. Teachers, if they are not aware of the consequences of employing fixed-interval reinforcement schedules (or even not aware that that is what they are using), may complain that students "wait until the last minute to do their work." Students, however, are responding in a manner consistent with the reinforcement schedule the teacher has chosen. To obtain different responses, another type of schedule should be used.

A variable-interval schedule is also time dependent, but reinforcement occurs at varying, rather than fixed, intervals. The teacher using this schedule would take up worksheets for a grade at different times during the week. If the grade on these assignments is important to students, then students will keep up with daily work, not knowing when the teacher may choose to grade them. If the teacher wants students to spread their effort out evenly over a period of time rather than waiting until just prior to reinforcement, a variable-interval schedule is more effective. In general, variable-reinforcement schedules, in particular variable-ratio schedules, are more effective at sustaining student effort during tasks.

Look at the following example and try to determine what kind of schedule is being used:

> *A Spanish teacher uses a deck of cards with students' names on them as a strategy for calling on all students. She goes through the deck one-by-one to make sure everyone has an opportunity to speak.*

What are the advantages and disadvantages of this schedule? Would another schedule be more effective? If so, what could the teacher do so that she can still use the deck of cards but employ a different reinforcement schedule? The use of cards illustrates one method of reinforcing student behavior, and there are several reasons it will be successful.

Understanding and being able to use reinforcement schedules provides teachers with a means of managing individual and class behavior (see Chapter 7). Teachers can also use four processes associated with operant conditioning—shaping, chaining, cueing, and fading—to understand how students acquire complex skills and to design instruction to help them learn skills. *Shaping* involves reinforcing successive approximations of a desired behavior until students can produce the behavior. For example, if a teacher wants students to write a paragraph, the teacher might initially reward students for even taking out paper and pencil. As students move closer to mastering the target behavior, the teacher eliminates rewards for the approximate behaviors. How would you use shaping to solve the following problem?

> *Mr. Smith usually gives his sixth-grade students math assignments in class to provide an opportunity for guided practice. When given an assignment of ten problems containing fractions, Avery put his head down on his desk and moaned, "I can't do this!"*

Chaining involves integrating the component skills of a complex skill or task. Behavioral theory dictates that complex behaviors be broken down into their component parts so that each part can be taught and reinforced. To shape behavior, teachers must first understand the smaller steps or component skills that make up a more complex behavior and then break the task down for students. However, to accomplish integrated performance of the behavior rather than performance of a series of component skills, the components must ultimately be linked. A common mistake in classrooms is the conviction that if we teach the subcomponents to students they will automatically be able to integrate them.

Cueing and *fading* also play important roles in teaching and learning complex skills. Skinner found that pigeons could learn when to perform behaviors by discriminating certain cues in the environment. Reinforcement occurred in the presence of some cues but not others. For example, Skinner's pigeons "danced" in the presence of some kinds of light sources but not in others. Similarly, a red light at an intersection cues us to put on the brakes; a green light cues us to press the gas pedal. Likewise, students in classrooms are cued to appropriate behavior by teachers' direct statements ("Remember, no talking while another student is reading"), physical presence or movements (walking up and down the aisles during seatwork cues students to work on assignments), nonverbal expressions (frowns or raised eyebrows), or other signals (flipping the lights on and off to signal a change of activities). Although teachers often use cues purposively, they are sometimes unaware of the cues they give or the way students interpret them. For example, a teacher may want students to engage in deep processing of the text they are reading but may not give them adequate time to do so. The amount of time given becomes a cue that students use to judge whether they should read at a surface level or for deeper meaning (Knight, 1990; Knight, Waxman, & Pedrone, 1989).

One of the ultimate goals of schooling is to enable students to become independent learners. Fading is one process that can be used to accomplish this goal. If students perform academically only in the presence of certain teacher-controlled cues, they will not perform when the teacher is no longer present. Therefore, controlling cues need to be gradually withdrawn while at the same time continuing to reinforce the behavior. For example, a teacher who cues students to engage in interactive discussion of readings by standing in front of the whole group and asking thought-provoking questions about the text might gradually diminish her presence as the cue by having other students take over the role of "teacher" (see, e.g., Palincsar & Brown, 1984).

Observational Learning

Operant conditioning has provided teachers with an understanding of many classroom behaviors and with mechanisms for changing student behaviors. Nevertheless, the theory fails to account for learning in the absence of direct

Teaching is more than standing in front of a classroom. Children learn from observing teachers and modeling is an important teaching strategy.

experience. We know that some students learn behaviors that were not directly reinforced. Bandura (1982) proposes a variant of conditioning that explains this phenomenon. From his perspective, students learn new behaviors or continue to perform existing behaviors through vicarious conditioning. They watch others and observe the consequences of their behavior. The example at the beginning of this section of the scratch 'n' sniff stickers awarded to a group of students is an attempt by the teacher to obtain similar behavior by others in the classroom. The four students receive positive reinforcement from the teacher. The remaining students have observed this and are likely to perform similarly if they also have hopes of obtaining stickers.

Depending on the status of the model and the conditions of reinforcement, modeling serves to (1) focus attention on behavior or aspects of behavior, (2) change inhibitions that observers might have about performing certain behaviors, and (3) arouse emotions. Students may learn from models directly by attempting to imitate a model's behavior, as when a kindergarten student makes a "B" sound after the teacher demonstrates the sound. Students may also learn in less direct ways. Symbolic modeling refers to imitating behaviors displayed by fictional characters in books, movies, or television. Although this may be harmless, as when teens dress like popular TV personalities, some educators fear that televised violence may prompt aggressive behavior on the part of students. Students may also develop behaviors by synthesis, or combination, of parts of observed behaviors. For example, teens may combine movements they have seen two different rock stars use to create a new dance step. Abstract modeling is even more complex and involves extraction of rules or patterns from observing different examples. For example, by observing the speech patterns of the teacher or the models on tape, students taking Spanish may learn that adjectives usually follow nouns.

For observational learning to happen, however, certain characteristics must be present (see, e.g., Schunk, 2000). Students must relate or feel some degree of similarity to the model and must perceive that they are capable of performing the behaviors. For example, misbehavior of a well-liked classmate that goes unchallenged in the classroom may result in similar incidents of misbehavior by others in the class. Likewise, rewards for desired behavior to one classmate may result in an increase in the same kind of behavior by other students. However, a person must feel capable of performing the behavior. A short person might relate to Michael Jordon and observe the accolades that he receives for his slam dunk of the basketball. Nevertheless, the person who is five feet three inches tall, with no hope of growing taller, might not perceive that he or she is capable of ever performing a slam dunk and therefore might not play basketball.

Several processes determine the success of modeling as a classroom strategy. Observers first must attend to the desired behavior and retain it in memory so they can subsequently perform it. Then they must reproduce the behavior. Finally, they must be motivated to performance of the behavior. Motivation, in this case, refers to the reinforcement received by the model for performance. If the observer does not view the reinforcement as desirable, motivation to perform will be low. For example, middle school students may not view a teacher's public praise of a fellow student's assistance with chores in the classroom as desirable. For this reason, they would not assist the teacher for fear of receiving similar praise. Look at the following example and try to identify the processes involved in observational learning:

> *A ninth-grade English teacher passes out graded essay exams. She then places one of the answers copied onto a transparency on the overhead projector. She says: "Look at the answer one of your classmates wrote [no name appears on the example]. I gave this an A grade. Let's look at it together and see why. First notice the thesis sentence . . ."*

What does the teacher do to enable her students to learn from the example? How does she focus attention? What reinforcement does she provide? Would students likely be motivated to reproduce this behavior? Why or why not?

Educators often fear that sports or music heroes who behave in an immoral or unethical manner but retain their standing and wealth in society may reinforce undesirable behaviors by our youth. Because identification with the model is an important aspect of vicarious conditioning, the shortage of females and minorities in certain professions also becomes a source of concern to educators who want to raise the aspirations of underrepresented groups.

Applying Behavioral Theory in the Classroom

Behavioral learning theory has had considerable impact on the strategies teachers use in classrooms because it provides tools for planning for instruction, teaching skills and knowledge, managing student behavior, and assessing the effectiveness of teachers' classroom behaviors. Planning tools include guidelines for formulating behavioral objectives that explicitly describe the observable, measurable behavior targeted, the conditions under which this behavior will be performed, and the criteria by which success will be judged. In addition, behavioral theory contributes procedures for task analysis to aid teachers in breaking down tasks into sequential, component skills that they can teach by using shaping and chaining processes. The creation of token economies, use of the Premack principle, and adherence to appropriate reinforcement schedules, all described previously, enable teachers to strengthen desired behaviors.

Rosenshine's Direct Instruction Model

The teaching model presented in Figure 6.1 has been used extensively in the classroom and as a basis for evaluation of teachers. The model's teaching functions are consistent with behavioral learning theory. Look at each of the functions. What principles that you have read about in this section are embedded in these functions? What kinds of outcomes would use of this model be likely to facilitate in students?

World Wide Web Site

You may learn more about direct instruction at: http://www. parentscoalition.org/resources/fact-sheets/directinstruction.htm

Figure 6.1   Teaching Functions

1. *Daily Review and Checking Homework*
   Check homework (routines for students to check each other's papers).
   Reteach when necessary.
   Review relevant past learning (may include questioning).
   Review prerequisite skills (if applicable).

2. *Presentation*
   Provide short statement of objectives.
   Provide overview and structuring.
   Proceed in small steps but at a rapid pace.
   Intersperse questions within the demonstration to check for understanding.
   Highlight main points.
   Provide sufficient illustrations and concrete examples.
   Provide demonstrations and models.
   When necessary, give detailed and redundant instructions and examples.

3. *Guided Practice*
   Initial student practice takes place with teacher guidance.
   High frequency of questions and overt student practice (from teacher and/or materials).
   Questions are directly relevant to the new content or skill.
   Teacher checks for understanding (CFU) by evaluating student responses.
   During CFU, teacher gives additional explanation or process feedback, or repeats explanation—where necessary.
   All students have a chance to respond and receive feedback; teacher ensures that all students participate.
   Prompts are provided during guided practice (where appropriate).
   Initial student practice is sufficient so that students can work independently.
   Guided practice continues until students are firm.
   Guided practice is continued (usually) until a success rate of 80 percent is achieved.

Use of behavioral theory for assessment of the effects of instruction provides teachers with a means of improving their own teaching and assisting others in improvement. The focus on observation and measurement of observable behaviors has resulted in a number of behavior checklists or observation instruments that can be used by teachers in their own classrooms or in the classrooms of their

4. *Correctives and Feedback*

Quick, firm, and correct responses can be followed by another question or a short acknowledgment of correctness (e.g., "That's right").

Hesitant correct answers might be followed by process feedback (e.g., "Yes, Linda, that's right because . . .").

Student errors indicate a need for more practice.

Monitor students for systematic errors.

Try to obtain a substantive response to each question.

Corrections can include sustaining feedback (i.e., simplifying the question, giving clues), explaining or reviewing steps, giving process feedback, or reteaching the last steps.

Try to elicit an improved response when the first one is incorrect.

Guided practice and corrections continue until the teacher feels that the group can meet the objectives of the lesson.

Praise should be used in moderation, and specific praise is more effective than general praise.

5. *Independent Practice (Seatwork)*

Sufficient practice.

Practice is directly relevant to skills/content taught.

Practice to overlearning.

Practice until responses are firm, quick, and automatic.

Ninety-five percent correct rate during independent practice.

Students alerted that seatwork will be checked.

Student held accountable for seatwork.

Actively supervise students, when possible.

6. *Weekly and Monthly Reviews*

Systematic review of previously learned material.

Include review in homework.

Frequent tests.

Reteaching of material missed in tests.

Source: Rosenshine, B., & Stevens, R. (1986). Teaching functions. In M. C. Wittrock (Ed.), *Handbook of research on teaching* (3rd ed., pp. 376–391). New York: Macmillan. Reprinted by permission of the Gale Group.

peers (see, e.g., Good & Brophy, 1999). The use of instruments that simply record behavior, without providing an inference or judgment, provide objective data about students as well as nonthreatening data about teacher behaviors. Teachers can use the data in reflection about their own practice, in teacher research, in peer coaching, or to identify and resolve instructional and managerial problems in the classroom. The Interactive Seating Chart in Figure 6.2 is one example of an instrument designed to provide teachers with information about teacher and student behavior.

Learning as Cognition

Mr. Garcia is teaching the concept of density to his science students. He provides groups of students with a number of different types of clear liquids (e.g., water, alcohol) and a bucket of ice cubes. He asks students to drop ice cubes in each of the liquids, record what happens, and discuss their findings in groups. Many students are surprised to find that the ice cubes float in some liquids but sink to the bottom in others. The next day he engages the entire class in a discussion of their findings and elicits their theories concerning the experiment.

Ms. Lee teaches secondary economics. Prior to beginning a series of lectures on international trade, she describes the different kinds of bartering for playthings that might take place among children at a playground and relates this to some of the concepts they will encounter in her lectures.

Mr. James is teaching his fifth-grade students about the Civil War. He puts a chart on the overhead projector that has Political Beliefs, Social Beliefs, and Economic Beliefs as column headings, and Northern Leaders and Southern Leaders as row headings. He assigns groups of students to gather information about each of the cells in the chart and to fill them in. During the discussion following the group work, they look for similarities and differences in the two groups and predict how that might affect the struggle. Mr. James also encourages the class to change the chart to better capture the information they have gathered.

What do all these examples have in common? Each vignette provides an example of a different type of cognitive theory about how people learn. As was true for behavioral theory, cognitive theory consists of many different approaches. However, they all share certain underlying principles that make them look somewhat alike when they are applied to classroom instruction. In addition, they all differ from behavioral theory in ways that are evident in classroom applications as well. As was true for behavioral learning theories, this section will review only a few of the many cognitive learning theories that might help you make decisions about instruction. In addition, we will discuss how these theories are similar and different from one another and how they are different from behavioral learning theories in their application. Then we will provide a rationale for using both in the classroom, depending on the kinds of student outcomes you want.

Figure 6.2 Interactive Seating Chart

This chart provides a means for recording student and teacher interactions in the classroom. To use it, first familiarize yourself with the codes for certain behaviors listed at the top of the chart. Then make a seating chart for students in a class you plan to observe. Using the codes provided, record next to the names of students on the chart the type of interaction each has with the teacher as it occurs.

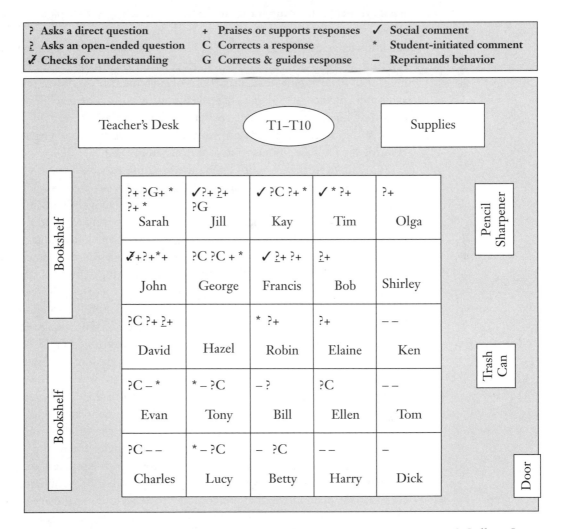

?	Asks a direct question	+	Praises or supports responses	✓	Social comment
?	Asks an open-ended question	C	Corrects a response	*	Student-initiated comment
✓	Checks for understanding	G	Corrects & guides response	–	Reprimands behavior

Teacher's Desk   T1–T10   Supplies

Bookshelf

?+ ?G+ * ?+ * **Sarah**	✓?+ ?+ ?G **Jill**	✓ ?C ?+ * **Kay**	✓ * ?+ **Tim**	?+ **Olga**
✓+?+*+ **John**	?C ?C + * **George**	✓ ?+ ?+ **Francis**	?+ **Bob**	**Shirley**
?C ?+ ?+ **David**	**Hazel**	* ?+ **Robin**	?+ **Elaine**	– – **Ken**
?C – * **Evan**	* – ?C **Tony**	– ? **Bill**	?C **Ellen**	– – **Tom**
?C – – **Charles**	* – ?C **Lucy**	– ?C **Betty**	– – **Harry**	– **Dick**

Bookshelf

Pencil Sharpener

Trash Can

Door

Source: Stallings, J. A. (1997). *Learning to teach in inner city schools training manual.* College Station: Texas A&M University, College of Education.

Comparing Behavioral and Cognitive Approaches

Earlier, we discussed some common features of behavioral learning theory. All shared an emphasis on observable, measurable behavior and the importance of reinforcement in the strengthening desired behaviors. From this perspective, teachers need to break tasks, skills, and knowledge into smaller components and teach and reinforce performance of component behaviors. Repetition or practice of these component skills is a key feature of most of the models drawing on behavioral theory. In many ways, the learner emerges as rather passive, reacting to the environment in ways that respond to the reinforcement received. Behaviorists see knowledge as learned patterns of associations and define learning as acquiring new associations. Applications derived from this theory will be particularly helpful in determining basic classroom management procedures, teaching basic skills and knowledge, and teaching psychomotor skills. The teacher's role consists of arranging the environment so that students make the desired associations. Because motivation depends on external reinforcement for behavior, extrinsic rewards such as food, money, and grades are important.

Cognitive learning theories view the learning process from a very different perspective (see, e.g., Phye & Andre, 1986). They focus on covert activities of the mind rather than on overt behaviors. The learner actively tries to understand what is going on in the environment rather than passively responding to associations between stimuli and responses. Cognitivists define knowledge as organized sets of mental structures and procedures and learning as the change in these mental structures brought about through mental reasoning. Students do not merely receive information—they construct knowledge by incorporating new information into existing knowledge. This may require them merely to add on to existing knowledge or to change either the existing or the new knowledge in some way. (This may sound familiar to those of you who have studied child development; Piaget's conceptions of assimilation and accommodation describe these processes.) When students alter incoming information to fit with what they already know, misconceptions often occur. Applications from this theory emphasize the active role of the learner in exploring the environment and tend to focus on learning complex skills and knowledge. The role of the teacher consists of providing students with opportunities to explore their environment and facilitate this discovery. Because motivation is related to the need for learners to make sense of their world, intrinsic rewards connected with successful problem solving, accounting for phenomena that are contrary to expectations, and accomplishment of tasks are important in this theory. The experiment with the ice cubes and the liquids described in the vignette about Mr. Garcia's science class should be intrinsically motivating to students because they observe a puzzling situation that they cannot initially explain.

Experienced teachers learn how to use numerous teaching and learning strategies and will select activities that motivate their students and meet individual needs.

Traditional Cognitive Theory

Traditional cognitive learning theory has often been associated with discovery learning, but discovery is not a requisite element of applications of this approach. The issue is how to make learning meaningful. Two cognitivists who have had considerable influence on elementary and secondary classrooms disagree about how meaningful learning occurs, but they concur that the emphasis should be on meaningful understanding of the substance of material rather than on verbatim recall. They both accentuate the importance of seeing relationships among ideas, learning generalizable concepts and principles, and organizing information both in written and oral text as well as in the mind of the learner.

However, Jerome Bruner (1966) advocates student discovery of concepts and principles through experiences in which the student observes specific instances of the concept or principle. In other words, he suggests that students engage in more meaningful learning when it is accomplished inductively. The way Mr. Garcia "teaches" density to his science students is an example of discovery learning in which students inductively discover scientific principles through exploration of specific instances.

David Ausubel (1968) advocates presentation of information to students in a deductive manner, often referred to as reception learning. In other words, students should be able to infer specific instances from a general principle or rule presented by a teacher during lectures or text. The key to making learning meaningful lies in enabling students to connect new information with what they already know rather than merely memorizing information. He counters Bruner's assertion about discovery learning by claiming that both discovery learning and reception learning can be either rote or meaningful depending on students' ability to connect the new learning to something they already know. From this perspective, rote discovery learning is just as likely to occur as rote reception learning without specific attention to meaning. For example, have you ever participated in a science lab experiment in which you were able to fill in the blanks of the lab sheet but had absolutely no idea what you were supposed to have "discovered"? Discovery learning can require a great deal of time and effort and often results in mere rote learning or the discovery of incorrect principles. To overcome this problem, Ausubel suggests incorporating advance organizers in lectures or texts to enable students to make connections during the more efficient reception learning.

Advance organizers present information at a higher level of abstraction than will be utilized later, so that subsequent subordinate concepts can be incorporated in the more general concepts presented in the organizer. The organizer uses language that is easy for learners to understand. In the work of Ausubel, advance organizers generally take the form of shorter, more abstract readings or oral summaries prior to a lecture or reading, but other research has supported the use of concrete models, analogies, examples, organizing principles or rules, and discussion of primary themes (Mayer, 1983). In the vignette presented at the beginning of this section, Ms. Lee used the playground analogy as an advance organizer for the less familiar concepts and principles to be introduced in her international trade lecture. Graphic organizers such as Venn diagrams, wherein two overlapping circles illustrate common features, or webbing, in which circles connected by lines illustrate relationships, may achieve the same objectives.

Cognitive Information Processing Theory

One of the most useful approaches to learning is also one of the most recent. Based on cognitive theory but with several elements compatible with behavioral theory (including an attempt to make covert processes overt so they can be observed and measured), cognitive information processing (CIP) theory uses the computer as its model for how humans process information. CIP theorists (there are actually various theories, but for the sake of simplicity, they will be treated in this section as one) are interested in how humans acquire, store, and retrieve information. Examination of mental structures and processes has implications for the design of effective instruction and may help us better understand instructional failures as well.

Early theory characterized the human mind as a multistore model that was selective in the type of information acquired and stored (Klatzky, 1980). Although this theory has been replaced with other, more current theories, the implications for instruction remain similar. Data from our environment enters our sensory register (SR) through our various senses. However, due to the sheer volume of environmental data, we understandably must screen and reduce these data. Teachers can help ensure that students attend to desired information by providing visual and verbal cues that some information is more important than other information. Cues such as "Listen carefully to the following because . . ." or underlining or highlighting important information on overheads or on the board help focus attention. Discrepant events also attract our attention because we tend to try to make sense of our world. Mr. Garcia's ice cube experiment would tend to direct student attention to the behavior of ice cubes in liquids because they behave in a manner inconsistent with our typical experience with ice in water.

Despite their utility, external cues are not sufficient to focus attention. What we attend to in the environment is influenced by our previous experiences as well as by the context of the situation. The tendency for humans to try to make new information meaningful may result in different perceptions of the same environmental stimuli by different people or revisions of what they hear or see in order to make the information more compatible with what they already know. For example, I observed a group of kindergarten students learning the "Pledge of Allegiance to the Flag" in a Houston, Texas classroom. The teacher recited the pledge slowly, phrase by phrase, emphasizing key words. The young students immediately repeated what she said. When they came to the part that says "with liberty and justice for all," one young girl loudly repeated "with liberty and Joske's for all." At that time, Joske's was a large department store in Houston near the elementary school the students attended. Although justice was not a familiar term, the idea that everyone should have a Joske's seemed perfectly reasonable to this little girl, and that is what she thought she heard!

This tendency to perceive information in a personally meaningful way means that we cannot assume that each student perceives messages, information, or experiences in the same way. Knowing our students' backgrounds and previous experiences in an area, consciously creating a context that will bring out related experiences or information, and continually checking student perceptions will help students learn and perhaps prevent development of misconceptions.

Field-Based Activity 6.4

Teachers call attention to important information and focus student attention in many ways. Here are some categories that provide a framework for thinking about strategies that focus attention.

Verbal statements   Thought-provoking questions

Visual displays   Emphasis—verbal or visual

Demonstrations   Use of student names

Unusual or puzzling events

As you visit classrooms, look for examples of the ways teachers focus attention, and list as many of these as you can under the category headings. Which ones seem to be most effective?

However, directing students' attention to important information and determining whether their perceptions of information are consistent with the teacher's intent is only part of the process.

Data selected for attention in the SR are transferred to short-term memory (STM), also referred to as working memory or consciousness. This is the site of conscious thought and processing of data. STM has a limited capacity of seven plus or minus two "chunks" of information (Miller, 1956). These chunks will be lost within thirty seconds unless they are rehearsed (repeated over and over as we might do when we have looked up a telephone number and need to remember it long enough to get to a phone and dial it) or transferred into long-term memory (LTM) for later retrieval. Long-term memory has, for all practical purposes, an unlimited storage capacity. One of the teachers' goals, then, is to enable students to retain important information in STM long enough to be able to process and transfer it to LTM. To do this, the teacher must focus students' attention on appropriate information in their environment, provide information in a way that does not overload the capacity of STM, and facilitate students' acquisition of strategies that aid in processing information for storage.

Understanding how to help students overcome some of the limitations of STM related to the amount of information that can be processed is important for teachers. A chunk of information refers to a meaningful piece of information. For example, the numbers 1, 4, 9, and 2, considered separately, would constitute four chunks of information. However, considering them together as a date that has meaning to us, such as 1492, would constitute only one chunk of information. Therefore, we can improve the capacity of our working memory by organizing smaller pieces of information into meaningful chunks.

Students who do not possess strategies for organizing information in meaningful ways or for making connections between new and existing information can be taught to do so with a resulting increase in memory capacity and problem solving (Pressley, Johnson, Symons, McGoldrick, & Kurita, 1989). Teachers can model strategy use for students as well as teach strategies explicitly to students. Knowledge about students' existing strategies and the strategies most successful for a given task enable teachers to integrate strategy instruction into specific content areas. Figure 6.3 provides a list of the kinds of strategies students may use to facilitate learning and problem solving.

Figure 6.3   Sample Learning Strategies

Reading Comprehension
> Looking up unknown words in the dictionary/glossary
> Guessing at the meaning of unknown words by examining the context of the sentence
> Stopping and rereading when a passage is difficult to understand
> Asking yourself questions about the passage
> Predicting what will come next in a passage
> Summarizing passages/portions of text when reading for extended periods of time

Main Idea
> Searching for and identifying the main idea of a lecture or passage
> Determining what is the main idea of a passage or assignment

Mathematical/Science Problem Solving
> Defining the problem (clear idea of the concepts involved)
> Selecting important information in the problem
> Mentally representing the problem (draw a diagram)
> Applying appropriate heuristics
>> Work backward
>> Work forward
>> Means-ends analysis
>> Solving a simpler problem within the problem
>> Relating to a similar problem
>> Trial and error
> Applying appropriate algorithms

Continued on next page

Continued from previous page

Knowledge Acquisition

Mentally linking new material to previously learned material

Using visualization techniques to help remember new material

Using mnemonic devices

Summarizing information mentally to self

Teaching information to someone else

Keeping up with reading and assignments so that new information is gained gradually

Asking questions during class

Attention/Concentration

Studying in an area that is free of external distractions

Clearing the desk of unneeded items while working or studying

Refocusing when your mind "drifts" during a lecture or while studying/reading

Maintaining your focus while completing a task

Motivation

Reminding yourself of the importance of completing a task

Looking for something interesting in assignments/tasks

Rewarding yourself when successfully completing a task

Study Skills

Having a designated place in which to study

Taking notes during a lecture

Reviewing notes as soon as possible after a lecture

Using underlining, note-taking, highlighting, outlining, concept mapping during studying/reading

Skimming over material or readings before a lecture is given

Time Management

Beginning an assignment soon after it is assigned

Keeping a systematic record of tasks that need to be completed

Being aware of which tasks need to be completed first

Being aware of how long tasks will take to complete

Test-Taking

Brainstorming possible questions that might appear on a test

Underlining key words in a test question

Crossing out possible incorrect answers to a multiple-choice question

Marking difficult items and returning to them after attempting other items

Source: Knight, S., & Boudah, D. (1998). *Teacher research training manual.* College Station: Texas A&M University.

Lack of strategies may have a negative impact on student learning, but another reason we may not achieve the learning results we intend in the classroom relates to the way we present information. Due to the limitations of STM, students may not be able to handle the amount of information we present at one time. For example, consider this dilemma and try to explain it in terms of information processing theory:

A math teacher complains, "I stood there for fifteen minutes and explained the procedure for dividing fractions until my throat hurt from talking! I know fractions are hard for fifth-graders—and it took a long time for me to describe the process— but this morning they came in and it was as if they hadn't even been there—or had only been there for part of the time! They just have no initiative! I just don't get it—what do I have to do to get them to pay attention?"

This math teacher was frustrated because she thought the students were not listening. In reality, she may have overloaded their working memory and caused an STM bottleneck that prevented them from being able to retain the information long enough to transfer it to LTM. The students also may not have had strategies to organize this incoming information, and there is no clue that the teacher helped them by providing the material in an organized fashion or in a way consistent with STM capacity.

Another way of overcoming limitations of STM can be achieved by making some of the operations that are typically carried out in STM automatic or externally supported so they do not take up limited processing space. For example, students working on math word problems may not have enough processing capability for understanding the problem and for determining and implementing appropriate algorithms or strategies to solve the problem if they also must perform certain computations (e.g., addition, subtraction, multiplication) simultaneously. If computation is automatic, as in retrieval of products of the multiplication of two numbers, space becomes available for other processes. For students who have not yet mastered these basic skills, external supports such as calculators or computers may free up processing capability so that higher order tasks such as solving word problems can be accomplished concurrently with acquisition of basic skills.

The manner in which information is transferred, or encoded, into LTM is important because it will affect how we retrieve it. The more connections that exist among pieces of information, the more likely we will be successful in retrieving what we need. Encoding is the process of forming internal mental representations, or schema, by making connections in LTM between new information and existing information. As described earlier, meaningfulness is one of the characteristics of learning considered desirable by cognitive learning theorists.

Meaningfulness, from an information processing perspective, refers to the number of connections between ideas in LTM. Therefore, increasing connections among ideas or pieces of information serves two purposes: We have a more complex, or meaningful, representation of information, and we are more likely to be able to retrieve relevant information when we need it because we have increased the number of means of access.

The information within a schema may be differently arranged depending on the learners' prior experiences. Culture and language histories, unique environmental contexts and experiences, interactions with various adults, and individual abilities are some of the many influences on schema. Humans construct knowledge in ways that are uniquely theirs. Although students in classrooms may be taught the same basic concepts, all children will not learn exactly the same thing, in the same sequence, or in the same way.

A very simple interaction can illustrate how a young child becomes an active participant in learning and predicts, confirms, or integrates new information. A young child looks out the window and sees something flying through the sky. Using prior knowledge available in established schema, the child points to the airplane and predicts by saying "bird, bird!" The mother standing close by provides a reaction to the prediction by saying, "It looks like a bird doesn't it, but hear the noise; that is an airplane." The child is unable to confirm the original prediction but has modified his or her schema to include flying objects that are not birds but that are noisy and called airplanes. The existing schema is modified, and a new category of flying objects is added.

Applying Cognitive Theory in the Classroom

Given the manner in which we process information, the teacher's goal in the classroom is to facilitate construction of meaningful representations by arranging instruction so that students make appropriate connections and increase the number of connections between old and new information. To do this, we need to ensure that students actively process information rather than merely memorize material. The notion of active student involvement in processing information differentiates behavioral from cognitive approaches. Although few behaviorists would deny the need for active engagement in academic tasks (see, e.g., Brophy & Good, 1986), the nature of that engagement is different from a CIP perspective and may not always be visible to external observers. To actively engage students mentally, the teacher can employ strategies that prevent mere rote association or memorization of information: Asking questions or having students ask questions that cue students to think about connections or to analyze examples or applications, asking students to paraphrase content, giving them opportunities for problem solving, having students write about what they are learning, and engaging them in hands-on activities as often as possible are ways to initiate active involvement and discourage rote memorization.

In addition to providing opportunities for active mental processing of content, teachers can also use and teach students to use strategies for organizing information in ways that expose possible connections between existing pieces of information and between prior and new knowledge. Strategies for organizing information into patterns or categories can be used by teachers to present information in a way that makes connections clear and by students to make sense of material from lectures or text. For example, providing graphic organizers that show relationships among concepts, such as concept maps, flow charts, graphs, diagrams, and tables, may help students see connections that might otherwise not be seen. Having students use graphic organizers helps them discover patterns and relationships.

The vignette depicting Mr. James teaching his class about the Civil War provides a concrete example of several teaching strategies compatible with cognitive approaches. Mr. James actively involves students in using a chart to discover patterns and relationships. He provides some initial structure, but students are responsible for seeking information rather than passively receiving it. Because Mr. James gives students the initial structure for the categories, he reduces the difficulty of the organizing task that their age and prior knowledge might have made too difficult. The partial assistance he provides, which will be gradually removed or reduced as students gain competency in the use of graphic organizers, is referred to as *scaffolding*. Just as scaffolds are used to support the erection of a building and then removed as sections of the building are completed, assistance provided to students can be reduced when no longer needed. In addition to providing scaffolding, the teacher systematically addresses both the content of the activity and the process used to organize information in the following discussion. Engaging students in a discussion about how the categories of the chart might be revised to better fit the information they collected will encourage students to explore and develop their own organizational strategies.

Actively engaging students in processing information and using and teaching organizational strategies may facilitate meaningful connections, but other teaching strategies may also be necessary to consciously increase the number of connections within existing knowledge frameworks and between new and old knowledge. Teachers may need to help students make connections by explicitly pointing out differences and similarities. For example, a second-grade teacher may need to show a series of examples of problems that require subtraction without regrouping and a series of problems that show subtraction with regrouping and make the differences explicit. Teachers can also use and have students use analogies that show the similarities in dissimilar objects or ideas. Strategies to create meaning where none exists initially for the student may also be necessary at times. The use of verbal mnemonics (using an acronym such as HOMES to remember the Great Lakes) or imagery (using a method that associates words or ideas with familiar places that are easily recalled) can aid both encoding and later retrieval of information that students want to remember.

From an information processing perspective, perhaps one of the most important tasks of the teacher is to provide students with the means to improve their own learning. Metacognition is the term used to refer to conscious awareness of the way in which we process information, our effectiveness in doing so, and the means for improving effectiveness when needed. As with strategy use, teachers can have a direct impact on students' metacognitive abilities. "Thinking out loud" for students while demonstrating procedures or solving problems, including modeling difficulties encountered while doing so, provides students with a model for strategy use as well as diagnosis and repair of errors in thinking. Having students "think out loud" while they are performing tasks or solving problems, either with you or with a peer, makes thinking processes public and available for discussion. Figure 6.4 provides a protocol for using this technique. Often the students themselves will become aware of the effectiveness of specific strategies as they are engaged in thinking aloud. Asking students to explain how they arrived at an answer or if they can provide an alternate way of arriving at a similar or different conclusion or answer emphasizes the importance of the process used to arrive at answers and provides additional models of thinking. Metacognitive awareness provides a valuable first step in enabling students to become independent learners in an era in which the sheer volume of information available makes efficient and effective information processing a priority for our schools.

In summary, cognitive theory has replaced behavioral approaches in the past decade as the dominant theory underlying the development and implementation of new instructional models and strategies. Educators have found both traditional and information processing cognitive approaches particularly useful in providing students with opportunities to acquire meaningful knowledge and to develop higher order skills such as problem solving and reading comprehension. In addition, information processing theory has focused attention on the importance of understanding students' prior knowledge, the strategies they use to process information, and the way they approach and solve complex problems. Information processing theory has also emphasized the importance of "thinking about our own thinking" and provided the tools to make our own as well as our students' intellectual processes more visible and more effective.

Figure 6.4   Think-Aloud Protocol

Phase I. General Instructions

I'm going to ask you to solve some problems about (social studies, science, reading, math). You can solve these problems any way you like. In fact, I'm really not even interested in whether you get the right answers. But I am interested in what you do when you read passages, answer questions, or solve the problems—the strategies you use. For this reason, I'm going to ask you to talk aloud as much as you can while you work. I'm going to turn on the tape recorder when you begin in order to help me remember what you are saying (optional). OK?

You won't have to do anything special. Just work like you normally would. Some students tell me that they "mumble to themselves" when they're reading or solving problems. If that's what *you* do, then all you'll have to do today is mumble a little louder. In any case, try to talk constantly when you're not reading silently. Say what you're thinking and doing even if it doesn't make sense.

Phase II. Problem Solution and Student "Think-Aloud"

Read the instructions to the student and ask him/her to begin. Turn on tape recorder (optional). Say as little as possible, being careful to use only neutral, nondirective phrases. Use *only* the following prompts:

Can you say what you're thinking?

That's very clear.

Please tell me what you are writing.

Mmm.

OK.

I see.

Continue this until the student has answered the questions following the passage.

Phase III. Debriefing

Even if the student talked continually, there may be many unclear points in the protocol. Ask the following clarifying questions after the student has finished:

Could you summarize for me how you got your answer?

Can you say some more about it?

Can you explain to me what you were thinking when you (asked yourself that question, got that picture in your mind, made those notes, etc.)?

Is there anything else you can think of?

Source: Knight, S., & Boudah, D. (1998). *Teacher research training manual.* College Station: Texas A&M University.

Learning as Constructivism

A third approach to learning theory that holds promise for classroom instruction, but that does not yet have the strong research base that the previous two approaches offer, focuses on the role of social interaction in learning (see, e.g., Von Glaserfield, 1997). Compatible with cognitive approaches that emphasize the active, constructive nature of learning and development of meaningful connections, social constructionist approaches focus on the role of peers and adults in the construction of knowledge. This theory suggests that cognitive abilities are acquired through interactions with others, particularly through assistance provided by others that enables us to accomplish tasks that we may not be able to do on our own. As the learner actively transacts, interprets, and interacts with the environment and with other people, understandings and knowledge that reflect the learner's background begin to guide the learning process (Strickland, 1995). A great deal of learning occurs in social contexts, and learners' relationships with others serve a vital function in communication. How people interact, what comments they provide, and how they view the world become part of learning. The Voice of a Preservice Teacher feature presents one teacher's view of a classroom that takes a constructive approach to learning and instruction.

The work of Vygotsky (1962, 1978) has been particularly influential in the development of constructivist theory. From this perspective, students learn best when provided with tasks that are within their zone of proximal development. This zone encompasses behaviors that the student cannot yet perform alone but can accomplish given assistance. Peers, teachers, or other adults who are more competent provide prompts and assistance as needed in the course of interacting toward accomplishment of a meaningful task. This concept is similar to the notion of scaffolding discussed earlier in relation to cognitive information processing theory.

Apprenticeship models best reflect the type of instruction consistent with a Vygotskian approach to learning. Apprenticeships have long been common means of learning and acquiring skills in medical schools, doctoral institutions preparing

---

World Wide Web Sites

You may learn more about Vygotsky and metacognition at:

http://www.massey.ac.nz/

http://www.oise.utoronto.ca/

Voice of a Preservice Teacher

The classroom looked as though some catastrophe had occurred and everyone had made a mad dash for the exit—collecting and dropping valuable and unvaluable items along the way. The desks were in disarray. I couldn't quite determine whether they were arranged or disarranged that way. No desktop was visible. Books stacked on books, stacked on paper, game pieces and other indescribable objects covered each desk as well as much of the floor. Five birds filled the air with song and the splats of birdseed dropping to the floor. A ship's sail, made from a bedsheet, hung from the ceiling, a wooden plank stretched from one desk to another, and a wicker basket lid resting on a desk looked as though it might be used for a helm. What a mess, I thought to myself. How could children possibly learn among all of this?

And then the children came in, filling the room with third-grade talk. Mostly I heard, "Mr. Landmann, Mr. Landmann" as they asked question after question. The class began with the activity of rewriting the script of The Tempest. *Each child had been assigned a character he or she was going to portray in a video filming of the play at a later date. Children simply began calling out their invented script lines and asking questions such as, "Will the audience know what a sprite is?" Then someone said, "Ariel should say, 'Father, don't get so overheated.'" I was surprised at their maturity, cooperation, and wonderful ideas. They conducted themselves much like a team of writers might behave working on a movie script or Broadway play. Mr. Landmann's position was that of coordinator and editor, reminding the students of time restraints and prop limitations. Again, I was dumbfounded and very impressed.*

Two words describe best the reasons for successful learning—autonomy and interaction. The children were involved. They—not the teacher—were the creators of almost every activity that took place. Mr. Landmann had only to initiate and then the students took over the responsibility to make it work.

I wonder if I'll be a teacher like Mr. Landmann. One who is open to all kinds of possibilities for teaching and learning. One who raises expectations and limits for teaching and learning and who provides opportunities for children to excel beyond what the curriculum expects of them. I hope to teach lessons that require students to discuss and interact with each other so that talking and listening is not considered disruptive chatter but reflective thinking.

future professors, and trades such as carpentry or tailoring. Students learn by interacting and working with those skilled in the profession or trade, and they learn in an authentic context, such as a hospital or factory, as opposed to a simulation of the context. Although this is possible only to a limited extent in elementary or secondary schools, the challenge is to create an environment as similar to the real world as possible so that tasks are tied to real-world situations.

The work of several theorists who have studied the elements of successful apprenticeships may facilitate transfer of the apprenticeship model to school settings (Collins, Brown, & Newman, 1989; Rogoff, 1990). Students need to have opportunities to observe skilled peers and adults as they are modeling the skill—in other words, as they are engaged in the skill or learning to be acquired. Students need to perceive that the mentor's engagement in the task is actually connected to real-world settings rather than to artificial tasks performed only in schools and classrooms. Beyond mere observation, more skilled adults or peers need to provide coaching in the form of direct instruction and feedback in the skill or learning. In conjunction with coaching, students need opportunities to practice and to receive assistance as they practice commensurate with their skill level at the time. Earlier, we labeled this activity as scaffolding, but Rogoff refers to it as *guided participation* and stresses the importance of the role of the skilled mentor in assessing the demands of the task in relation to the skills of the apprentice and in structuring tasks so that apprentices are constantly increasing their skill level. Mentors encourage apprentices to reflect on their performance in compari-

6. Preservice teachers will develop advance organizers for a science unit they will teach to secondary students.   _____   _____   _____

7. The junior English students will design a children's book and share it with nursery school students at the local Head Start program.   _____   _____   _____

8. Physical education students will be able to jog a mile in less than fifteen minutes.   _____   _____   _____

9. Second-grade students will be able to edit their own stories for publication in the class anthology after working with a fourth-grade writing partner.   _____   _____   _____

Do you have three checks in each column? Be sure that you matched the goal with the learning theory that would provide the most appropriate instructional approach.

If you had any difficulty matching the goal and the learning theory, go back over the chapter, discuss your responses with a peer, or read some additional information about learning theories.

Answers: Behaviorist theory is best applied to goals 1, 5, and 8. Cognitive theory is best applied to goals 3, 4, and 6. Constructivist theory best matches goals 2, 7, and 9.

son with experts and peers and may require apprentices to articulate what they are doing as a means of testing their knowledge. This practice should not be limited to mere imitation, however, but should provide opportunities for apprentices to explore new ways of approaching and accomplishing tasks.

Putting It All Together: Using Behavioral, Cognitive, and Constructivist Theories

The three theories discussed in this section define learning from three very different perspectives, and the skilled classroom teacher will find value in the use of all three, depending on the needs of the students in the classroom and the kind of learning outcomes desired. Behavioral theory provides ways to manage classroom behaviors and to teach basic intellectual and motor skills. Instructional strategies based on this theory have been particularly helpful with younger students, students with learning or behavioral disorders, and students of low ability. Cognitive theory suggests ways of promoting student acquisition of dispositions and skills associated with complex tasks or tasks that have multiple solution paths or right answers. In addition, information processing theory enables us to understand and assess students' cognitive processing so that we can encourage more effective processes and ultimately transfer control of the learning process to the student. Finally, constructivist theory suggests ways we can take advantage of the social nature of the classroom and provide meaningful experiences for students that may be more likely to transfer to the world outside of the classroom.

Portfolio Reflections and Exhibits

Throughout this chapter you completed a series of field-based activities. The activities may serve as the basis for a portfolio representation, you may develop your own exhibit, or complete one of the suggested portfolio activities listed here:

1. Use the Interactive Seating Chart (see Figure 6.2) while observing in a classroom. Analyze your findings, and ask the classroom teacher to comment on it. How were your analyses similar and different? Would you revise your interpretation in any way after talking with the classroom teacher? If this were your class, what would you do based on the data obtained? Include your data and a summary of your analysis with the teacher's comments in your portfolio.

2. Discuss problems of classroom management or motivation with one of the teachers in your school. Together, select a target behavior of a student (or students) that needs changing. Define the behavior clearly. Choose a period of time during which the behavior is likely to occur, and keep a baseline record of the behavior. In other words, make a note each time the behavior occurs during that time period. Share your data with the teacher and discuss possible cues or reinforcements that contribute to the behavior. Include in your portfolio the data, a summary of your interpretation of the data, and possible ways to extinguish the behavior or strengthen a positive behavior.

3. Conduct a think-aloud interview with a student to determine what strategies the student is using to approach and solve a complex task. Choose a task requiring higher level thinking typical of the content area and age group of the student you plan to interview (i.e., math word problem, science experiment, summary of a reading). Interview the student, transcribe the tape of the interview, and analyze the kinds of strategies the student uses in relation to their success on the task provided. Figure 6.4 may help you identify some of the strategies used.

InfoTrac College Edition Extension

Log on to the InfoTrac College Edition Web site, and use a keyword search to find an article about how learning theory relates to you. Type in "learning theory and preservice teacher."

Alternatively, look for more information about constructivism and how it is defined. Using a keyword search, type in "constructivist and teaching" or "constructivist and classroom" and read about applications of constructivist approaches.

Related Readings

Aaronsohn, E. (1996). *Going against the grain: Supporting the student-centered teacher.* Thousand Oaks, CA: Sage.

> *This book tells the story of a new teacher who tries to use new theories in her class-room. It describes her efforts to overcome the resistance from other teachers in her new school as she learns how to handle her own uncertainties about her nontraditional curriculum.*

Brooks, J. G. (1993). *The case for constructivist classrooms.* Alexandria, VA: American Association of Curriculum Development.

> *This book describes activities and teaching principles in which a constructivist theory is applied to classroom contexts. Some of this book focuses on research and inquiry, but there are some good examples of how constructivist learning theory translates to teacher practice.*

References

Alexander, P. A., & Knight, S. L. (1993). Dimensions of the interplay between teaching and learning. *Educational Forum, 57*(3), 232–245.

Ausubel, D. P. (1968). *Educational psychology: A cognitive view.* New York: Holt, Rinehart & Winston.

Bandura, A. (1982). Self-efficacy mechanism in human agency. *American Psychologists, 37,* 122–148.

Brophy, J. E., & Good, T. L. (1986). Teacher behavior and student achievement. In M. C. Wittrock (Ed.), *Handbook of research on teaching* (3rd ed., pp. 328–375). New York: Macmillan.

Bruner, J. (1966). *Toward a theory of instruction.* Cambridge, MA: Harvard University Press.

Collins, A., Brown, J., & Newman, S. (1989). Cognitive apprenticeship: Teaching the craft of reading, writing, and mathematics. In L. Resnick (Ed.), *Knowing, learning, and instruction: Essays in honor of Robert Glaser* (pp. 453–494). Hillsdale, NJ: Erlbaum.

Gage, N. (1984). *Hard gains in the soft sciences: The case of pedagogy.* Bloomington, IN: Phi Delta Kappa.

Good, T., & Brophy, J. (1999). *Looking in classrooms* (8th ed.). New York: Longman.

Klatzky, R. L. (1980). *Human memory: Structures and processes* (2nd ed.). San Francisco: W. H. Freeman.

Knight S. (1990). The effort of cognitive strategy instruction on elementary students' reading outcomes. In S. McCormick & J. Zuttell (Eds.), *National reading conference yearbook* (Vol. 38, pp. 241–251). Chicago: National Reading Conference.

Knight, S., & Boudah, D. (1997). *Participatory research and development for the improvement of teaching and learning.* Paper presented at the annual meeting of the Southwest Educational Research Association, Austin, TX.

Knight, S., Waxman, H. C., & Pedrone, R. N. (1989). Examining the relationship between classroom instruction and elementary students' cognitive strategies in social studies. *Journal of Educational Research, 82*(5), 270–276.

Mayer, R. E. (1983). *Thinking, problem solving, and cognition.* San Francisco: W. H. Freeman.

Miller, G. A. (1956). The magical number seven, plus or minus two: Some limits on our capacity for processing information. *Psychological Review, 63,* 81–97.

Palincsar, A. S., & Brown, A. L. (1984). Reciprocal teaching of comprehension-fostering and monitoring activities. *Cognition and Instruction, 1,* 117–175.

Phye, G. D., & Andre, T. (1986). *Cognitive classroom learning: Understanding, thinking and problem solving.* San Diego: Academic Press.

Premack, D. (1965). Reinforcement theory. In D. Levine (Ed.), *Nebraska symposium on motivation* (Vol. 13). Lincoln: University of Nebraska Press.

Pressley, M., Johnson, C., Symons, S., McGoldrick, J., & Kurita, J. (1989). Strategies that improve children's memory and comprehension of text. *Elementary School Journal, 90*(1), 3–32.

Rogoff, B. (1990). *Apprenticeship in thinking: Cognitive development in social context.* New York: Oxford University Press.

Schunk, D. (2000). *Learning theories: An education perspective.* Saddle River, NJ: Prentice-Hall.

Skinner, B. F. (1954). Science of learning art of teaching. *Harvard Educational Review, 24,* 86–97.

Skinner, B. F. (1958). Teaching machine. *Science, 128,* 969–977.

Skinner, B. F. (1963). *Science and human behavior.* New York: Macmillan.

Becoming a Teacher in a Field-Based Setting

Skinner, B. F. (1968). *Technology of teaching.* New York: Appleton Century Cross.

Skinner, B. F. (1969). *Contingencies of reinforcement: A theoretical analysis.* New York: Appleton Century Cross.

Stallings, J. A. (1997). *Learning to teach in inner city schools training manual.* College Station: Texas A&M University, College of Education.

Strickland, K. (1995). *Literacy not labels: Celebrating students' strengths through whole language.* Portsmouth, NH: Boyton/Cook.

Thorndike, E. L. (1913). *Educational psychology: The original nature of man* (Vol. 1). New York: Teachers College Press.

Von Glaserfield, E. (1997). Amplification of a constructivist perspective. *Issues in Education, 3,* 203–210.

Vygotsky, L. (1962). *Thought and language.* Cambridge, MA: MIT.

Vygotsky, L. (1978). *Mind and society.* Cambridge, MA: Harvard University.

Wang, M., Haertel, G., & Walberg, H. (1993). Toward a knowledge base for school learning. *Review of Educational Research, 63*(3), 249–294.

CHAPTER 7

Establishing a Successful Classroom Environment

IN THIS CHAPTER

- **Establishing a Personal Management Style**
- **Factors Influencing Classroom Procedures**
- **Developing Effective Classrooms**
- **Organizing Students, Time, and Materials**
- **Discipline**
- **Classroom Environments and Decision Making**

I took Steven aside during a calm interval and told him I was very unhappy about all the hitting he was doing. I thought he would stop it because there are so many things he does well. Now, however, when he hurts someone, he will have to sit alone, away from the class, in a "time-out" chair, and do nothing for ten minutes. I showed him the chair, and he nodded.

He wandered around the room, looking at the chair. I became involved in writing down a story Jan was dictating. Suddenly Steven pushed Jimmy down and began kicking him. I jumped up, grabbed Steven, and dragged him to the chair. He would not come by himself and he would not remain seated. He screamed furiously. I said nothing, but held on to both his arms and sat next to him. He struggled and tried to kick me. I said, "Steven, don't even think of kicking me. I can't ever let you do that. I have to make you sit here because you won't do it by yourself. Every time you hurt someone you must sit here."

I told the children, over his screaming, that Steven needed me to sit here with him. They must have understood that I was upset and Steven was upset, and we were trying to work something out. They stayed away from us and their play was subdued. They were upset too.

This was a Monday. We did this twice on Monday, and twice on Tuesday. On Wednesday, Steven sat on the time-out chair by himself with no complaint. After that, he stopped hitting children. I had won because of superior strength and size. I was not sure what was won and what was lost.

—Vivian Gussin Paley, *White Teacher**

Establishing effective learning environments is a demanding task. The most successful teachers are recognized for their ability to fashion environments where all learners have the potential to succeed. To have everyone benefit from educational opportunities, competent teachers must orchestrate many factors and make multiple decisions. In addition to only one teacher dealing with twenty or thirty students, instruction involves factors such as managing materials, scheduling activities, moving from activity to activity, and managing behavior. Management approaches and decisions reflect beliefs about learning, student development, and the roles of teachers and students. Managing classrooms is an extremely complex task that requires a great deal of effort, thought, and reflection on the part of the teacher.

Organizing and managing classrooms is a major concern of both beginning and experienced teachers. Many strategies have proven successful, and knowledge in this area is expanding. Nevertheless, classroom management also involves a personal approach that reflects the personality of the teacher and the students who are in the classroom. Some techniques will emerge from experience, but you can learn a great deal by observing veteran teachers who maintain effective and well-ordered classrooms, by acknowledging your own beliefs about power and control, by participating in field experiences that provide opportunities for you to plan and manage instruction, and by reflecting on your perceptions and experiences.

---

*From *White Teacher*, by Vivian Gussin Paley (pp. 17–18). Cambridge, MA: Harvard.

Effective teachers coordinate and balance a complex set of learning processes, interpersonal relationships, individual differences, and instructional strategies to establish a successful learning environment for their students.

In this chapter we discuss several aspects of classroom environment, organization, and instructional planning and specifically answer these questions:

- What factors must be considered when establishing effective learning environments?

- What factors contribute to a teacher's personal view of effective learning environments?

- How does a teacher encourage student involvement and positive behavior?

- What are ways that students can be grouped for maximum instructional effectiveness?

- What instructional arrangements, approaches, and strategies can contribute to effective learning environments?

Careful planning encourages and motivates students and helps avoid behavior and discipline problems. Planning and organization should result in predictable classroom procedures, a comfortable environment, and realistic teacher expectations. Teachers who plan and organize daily routines and schedules based on the needs of their students, the nature of the learning process, and the desire to provide motivating instructional strategies and materials are more likely to have successful classrooms.

Establishing a Personal Management Style

A teacher can select from a wide range of management styles. When you think about your own education, you may remember some teachers who were extremely strict and enforced rules and regulations and others who were very warm, interactive, and flexible. One teacher might have encouraged a great deal of drill and memory work, whereas another teacher focused on exploration, multiple responses, and active participation in interpreting and solving problems. Some teachers avoid controversial issues, choosing to focus their students on teacher-selected topics. Other teachers include a wide range of issues, encourage debates and ambiguity, include current topics, and capitalize on the curiosity of students. Almost all of these approaches can be successful with most students and in some situations.

Although there are many ways to describe effective classrooms, establishing healthy learning environments means that students will learn designated content, misconduct is diminished, and worthwhile academic activities occur (Brophy, 1988). Effective classrooms do not emerge by chance. Classroom environments that work require personal reflection about teachers' roles, an understanding of what works in classroom organizations, a view of the relationship between management and instructional decisions, and the ability to use multiple methods while organizing classroom components of classroom organization.

The manner in which a teacher goes about establishing a positive classroom climate is a central issue in learning to be a teacher. Although a wide variety of processes and techniques are used to set up learning situations, teachers' authority is most effective when based on respect and caring for students. Classrooms require structure and rules designed to produce situations in which all students feel safe and look forward to academic success. Care and control in the classroom can be blended. The combination of these two important elements empowers students and clarifies their roles. In addition, classroom interactions can demonstrate and teach caring, communication skills, and democratic principles (Ames, 1992; Noddings, 1995). A balanced approach to classroom management includes respectful treatment and avoids producing situations in which students feel alienated and disenfranchised.

Field-Based Activity 7.1

Describe the learning environments in the school setting where you are currently working. Are they structured, highly defined classrooms where teachers deliver traditional lectures and make assignments that are graded and returned? Or are they more relaxed, in that there are discussions, small-group activities, and student-directed lessons? Which of these provides a more comfortable learning environment for you? Develop a list of descriptors that make you the most comfortable, keep you interested, and help you learn most effectively.

Factors Influencing Classroom Procedures

Many factors must be considered when a teacher is setting up the classroom for instruction. Teachers implement some factors, and other factors exist independent of teachers' actions. Outside influences have an impact on establishing a positive learning environment in numerous ways. Recognizing the various influences on classroom environments is important, even though teachers are not always able to control or change the life situations involving their students. Chapters 3 and 5 provide an in-depth review of societal conditions that affect classrooms today. In this chapter, we focus on providing a context for considering classroom learning environments.

Home and Social Contexts

Some student behavior and attitudes can be traced to factors outside the school environment. Violence, gangs, drugs, poverty, and homelessness have an impact on some students directly and on others in more subtle ways. These factors have traditionally been associated with inner-city schools, but they are now more and more evident in small cities, rural communities, and suburbs. Children are being exposed to some tough situations at younger and younger ages. Reports of gang activity among fourth-grade students, alcohol abuse among eleven- and twelve-year-olds, and pregnancy among young teenagers are not uncommon. There is some evidence that young people's attitudes and beliefs are influenced by the representation of society on television, in movies, by email, and on the Internet.

Family life can have an impact on students' school behaviors and responses. Families have changed a great deal, and students may live in situations that are different from traditional ideas of family life. Aunts, uncles, grandparents, or older brothers and sisters may be the heads of some households. Homes where children live are headed by single or divorced parents or by two parents who both work, so parents are not always present to oversee their children. Some school-children leave school and let themselves into an empty, unsupervised home. Almost all families care and want the best for their children, but changing family structures have had an impact on the educational system. Schools are assuming more and more responsibility for teaching lessons once taught by parents and for providing after-school care and other support systems.

Probably no other circumstance affects children and their learning as much as poverty and the resulting conditions. Nearly one-third of the nation's children are living in poverty. Not all poor children live in inner cities or are members of minority cultures, but there are large pockets of poverty in large cities and an overrepresentation of family poverty in minority groups. Poverty inevitably affects the health and well-being of children. Children from poor families may not receive the nutrition or health care necessary to maintain good health. They may come to school hungry or sick. Poverty can affect the experiences and resources that a family can provide for its members. Experiences taken for granted by middle-class parents—vacations, visiting zoos and museums, attending cultural events—may be beyond the reach of poor families. Even more dramatic is that schools located in poverty areas may not have the same access to resources as schools in affluent areas. Poor schools do not have the textbooks, computers, or a wide variety of class offerings found in schools with more adequate resources. So, in one way or another, poverty makes a substantial difference on the school experiences of some children.

Many students and their families overcome great odds to succeed. Stories of success usually occur where there is a strong community and family support system and role models that encourage students to value their school experiences. Many students from all economic groups do not receive the support they need to deal with societal issues, and teachers are usually well aware of their plight. Students make decisions each day about their response to society, and schools can play a role in the way students respond to these issues.

Despite the difficult societal conditions educators may face, schools do make a difference in the lives of students. For example, positive, well-managed class-rooms and school environments have been connected to prevention of delinquency, teen pregnancy, and drug abuse (Dryfoos, 1990). Child-friendly schools have been suggested as possible mediators of risk factors that often lead to school failure (Bennett, 1998). Effective processes can enhance student self-understanding, self-evaluation, and self-control (McCaslin & Good, 1992). An effective learning environment provides students with a sense of community and with opportunities to develop interpersonal communication and conflict management skills and to take the risks necessary for learning.

Students' Characteristics and Needs

Students' characteristics are extremely varied. They may differ in developmental levels, culture, experience, gender, language, and intellectual and physical abilities. The differences represented in the classroom provide both the joys and the frustrations of teaching.

A key element in classroom management is paying attention to the developmental issues of students. In implementing classroom instructional procedures, one of the first considerations is that of age and maturity of students. Older students, for example, may be much more sensitive to issues of power and control and may need more experiences with choice and negotiation (Glasser, 1988). Younger children will need more opportunities to learn how to make good decisions. The nature and complexity of the content presentation changes as children gain more academic experiences. Most teachers focus on a particular age—primary or high school, for example—study the behavior, and become experts of learning abilities of children at that age. Consideration of age differences appears to be one of the most natural factors in instructional processes.

Students' cultural and experiential backgrounds also need to be considered when developing instructional and management methods (Kuykendall, 1992). The diversity represented in today's classrooms requires teachers to consider multiple ways of interacting. Teachers who are aware of the diverse characteristics in their classrooms will take responsibility for how teacher behavior is interpreted and internalized by students who come from different backgrounds and have different experiences than their teachers (Dana, 1992). (See Chapter 5 for a complete discussion of student differences.)

With our entry into the twenty-first century, teachers will have more chances than ever before to hear many different languages in their classrooms. All children who come to school speaking languages other than English are not the same and will possess different levels of fluency and literacy. Bilingual and bicultural education is designed to meet the needs of students who do not speak English. Programs run the gamut of teaching skills needed for transition to English, maintaining support for continued growth in the native language, and providing intense study in English language. Bicultural, bilingual programs help build pride in native culture while preparing for success in English-speaking schools and society.

There are also gender differences in the ways students respond to classroom procedures. Both the 1992 and 1998 reports by the American Association of University Women (AAUW) made a case for the different learning styles and requirements of boys and girls. Some differences in classroom experiences between genders are caused by how teachers respond to girls and boys. Class-

Voice of a Teacher

There has been so much written about how teachers treat girls and boys differently, and I worry that I am not conscious enough of what I do in the classroom. I try to call on everyone equally. I use girls and women as examples during my teaching. I also try to select literature that shows women in strong roles. But it's hard to do this all the time. Textbooks aren't always helpful. Media, television, and newspapers don't always provide female role models. When I make an explicit attempt to be gender conscious, I find it takes additional time to add examples, watch my own behavior, and rethink my actions. I am not sure that I am gender conscious in everything I do. It's easy to forget this concern when things are moving quickly in the classroom.

room contributions, the feedback the two genders receive, the representation of both genders in content areas, and the interactions between teachers and the two genders establish and support lifelong beliefs about the capabilities of men and women (Orenstein, 1994). All of this has a great deal to do with how teachers set up and manage the classrooms where boys and girls are learning.

World Wide Web Site

You may learn more about the American Association of University Women at: http://www.aauw.org

Specific management skills are required for students with special intellectual and physical needs, including gifted and talented students, special education students, and students with behavior disorders. With the passage of Public Law 94-142, special education students were given the right to receive public education in the least restrictive environment. Originally, the law was interpreted to provide special teachers, classrooms, and conditions for students who might have special needs. This practice isolated students from their peers, and the label "special" often reduced expectations of their performance. A more recent approach, often referred to as "inclusion," is to include special students in regular classrooms, mainstreaming them with other children and providing additional support such as modified inclusion or special teachers to help them succeed in classrooms with their peers. Students participate in specialized and limited environments only when their needs cannot be met in regular classrooms. This approach can put a great deal of pressure on regular classroom teachers who will

World Wide Web Site

You may learn more about Public Law 94-142 at:
http://www.ridgewater. mnscu.edu/

need to plan and implement many types of instruction for a diversity of student characteristics, including those with handicaps or gifts.

Expectations of Teachers and Learners

Researchers have recently demonstrated that the expectations related to what it means to be a teacher and a student in a particular classroom are established within the first few days of school (Fernie, Kantor, & Klein, 1990). However, classroom expectations and perceptions reflect more than the immediate interactions between students and teachers. Teachers enter the classroom with preconceived expectations, beliefs, and attitudes about classroom life (Chandler, 1992). Students, like teachers, come to the learning context with certain expectations, beliefs, and attitudes developed through messages from society and family that enhance or detract from their cognitive, physical, linguistic, and problem-solving abilities. Children gain ideas of what should happen in a classroom from their brothers and sisters and from television and other media. Parents' attitudes toward education have an impact on students' views of what should happen in classrooms. As students proceed through school, their own life experiences teach them what they should expect from school and what teachers' expectations of student behavior and academic achievement might be. Both student and teacher expectations can influence the curriculum, the organization, and the everyday events of a classroom.

Teachers' expectations of students' achievement is an important influence on classroom behavior (Good & Brophy, 1999). Expectations affect what is taught, how it is taught, and the attitudes of both teacher and learners. General expectations may emerge from personal beliefs about gender, race, and other equity considerations, or expectations can be personally directed toward one learner. What and who learns particular content can be greatly affected by socialization processes. Expectations can override teacher effectiveness as well as student abilities. When teachers hold low expectations for the learning achievement of some students, the most advanced teaching strategies are sure to be ineffective (Bartolome, 1994).

Becoming a Teacher in a Field-Based Setting

The problem of low teacher expectations for various socioeconomic, ethnic, and language minority students is pervasive. Some teacher behaviors and school practices reflect a belief that minority students or poor students will not have the experiences, language, or support to succeed in school. Often this results in lower expectations for poor or minority students. For many years, there has been a discrepancy between the achievements of some minority students and white students (Jeneks & Phillips, 1998). This can be seen in the high minority representation in low ability and remedial groups versus the white middle-class membership in gifted programs. Some prejudices, perceptions, and misunderstandings can be overcome in classrooms where activities are well planned and highly organized. Teachers can counter the problem of low expectations by providing learning environments that facilitate successful teaching of students who typically do not succeed in schools.

The most effective contexts leading to optimum student achievement are classrooms where all students feel valued, respected, and capable of succeeding despite their differences (Olsen & Mullen, 1990). Effective classroom organization is built on the understanding that children have different interests, learning styles, and abilities and will require different considerations during instructional planning. Understanding the potential differences and using that knowledge to organize instruction can improve the learning environment for all students.

The School Context

School contexts have a substantial impact on classroom processes. The climate, organizational structures, decision-making procedures, and types of professional support available will play a role in teachers' personal approaches to classroom management. Schools in which teachers work collaboratively and have developed a common vision of success will be able to offer support and establish healthy classroom contexts. An overall positive environment is established when a sense of belonging exists for all students. Some secondary schools are establishing different types of schedules to provide extended periods of time with one adult and one group of peers to help their students have time to develop healthy relationships. The quality of life within a school is an essential consideration for ongoing efforts to create healthy learning environments.

Instructional Tasks

Management procedures are most effective when tailored to instructional methods. What is being taught and how it is being taught are important when making decisions about classroom management and organization. Some information might be best delivered through direct instruction by the teachers, whereas other information may be learned effectively through discussion or independent reading. Using a variety of instructional tasks will ensure that differences in learning preferences will be taken into account, but changes in tasks can also require differences in management techniques. When teachers move away from lecture and presentation methods and rely on more interactive, small-group discussion practices, managing the classroom becomes more complex (McCaslin & Good, 1992). As a beginning teacher, you will need to consider various types of management methods to facilitate varied instructional methods such as whole language approaches or cooperative learning techniques. The use of various instructional methods will require teachers to help students be successful when working with groups, sharing ideas, debating issues, and providing peer assistance. Chapter 8 contains much more information about designing instructional processes.

Developing Effective Classrooms

Although an overwhelming number of factors influencing classroom environment cannot be changed or altered by schools and teachers, some fundamental factors related to classroom management can be fostered by teachers and can have a positive impact on the classroom environment. These factors include recognizing effective teaching behaviors, creating positive interpersonal relationships, and enhancing on-task behaviors.

Recognizing Effective Teaching Behaviors

What does a good teacher do? What behaviors do they display? There are many ways to answer that question. Classic educational research has described the behaviors of teachers who are most successful during traditional teacher-centered whole class instruction (Brophy & Evertson, 1976; Doyle, 1986; Emmer, Evertson, & Anderson, 1980). Although teacher behaviors have not been studied as much in more interactive, student-centered classrooms, these three proactive behaviors associated with early research seem to make sense in most settings and can serve as general principles to guide teacher behavior (Jones, 1996).

The teacher actions most associated with effective teaching include an explicit awareness of what is going on in the classroom, or "withitness" (Kounin,

An effective learning environment requires teachers' attention to many factors, including student relationships, on-task learning behaviors, student organization, time, and materials.

1970). Most good teachers know their students, understand interactions, and can usually predict behavior and responses from their students. Teachers who are "with it" know when students are not attending to instruction or when they are upset or happy and can redirect classroom activities to take advantage of or defuse classroom attitudes. A change of pace or activity can be made at a critical time if a teacher maintains close contact with what is going on in the classroom.

Good teachers also plan smooth transitions between activities. They understand that procedures for moving from one activity to another should be clearly understood by students. Routines are introduced to change activities and to move from small-group to large-group instruction. If rules for transitions are clearly articulated, students do not lose valuable time when making instructional transitions and disruptive behavior is avoided during transition.

Finally, good teachers find ways to hold students accountable for assignments and classroom activities. Teachers should expect assignments and activities to be completed in thoughtful and productive ways and should provide feedback when students respond or provide a product. The feedback should be appropriate, and students should understand how and when feedback will occur.

Each of these behaviors makes very good sense in any type of instructional setting. They have become the mainstay of expected teacher behaviors, although some educators encourage more consideration of instructional objectives and methods in defining good teacher behaviors (Jones, 1996). For example, the concept of "withitness" might change if a teacher uses a great deal of small-group work and independent work where students may find ways to deal with problem solving that are not as controlled as in traditional classrooms. Teachers may not control each aspect of problem solving and learning, and the smoothness of transitions may be interrupted when students are developing their own learning processes. A more modern approach to identifying effective teacher behaviors is to see how instructional goals guide the classroom management techniques as opposed to imposing specific teacher behaviors before the instructional outcomes are identified.

Creating Positive Interpersonal Relationships

The extent to which students will have their needs met in an educational setting is dependent on the relationships between teachers and students. Understanding that classroom organization and effectiveness are influenced by the beliefs and perceptions of teachers and learners suggests that roles and relationships of learners and teachers must be considered when planning for instruction (Green, Kantor, & Rogers, 1990). The relationships between teachers and students are dynamic and change with each new class or when a new learning strategy is introduced (Zaharlick & Green, 1991).

Teacher–Student Relationships   Interacting with young people is one of the major reasons individuals become teachers, but these same interactions can also be the greatest source of frustration and stress to teachers. Teachers report that much of the stress associated with their work comes from managing student behavior (Jones, 1996). Experienced teachers explain that students and their behavior have changed dramatically since the 1980s, making it more difficult to plan and manage instruction. Teachers are being asked to deal with a wide range of students in their classrooms, including students with special needs—academic, social, personal, and emotional characteristics that require a great deal of attention and can cause unpredictable results during class interactions.

The quality of interactions between teachers and students affects students as well as teachers. Since the 1960s, educators have known that positive relationships between teachers and students can improve academic behavior. Students do care about what their teachers think about them. When students believe that their teachers care about and respect them, they are more positive and have higher academic achievement (Phelan, Davidson, & Cao, 1992).

Students who are more at risk of failure in school environments need more support from teachers than do students who are more successful (Wehlage et al., 1989). At-risk students need to feel that they belong in the classroom and that their teachers care about them. Several educators have made this point regarding the relationships between teachers and minority students. Comer (1988) wrote that "no matter how good the administration, teachers, curriculum, or equipment; no matter how long the school day or year; and no matter how much homework is assigned, if students do not attach and bond to the people and program of the school, less adequate learning will take place" (p. 46). Most important, teachers should realize the importance of expressing a sense of optimism that all students can learn (Wehlage et al., 1989).

The feedback of teachers to students about their work plays an important role in positive learning environments. Clear and specific feedback that is immediate, focuses on students' performance and effort, and avoids comparisons with others is most effective. When grades and test scores establish environments where comparisons are made and success and failure is numerically calculated, providing feedback related to school achievement and promoting a cooperative as opposed to a competitive environment may be difficult. Standardized test-driven settings are becoming increasingly popular, and teachers must develop positive feedback strategies that focus on individual progress and achievement over time.

Peer Relationships   An important aspect not often discussed, but related to positive learning environments, is peer relationships. More effective classrooms are established when the students within the classroom get along and can work together. A classroom personality develops from the combination of students in the classroom. Classrooms offer an opportunity for prolonged contact with peers, and interactions serve more than an educational role in students' development. Interactions between peers in classrooms contribute to social roles, adult personality patterns, and future peer associations. Instructional strategies requiring students to accomplish tasks cooperatively and in small-group settings make positive peer relationships even more important in today's classrooms.

Some research has shown that students' achievement increases when they are accepted by their classmates, and students work together to establish norms

Field-Based Activity 7.2

Observe in the classroom setting and determine what types of behavior students display when off-task. What are they doing when not paying attention to their teacher or when they quit working on the classroom assignment? Are they reading, talking to each other, or distracted in other ways? Complete the chart in Table 7.1. Compare your findings in a class discussion and define task-oriented behavior. Are you tolerant or intolerant when students do not do what the teacher expects? What does this tell you about your view of teaching and authority?

related to how they perform and respond in the classroom (Jones, 1996). Teaching students to interact and collaborate more with each other may ultimately enhance classroom behavior, increase school achievement, contribute to positive learning environments, and develop important life skills (Jones, 1996). Attention to student relationships and developing a culture of cooperation encourages behavior skills that are valued in society and the workplace.

Enhancing On-Task Behavior

The amount of time that a student is actively engaged in learning tasks, known as on-task behavior, is related to successful learning. Consideration of the amount of time involved in learning is a classic way of looking at classroom management as well as instruction. To plan instruction that achieves the most on-task behavior, teachers must establish goals, design instruction to reach the goals, and provide immediate feedback to students during learning attempts.

Motivate   The ability to motivate, to engage students in learning, is a crucial element for establishing a positive learning environment. Children are born with the motivation to learn (Wlodkowski & Jaynes, 1990). The curiosity of infants, toddlers, and preschool children who ask questions, experiment, and acquire new information on what seems like an hourly basis is a joy to watch. Too often the child's entry into formal educational practices results in loss of the spontaneous joy of learning evident with younger children. Competition for a child's motivation, formalized approaches to learning, constant evaluation, and grading are a few of the factors that may change motivation related to school learning.

The motivation to learn must become a habit, a routine, and a priority in young people's lives that contributes favorably to learning in school (Wlodkowski

Table 7.1 Off-Task Behaviors

Behaviors	Descriptors	Observation Notes
Chatting	Student is talking with others.	
Disruptive Behavior	Students are making noises, teasing others, roaming around the classroom.	
Personal Needs	Students are sharpening pencils, being excused to go to the bathroom, getting a drink of water.	
Uninvolved	Students obviously are not listening or taking part in classroom activities, and are daydreaming, staring.	
Waiting	Students are standing in line, raising their hands, waiting on teacher.	
Sleeping	Students have their heads on their desks, eyes closed.	
Other Behaviors		

& Jaynes, 1990). Many school factors including the nature of the task, responsibility, rewards, use of groups, evaluation, testing, and teacher expectations affect motivation (Malhr & Anderson, 1993). Culture, family, school, organizational structures, and individual personality all come to bear on learners' motivational levels. Despite a large number of outside influences, motivation to learn can be taught and encouraged. A good teacher increases the potential for academic motivation to learn in various ways.

Provide Support for Success Students will work to accomplish learning tasks if a support system exists to help them avoid frustration and confusion. Teachers support student efforts by making tasks manageable, providing models for accomplishing tasks, and being sure that students understand explanations and processes (Blumenfeld, Puro, & Mergendoller, 1992). Additional support can be provided for learning demanding material through small-group collaboration and opportunities to share learning. Scaffolding, initially giving a great deal of help and facilitative encouragement and gradually requiring students to do more and more on their own, is also an important way to provide support during learning activities.

Successful teachers make sure that their students can take part in the learning activities. When introducing a particular routine or strategy, everyone should know how to participate and what is required for successful involvement. Even students at the secondary level must often be taught instructional procedures that will help them succeed in the classroom. They may not automatically know how to do what is required for academic achievement. For example, if the teacher is using a particular cooperative learning technique and students are taking on roles such as leader, timer, and question poser, students should be taught what is expected of each role.

Communicate High Expectations   Teachers' expectations and student motivation are linked. Teachers and students must believe that success is possible, that tasks are reasonable, and that all students can do the work. Students are willing to attempt difficult tasks if it is clear that those around them believe they can succeed. All students should be expected to do their best, and no exceptions should be made because of gender or culture. Developing the perspective that all students can and will achieve, no matter what their gender, ethnic, or linguistic background, is a belief fostered throughout teacher careers.

Provide for Flexibility and Variation   An important factor related to motivation is having available a multitude of tasks at appropriate levels of difficulty. Students who are able to select their mode and method of learning in various situations will be more motivated to focus on their learning tasks. Some tasks must be completed by all students, and there will be times when the teacher will select the focus. But when it is appropriate for students to learn different information or in different ways, they can be given choices. If students are allowed to select from a range of tasks, they will come closer to selecting the activities that are most motivating to them. The tasks should be challenging but at the same time realistic and should provide choices for learning in different ways.

Ability grouping and other comparative and competitive approaches can have a negative impact on motivation in some circumstances. Whenever possible, teachers should minimize processes that compare students or require them to compete against each other. The practices associated with comparison and competition can send the message that not everyone is expected to succeed in the same way. Teachers who use flexible grouping techniques based on achievement of specific skills or knowledge as opposed to grouping by ability, for example, treat their students as if they all can learn. Several types of flexible grouping arrangements are described later in this chapter.

Plan Relevant and Meaningful Activities   A most important contribution to the motivation of student learning is how much students value and are interested in the material. Learning activities that offer opportunities for students to relate their ordinary life experiences to the content presented in schools and that encourage students to use their real-life experiences to understand new information are meaningful to students. Learning does not occur in a vacuum. Connections to students' lives and opportunities to transfer their knowledge and strategies to new learning situations will motivate their learning.

Relevant learning activities produce the active and personal engagement that demonstrates motivation. Individual contributions, discussions, and sharing of life experiences are simple ways to make learning relevant. Focusing on topics that students find interesting, such as current events, popular culture, and media, will also increase the relevance of learning activities. Sometimes the teacher must help make connections to develop interest and relevance. Presenting Shakespeare as an analogy for a contemporary problem is an example of connecting topics to relevant issues.

Stress Cognitive Engagement   Students must be encouraged to answer questions and complete assignments and, as a result of their work, receive feedback (Blumenfeld et al., 1992). Cognitive engagement is encouraged when students synthesize, represent, demonstrate, and apply their knowledge in a variety of ways. Feedback requirements should be more than coming up with one right answer; they should involve manipulating the information, considering multiple answers, and sharing predictions and hypotheses.

Provide Feedback   To motivate continued learning, students need to know when a learning component ends and to be able to make some judgment about the impact of the activity on their own personal learning (Brophy, 1988; Lepper, 1983). The more learner goal-setting and self-monitoring that can be implemented, the more motivated students will be. Students should be held accountable for learning and understanding material, not just for getting the answers correct or making good grades. The frequency and form of teacher feedback play an important part in the classroom motivational process (Good & Brophy, 1999).

The teacher is key in motivating students. In addition to using all the techniques described, teachers can do a great deal to motivate students by being enthusiastic learners themselves. Providing a good example for motivated learning is one of the most successful techniques teachers can use to encourage attention to learning. Students want to know what activities and abilities interest adults. Reading, for example, is very easy to model. Sharing information and personal reading can be a powerful lesson in motivation to read and learn. When teachers share their excitement about learning new information, students are intrigued and interested. When teachers demonstrate that learning is important, motivating, and relevant, students will become increasingly self-motivated to be active learners. One way for teachers to demonstrate their enthusiasm for learning is to involve students in collaborative learning. Working and learning together is an excellent way to involve students in the learning process.

Organizing Students, Time, and Materials

Schools provide some students with a structure not present elsewhere in their lives. Other students will find that the regular routines of home life are consistent with school schedules and routines. This adherence to a certain structure does not mean that the plans and organizations of the classroom cannot be responsive to children's needs. On the contrary, effective teachers are willing to incorporate their students desires, interests, and concerns into the daily routine. Teachers who demonstrate flexibility with daily plans and routines will better meet the needs of their students. Personal events, such as neighborhood or family emergencies or crises within their peer groups, affect students' interest and attention. Worldwide events such as wars, national disasters, and presidential elections have an impact on the classroom. Sometimes teachers may abandon regular routines and refocus instruction to recognize relevant and current student interests. Generally, however, students should know what to expect from classroom instructional routines.

Organizing Students

There are several ways to organize a classroom full of students. When planning for instruction, the teacher must consider the goals of instruction, the desired nature of interaction, and the responses required during lessons. Small groups, large groups, or individual student arrangements are all viable grouping procedures depending on the instructional objectives.

Grouping Learners   Students can be arranged and grouped in many different ways during instruction. Different activities and goals, of course, will require various groupings. Distinctive classroom mixtures will require a variety of arrangements because the way individuals work together commands various organizational patterns. The key to arranging and managing the classroom is to be flexible and to experiment with different groupings to find the best one for the students, the activities, and the materials involved.

Students can benefit from varied grouping arrangements; different reactions and responses are produced when students interact with small groups of peers, peer pairings, or large groups. Small-group arrangements may ensure that all students will have an opportunity to take part in discussions. Not all children will volunteer in large-group settings, and small groups can encourage a great deal of interaction. Large-group work can provide a good opportunity to hear many ideas or to summarize learning and new knowledge. Large groups can present a wider range of ideas and solutions than small groups. Small groups may be more manageable than whole classes and can be assigned special projects.

There are many ways to arrange students during the school day. Although a teacher can use most any method for making group assignments, the teacher should avoid any organization that labels the learner. It is much more beneficial and positive to organize the class based on student and instructional needs.

- *Ability Grouping.* Grouping by ability or special talents is a controversial issue in schools and classrooms. Placing students into groups according to their abilities, usually measured by some form of standardized testing, is designed to reduce the wide range of differences among students so that more effective instruction can be provided. Recently, however, ability grouping has come under intense scrutiny, and it is no longer viewed as the optimum method of organizing students for instruction. Although some benefit may be seen for high-ability students, ability grouping presents problems for low-ability students (Garmon, Nystrand, Berends, & LePore, 1995). More specifically, here are several detrimental practices associated with ability grouping:

    1.   Ability grouping labels students. Often the placement of students in groups will affect their perception of their learning abilities for years to come. The results of grouping have been shown to be long lasting; most adults can remember which group they were in during their school experiences.

    2.   The groups remain constant through several years of schooling. It is seldom that students move from one group to another.

    3.   Instruction varies among groups. Instruction directed at students identified with less ability is usually more focused on simple tasks, less reading

and problem solving, and more rote learning. Many of these differences in instruction only maintain the differences in school performance.

4.   Members of minority groups and poor children have been over-represented in low-ability groups for years. Students whose language, experiences, and culture are different seem to be at risk on achievement tests. Ability groups reflect this discrepancy.

Teachers may have reason to establish ability groups to help students learn a particular skill or strategy, but once the strategy has been learned the group should be disbanded.

• *Flexible Grouping.* One way to arrange the class in small, manageable groups is to establish flexible grouping practices (Good & Brophy, 1999). Membership in a flexible group terminates when the reason for establishing the group is accomplished. Small groups can be established for long periods of time or may be set up for short-term projects or objectives. The goals and objectives of the small groups should be explicitly delineated and understood by the teacher and the students, and follow-up activities should be carefully described and monitored. Several types of small flexible groups can contribute to successful learning environments:

1.   Special project groups can work on activities that accompany instruction. A teacher may arrange students in groups to conduct lab experiments, read similar content, or interview other students in the school about a particular topic. Small flexible groups can be assembled to complete problems or other skills related to content areas.

2.   Interest groups can be established to enable groups of students to read, discuss, and complete activities based on common interests. Interest groups provide students with more opportunity to make decisions about classroom activities. For example, some students may group together because they are all interested in science fiction. However, they may read different books and share their stories or identify common elements of the genre they are reading. Another interest group could be formed to study poetry and songs. They might all share poetry orally or write their own poetry as a result of their common interest.

3.   Research groups are established to locate, organize, and report information. Research groups are particularly appropriate for instruction in content areas. Before research groups set out to work on their own, they should be taught research skills needed in the small group. Many of the skills can

be demonstrated in whole class settings before children are placed in small groups.

4. Instructional groups are formed when more than one student could benefit from teacher-led instruction. For example, a group of children who are having difficulty with long division processes involving remainders could meet together to receive extra instruction. These groups are disbanded when all group members understand the strategy, skill, or concept.

5. Brainstorming and categorizing groups are usually short-lived and are established to begin reading, discussing, or writing. Students are placed in small groups to list everything they know about a concept or a topic or to design questions they would like to answer during study.

6. Expert groups may be formed and assigned a topic on which they are supposed to become "experts." After studying and researching, the group becomes a resource for the rest of the class. Expert groups may be required to do the research, be familiar with a particular portion of the text, or perfect some skill that can be taught to others in the class.

• *Cooperative Grouping.* Cooperative learning describes a certain type of student grouping arrangement that may or may not be used in conjunction with the flexible grouping options previously described. Table 7.2 outlines one way to use cooperative group work in the classroom. Activities from any content area are planned and common goals are established to be met by assigning responsibilities for learning within the group. In most cases, four or five students form a cooperative group that works together to solve a problem or complete a task. Individual evaluation may be included as in Slavin's (1987) cooperative grouping approaches. However, individual competition is downplayed, and the work of the entire group is recognized for evaluation. The entire team is responsible for motivating all in the group to complete their tasks. Although cooperative learning has been set up in many different ways, there are basic guidelines for introducing the instructional strategy:

1. Clarify rules and procedures before implementing the procedures. After a teacher decides what is to be accomplished cooperatively, demonstration and instruction should accompany the task so that students are assured of success. Students should be explicitly aware of the goals and intentions of cooperative groups. Sample rules for the procedure might include the following:

    Know your responsibilities.

    Understand one another's roles.

    Help others who need help.

Table 7.2   Sample Cooperative Learning Lesson

Task: Each group will compare two reading selections. The teacher will have discussed methods of comparison in advance.

Group Responsibilities
1. Be sure that all group members have a copy of the two reading selections.
2. Involve each group member.
3. Assign roles and responsibilities.
4. Use the format provided by the teacher.
5. Share group work with the rest of the class.
6. Evaluate group performance after completion.

Individual Responsibilities
1. Read the selections to be compared.
2. Contribute to the summaries of the two texts.
3. Contribute at least two ways the stories are alike.
4. Help the entire group complete the format provided by the teacher.
5. Help the group contribute information to the whole class activity.

Evaluation (by the teacher)
1. Review the small-group summaries.
2. Evaluate group skills in making decisions, achieving goals, and helping each other.
3. Evaluate each small group's contribution to the class summary.

Do your part and contribute to group activities.

Use rules for disagreements and discussions.

Ask the teacher for help only as a last resort.

2.   Organize the groups. Most cooperative learning activities arrange the class in groups of three to six students. Each student is assigned a specific role. The individual is responsible for that role, and his or her contribution is necessary to complete the tasks successfully. Some of the tasks that might be assigned include:

Encourager

Observer

Materials monitor (makes sure all students have materials)

Recorder (writes responses from group members during group activities)

Becoming a Teacher in a Field-Based Setting

Reporter (reports responses from group members during large-group discussions)

3. Clarify purpose. Describe the goals for the activity and describe the task that is to be completed. Cooperative learning groups can accomplish reading activities, discussion or problem-solving activities, research activities, or any other work that is logical for more than one person to do.

4. Explain and demonstrate procedures. Students must be clear about the procedures and logistics of the group work. It may take time to teach students what will happen in small groups. The small-group activity can be introduced through whole class discussion, role-playing, or demonstration. Some of the skills students may need to learn to work in cooperative groups include making space for people, communication skills, elimination of put-downs, taking turns, and active listening (Hill & Hill, 1991). Students may need time to practice these skills before working together in cooperative groups.

5. Observe student interactions. Cooperative learning teaches students how to be independent and to interact with others, but it requires careful monitoring by the teacher. During activities, the teacher moves from group to group, noting problems, suggesting solutions to any potential conflicts, and generally guiding activities. Even though students are held responsible for their own learning, the teacher is still involved actively in students' work.

World Wide Web Site

You may learn more about cooperative learning at:
http://www.memphis-schools.K12.tn.us/

Whole Class Instruction   Working with the entire class may not be the best arrangement for all types of instruction, but some activities can be very successful if the whole class is involved. Discussions, enrichment activities, concept introduction, reading aloud, and direct instruction and skills and procedures can be accomplished with the whole class. It is a useful arrangement for presenting information for several reasons:

1. Whole class instruction is efficient. Presenting the information to the entire class at one time can free the teacher to provide more attention to individuals and smaller groups who may need more intense and repetitive instruction. Whole class instruction can be more economical when presenting some strategies and information. It is an excellent way to present routines,

discuss new approaches, and respond to information. Small-group work can follow whole class instruction and focus on different aspects of the main theme of instruction.

2. Whole class instruction provides students with time to interact with those of differing abilities and opinions. Whole class approaches avoid labeling or focusing on special abilities and offer an opportunity for a wide range of interests and abilities to be recognized. Students at all levels of ability can participate easily in whole class sharing and instruction thus feeling that they are a part of the class. Even if all students do not participate in discussions, they can learn a great deal by listening.

3. Whole class activities contribute to establishing a classroom community. Students who share and interact together build common experiences, languages, stories, and procedures. This is a time when all students in the class can share their ideas and understand others' perspectives. It is a time to get to know each other.

Almost any type of activity that can be accomplished in small groups can be done in whole classes and vice versa. The activities for the entire class should offer something for everyone. In-depth discussions or strategy instruction that applies only to a few students should be saved for small groups.

Teacher–Student Conferences   Conferences are an instructional strategy that can be used to encourage, monitor, evaluate, and guide students. Conferences can be conducted for individual students, small groups, or whole classes. The teacher is responsible for planning and organizing the structure normally used in each situation.

Conferences are individual or small-group meetings that provide teachers and students with an opportunity to discuss a wide array of academic issues. The teacher has a different role during conferences than might be expected in other grouping arrangements. Although the structure for what happens during the conference is provided by the teacher, the activities are guided by students who are responsible for establishing the topic or focusing on strategies. A teacher must remember that students should do most of the talking during a conference. Conferences are a time for teachers to listen and support students during the learning process. The discussions provide teachers with information that can help and guide student learning.

Conferences may be regularly scheduled with students or can be initiated by the teacher or student if there is a need. The main objective is to provide students with an opportunity to discuss their individual learning with the teacher. Conferences have been used extensively in teaching reading and writing (Wise-

While others in the class work independently, a teacher provides one-on-one attention to this student. Student–teacher conferences provide opportunities for teachers to evaluate student learning and help them with specific learning needs.

man, 1992), but they could be adapted for use across the curriculum. Conferences have four parts: sharing, questioning, interacting, and guiding (Pappas, Kiefer, & Levstik, 1990).

1. *Sharing.* Conferences can begin by having children share what they have been learning or accomplishing in class. If students have been keeping journals or other written records of class work, they can be encouraged to share some examples of their work with the teacher.

2. *Questioning.* The teacher listens to the student and asks questions about what the student is sharing. If the teacher is meeting with more than one student, the other students are also invited to ask questions.

3. *Interacting.* The conference includes opportunities to share new information, read orally, provide examples of learning, or share favorite or interesting issues. During the conference, the teacher notes and records discussion topics and examples for later reference.

Field-Based Activity 7.3

Use the text to produce a list of different ways of grouping students. Invite some of the teachers or student teachers from your school into your classroom to talk about how they organize their students for instruction. Share the list with them, and ask them what grouping arrangements they have used. What classroom management concerns do they feel these different kinds of grouping arrangements present? What do they see as the pros and cons of different grouping procedures?

4. *Guiding.* The teacher and the students discuss future plans for learning. Students can identify what else they need to learn, and the teacher can guide them to the next steps. At the conclusion of a conference, students know their next step in relation to the learning activity.

A conference can be used at any grade level to encourage independent learning and to respond individually to students. Once students learn the logistics of a conference, they can conduct conferences with each other.

Peer conferences give students an opportunity to share their learning and may be effective at the secondary as well as elementary levels. Conferences can be arranged and encouraged by the teacher or may occur spontaneously when a collegial atmosphere is established in the classroom. In a classroom that values the learning of individuals, it is not unusual to have student-initiated conferences. Often, informal conferences between students mirror the components of teacher-led conferences (Graves, 1994).

Student Pairs Students can be paired in numerous ways to support instructional organization. Pairs can be used to accomplish a goal, clarify an instructional objective, or tutor each other in a particular strategy. Students will need to experience responses to their own work to develop ways to respond to each other. They need to have guidance in how to respond to the work and ideas of classmates, and this requires teaching and demonstration opportunities.

Students can be paired to accomplish a specific goal. Teachers can pair students to provide each with practice in a particular strategy. Sometimes students can explain a new idea more clearly to their peers than a teacher can. Pairing students can provide opportunities for each to share his or her understanding of a topic. One adaptation of student pairs is cross-age tutoring. Arranging for situations in which older students tutor younger students can provide teachers with some help and enable younger students to receive some individual attention. For example, a freshman English teacher and a junior English teacher might design activities that feature juniors working one-on-one with freshmen to produce stories or book reviews.

Individual, Independent Activity   There are many times when students work independently. Daily plans will include projects and assignments for students to complete on their own without direct teacher supervision. While students are working independently, the teacher can meet with small groups and individuals. Individual activity must be planned carefully because of the potential for off-task behavior.

Organizing Time

Scheduling requires consideration of many activities and school structures. The school day may be divided in different ways depending on the grade level or teaching arrangements within individual schools. The overall school schedule places some constraints on how a teacher organizes the day. At any grade level, the school day is full of many activities that limit instructional time: Class pictures must be taken, assemblies must be attended, and guest speakers heard. A teacher will make many decisions about how the remaining time is organized. Even though the master schedule of a school will influence how a teacher organizes classroom time, the amount of available time and the nature of the learning activity also will be major considerations for a teacher who is planning daily activities (Epanchin, Townsend, & Stoddard, 1994).

The modular scheduling concept, which establishes specific amounts of time for instructional blocks, has existed in secondary schools for many years. Usually it is set up around forty- to sixty-minute blocks. For example, we are all familiar with science period, math period, and band period. These time blocks remain constant regardless of learning requirements or learning demands. One of the difficulties of teaching in high school is to cover content in regimented time blocks. There are times, for example, when the content may require longer periods of attention or when the nature of learning is such that students do not need to be engaged for extended periods of time. Some subjects can be best taught in short time blocks, and other learning might be most effective in longer in-depth sessions. One of the innovations in high school scheduling is to block courses, providing longer time periods for some courses and teaching two or more subjects together in others. For example, history may be taught in a ninety-minute block on alternating days, and English and social studies or science and math may be taught in two- or three-hour blocks.

Scheduling for elementary schools is usually more flexible because there are no predetermined subject periods, but teachers have another problem when planning elementary instruction. "Pull-out" classes or other special classes may interrupt the daily schedule of an elementary classroom. Students may leave the classroom for physical education, music, art, library, and special classes. Elementary teachers work with special teachers in English as a second language, bilingual, or special education to plan for times when students with special needs are scheduled in multiple programs. Making transitions and guiding students through many interruptions can be particularly problematic for students who attend resource rooms where they receive special instruction.

An important element in scheduling the day for elementary students or the weekly class schedule for secondary students is that they learn a predictable schedule. Students want to know what to expect in their classes. At times they can be flexible, but overall predictability helps them feel in control and allows for some understanding about expectations during the school day. Most elementary school day schedules and secondary schedules viewed in the context of an entire week will include time for the following activities:

1. *Whole class activities*. The teacher should plan for time when the entire class works together on specific activities. This is the time when the teacher focuses class work and organizes the day, class period, or week. Whole class instruction is a time to teach new strategies, discuss new information, or talk about the behavior that is expected of each student. The teacher might use this time to lecture, read aloud, have students read, or have discussions of general or topical interest. This time is very flexible depending on the teaching objectives and the developmental level of the students.

2. *Independent work time*. There are scheduled times in a daily or weekly class schedule when students will work on their own, making independent selections of reading material, working lab problems, or writing responses to assignments. Even very young students will have some daily independent work time. Some independent work time can be assigned in response to assignments or discussions introduced during whole class activities. Independent work time may occur for the entire class or for part of the class working independently while the teacher works with small groups. The rules for independent work should be established early, and everyone should be aware of how this time is conducted.

3. *Discussion or sharing time*. Discussion or sharing sessions culminate the time allotted for planned instruction. Discussion provides opportunities to verbalize and talk about what students have read and written in their independent work. Sharing time provides opportunities to discuss books, share personal writing, check lab problems, reteach, and evaluate the effectiveness of instruction. Sharing time may be different from class focus time, when

Highly capable students can work on their own. A student's ability to engage in independent study is often dependent on a teacher's skill in organizing lessons and motivating.

teachers implement specific plans and objectives, because it may be guided by what the students wish to discuss or share.

Organizing Materials

Materials used in the classroom are diverse. Schools usually provide basic textbooks, some selected lab materials, and access to multimedia. Teachers may contribute some of their own books, references, and media equipment to the classroom. Students also may provide materials they have written and designed to classroom instructional processes.

Basals and Textbooks Instructional organization traditionally relies on textbooks, which are provided in most classrooms. There are textbooks for almost all content areas. Although lessons designed to accompany textbooks may vary somewhat from subject to subject, most lesson structures include before-reading, during-reading, and after-reading activities and discussions. The before-reading activities provide background information, develop vocabulary, and establish purpose and learning objectives. Skills instruction can be part of the introductory activities or part of the conclusion of a lesson. The skills emphasized in the introductory phase are subject-related. For example, social studies might focus on globe and map skills, and science might focus on laboratory skills. Teachers are given guidance in directing the activities through lesson plans suggesting discussions and activities that reinforce, reteach, or enrich the concepts and enable teachers to evaluate what students have learned.

Textbook publishers provide teacher's editions that have many suggestions for instruction as well as specific lesson plans for particular units and concepts and supplemental materials. For example, a social studies series might include maps, globes, and atlases. A science series might include lab manuals, microscopes, and charts.

Almost all states have approved textbooks and basal readers that school districts can select for use. These approved texts usually reflect the statewide curriculum and make sure that objectives and goals identified by the state are covered. The school districts select their texts from the list of textbooks on the state-adopted list.

Textbooks can play an important role in the instructional process as one source of material for teachers. The suggested plans accompanying the textbooks can be used as a framework for instruction. Suggestions can give teachers ideas about where to start their instruction, introduce and augment discussions of topics, serve as surveys to begin the study of a concept, and establish initial concepts about a topic before students begin a self-directed study. It is not unusual, however, to see a single textbook adopted and used in classrooms as the sole source of information on a subject. When there is total reliance on basal readers and textbooks, they control what is taught, how it is taught, and in what order instruction is presented to students. This total dependence may not be desirable for several reasons. One of the first problems that arises is that learners come to classes with differences in prior knowledge and interest in the topic. Sometimes children need different levels of motivation to encourage their interest in a topic, and textbooks do not always present material in an interesting way. The concerns associated with the misuse of textbooks are enough to demonstrate that textbooks alone are not adequate for teaching most subjects.

Students have more potential to read and learn concepts and information if a large variety of printed and other media is available. Effective use of textbooks suggests that teachers should make decisions, use their knowledge of the content, the student, and instructional methods, and select a variety of materials to support the instructional approaches used in the classroom.

Children's and Young Adult Literature   Teachers of elementary, middle, and high schools can take advantage of the wide range of children's and young adult literature available to teach almost any subject. Literature, both fiction and non-fiction, provides an excellent resource in planning instruction. Students can learn concepts, facts, and ideas from both expository and narrative literature. Literature can be incorporated into almost any subject taught in schools and can be used to build knowledge, motivation, and interest on a range of topics. Supplementing textbooks with literature increases opportunities to read about, write about, and discuss many different subjects.

Newspapers, Magazines, and Other Current Periodicals   Today's world is changing so rapidly that current periodicals will sometimes have the most up-to-date information about topics being presented in the classroom. Options for classroom reading material include materials that are regularly read in the home and workplace. Popular periodicals can serve an important role during instruction. Current periodicals can be written for school students or directed toward adult readership. *Weekly Reader* and *Scholastic Magazine*, written for young people, are two periodicals found in many classrooms. Daily newspapers and weekly newsmagazines can be used with older readers. Other available magazines and periodicals reflect a wide range of interests and concerns, including outdoor life, science, sports, and cultural activities. Use of magazines and periodicals enriches the classroom and assures that a wide range of interests, cultures, and perspectives are represented during instruction.

Computers and Multimedia   More and more teachers now have the opportunity to use computers and other multimedia technology in their classrooms. With modern methods of communication, such as CD-ROMs, email, and the Internet, the resources available in the classroom are greatly expanded. Teachers can use the technology to find new instructional approaches, access teaching units, and identify resources from all over the world. Students can use the technology to complete research projects, communicate with others and identify sources for further contact, and present projects in varied ways. Only the teachers' and students' imaginations will limit the ways that new technology can contribute to classroom planning.

Much information can be provided in print, film, and recordings, and there are many effective ways to use tapes, CDs, television, movies, and VCRs in instruction. These common technological tools can add a great deal to classroom instruction through enrichment activities to units of study or reading assignments.

Field-Based Activity 7.4

Sketch the design of the classroom where you are assigned. During classroom observations, watch carefully to see what student behavior is encouraged by the physical arrangement of the room. Watch what students do as they walk into the classroom and prepare for the day's activities. Watch how the arrangement of the room contributes to the ongoing instructional processes in the room. Share your observations in class, and associate particular types of classroom learning and interactions with various classroom physical arrangements. Can you identify a link?

Physical Arrangement

The physical arrangement of classrooms should support routines, grouping, and instructional activities. Arrangements will vary according to the amount of space, equipment, and furniture available. The room's size, space, and shape are relatively constant, but teachers can arrange the furniture and equipment to suggest an emphasis on group work, individual work, or whole class discussions. This may be more difficult for secondary teachers who share classrooms with other teachers or for teachers not assigned a specific classroom. In this case, the teachers may need to get together to discuss how they can best arrange rooms to reflect different needs and approaches. Classrooms should invite movement from small groups to individual work to whole class sharing. Materials should be easily available to students. If possible, quiet spaces for individuals as well as small-group work space should be provided during learning opportunities. The classroom becomes a space that reflects a teacher's philosophy and the students' work.

Some teachers will need a classroom with movable desks, chairs, and tables so that the room arrangements can be changed for certain activities. In general, a room should provide a large space for whole class instruction and sharing, a smaller area for small-group work, display and bookshelves, and individual work spaces.

The physical arrangement of the classroom, materials, and equipment can make a statement about the philosophy of instruction. Classrooms can be arranged to say "Let's read, talk, and write about what interests us." Classroom arrangements may also suggest a student-centered focus and a challenge to try things. Circular arrangements or round tables stimulate interactions. The arrangement of the classroom can reflect different instructional approaches and different student needs. Teachers will recognize what arrangements are most advantageous to their teaching style over time and with some trial and error.

Becoming a Teacher in a Field-Based Setting

Discipline

Teachers who attend to many of the aspects of classroom management identified as crucial to positive learning events will avoid a great many conflicts and have significantly fewer classroom disruptions. Even so, there will be times when students bring problems to the classroom, and even teachers who are very effective classroom organizers will be confronted with unproductive student behavior that requires intervention (Brophy, 1996). Disciplining students for disruptive behavior should be part of a continuous plan that is explicit to the teacher and students. Skills necessary for teachers during disciplining procedures are the ability to listen, knowledge of conflict-resolution techniques, the ability to work with teams of professionals who can focus on the disruptive behavior of a particular student, and the knowledge to develop and carry out management and discipline plans.

The most important aspect of attending to disruptive behavior is to return the classroom to a constructive atmosphere. Regaining control of the classroom quickly and avoiding involvement of more students than necessary is a goal following any type of disruptive behavior or confrontation. Several strategies are important for the teacher when responding to disruptive student behavior:

1. Try not to make unreasonable requirements or overreact to disruptive incidents. Teachers may contribute to the crisis at hand by exerting too much control or power, responding in a prejudicial or grudging manner, or not attending to students' behaviors (Seeman, 1988). Teachers should examine their own contributions to disruptive situations.

2. Be honest about your feelings. If you are upset, disappointed, or angry, explain that to students. They will be the first to know if you are trying to mask your feelings. They will respect you for your honesty and realize that you have emotions and reactions that are similar to theirs.

3. Be consistent and follow through with what you have said you will do. When rules of discipline are established, it is crucial that the teacher follow through with those processes. Threats should be avoided; they will only encourage student challenges.

4. Above all, be fair with your students. If you have made a mistake, applied rules indiscriminately, or have implemented actions that are not working or were not fair in the first place, apologize to your students. They will respect you for your honesty and openness.

When students' misbehavior is serious and teachers' efforts fail to result in appropriate behavior, more severe strategies are needed. Usually, this occurs with collaborative consultation between classroom teachers and other educational

Voice of a Teacher

Keeping a classroom on-task and involved is a complicated task. It's hard to explain to someone else about your own classroom discipline because it is such a personal thing. I have developed a discipline system that reflects my personality, experience, and philosophy. Students contribute to the organization in a classroom too. The makeup of the class makes a big difference in how I manage instruction and keep order and discipline. Some years my discipline is much easier to establish than others.

I believe that management and discipline are closely related. I have found that good organization helps reduce the discipline problems in my classrooms. When my students understand what is expected of them, know what work they need to finish, and how I will respond to them . . . most of them will work in class. They really want to be actively engaged—they like to interact with each other while engaged in interesting, meaningful activities.

Don't get me wrong. There are times my students don't go along with my planning. They may not be motivated to learn what I am trying to teach. Or they may need a great deal of structure to get them into the learning mode. Kids do need limits. I have to establish limits, rules, and follow through—do what I say I will do.

Another important aspect of classroom management and discipline is to figure out how you can show respect for your students. I try and listen to what they say and listen carefully to what they are telling me. I try to see the movies they see and read what they are reading. I can't always understand or enjoy their music—but I try. When I show that I know about some of these things, my students are really impressed. They know that I am interested in what they are doing.

I worried more about classroom management and discipline when I started teaching than I did any other thing. It didn't matter how much anyone talked to me about it—it's hard to know how to juggle all the aspects of classroom discipline and management—it is mostly learned while you are in front of a classroom. And each teacher will have his or her own individual way of approaching classroom organization. If I were to give a new teacher advice, I would suggest that the teacher read as much as possible and then approach his or her first classroom with the idea that it will be organized, well planned, and respectful. And then I would tell new teachers to remember that classroom management and discipline will get easier with experience.

resource staff. Consequences may involve corporal punishment in states where it is allowed and suspension from school.

Corporal punishment (spanking) is dreaded by all schoolchildren. Most educators believe the use of force does little to encourage compliance with rules or to promote good behavior because punishment may have unintended consequences that make it an undesirable option. Suspension from school is another severe response for violation of school rules. Except in cases in which students are dangerous to themselves or others, school suspension should be discouraged (Pinnell, 1985). In cases of corporal punishment and suspension, student behavior is controlled by outside forces and the student is not developing and internalizing self-controls. Some schools provide in-school suspension centers, which remove students from the classroom but enable them to continue their studies. Take time now to complete the Self-Reflection exercise and to think about what you have learned.

Classroom Environments and Decision Making

The management of a classroom requires a teacher to make numerous decisions in a fast-paced, complex environment. Decisions about the classroom range from the physical organization of desks and tables to intense personal interactions during teacher–student confrontations. Decisions about organizing and planning for instruction can seem overwhelming for beginning teachers, and they often must draw on numerous support systems to help with the task.

A new teacher's own experiences play an important role in how he or she organizes a classroom. How you were taught during your schooling will influence

---

Self-Reflection

WHAT MATTERS?

Think about what you value most in classrooms. Then rank order the following values from 1 (most value) to 12 (least value). (One space has been left blank for you to add any descriptor that you value that is not included in this list.)

____ Quiet	____ Equality
____ Laughter	____ Fairness
____ Respect	____ Self-direction
____ Orderliness	____ Caring
____ Creativity	____ Competition
____ Freedom	____ _____

Now look at your top three choices. What does this say about the rules you will enforce and the behaviors you will encourage in your own classroom? For example, if you chose quiet, orderliness, and respect as your top three values, you might not feel comfortable implementing activities that require considerable student movement and interactions. If you selected creativity, freedom, and self-direction, you might be more comfortable with high levels of student interaction and student-led activities.

Portfolio Reflections and Exhibits

Choose one of the field-based activities suggested in the text, develop an exhibit that represents what you have learned during the readings and discussions accompanying this chapter, or complete the suggested portfolio exhibit listed here. Your response to the activities or your exhibit may become part of your teaching portfolio.

Suggested Exhibit 7: My Emerging View of Classroom Management

1. Review your responses to each of the field-based activities in this chapter. Compile your personal list of the descriptors that emerged after each of the activities. Summarize in writing what your responses to each of the activities had in common. Identify the descriptors that were mentioned with each of the activities.

2. Represent your responses to classroom management and organization in some explicit and descriptive way. Use a graphic, such as a continuum, a computer program, a drawing, an essay, or a collage, to describe how you see yourself as a classroom manager. Will you be flexible, traditional, creative, structured, or eclectic? Describe your thoughts about classroom environments. Be prepared to share your representation with your classmates.

the way you feel that your classroom should be organized. In addition, what you observed in the classroom during your teacher preparation process will provide important information that will help you make decisions about your own classroom. But experience is not the only way to learn about classroom environments. Knowledge about classroom organization can also be accessed through reading professional books and journals. The topic of effective classroom environments has received a great deal of attention from thoughtful and experienced educators, and their insights provide well-founded information that will help a beginning teacher make informed decisions. Given the complexities of classrooms, the many needs of students, and the growing knowledge about good classroom management techniques, new teachers will experience great challenges as well as find much support as they establish their own classrooms.

 # InfoTrac College Edition Extension

Log on to the InfoTrac College Edition Web site. Choose an educational journal and a topic from the chapter and find articles of interest to you. Here are some suggestions to get you started:

1. Using the PowerTrac search, choose journal from the index and type in "Educational Leadership." Then choose subject from the index, and type in "classroom management." Your search expression should look like this: Jn Educational Leadership and su classroom management.

2. Do the same search for the Instructor journal.

Related Readings

Collins, M., & Tamarkin, C. (1990). *Marva Collins' way: Returning to excellence in education.* New York: Putnam.

> *Marva Collins, a successful Chicago teacher, presents some inspiring ideas about establishing a successful classroom environment. She talks about how she motivates children who might normally be unsuccessful in our schools.*

Paley, V. G. (1990). *The boy who would be a helicopter: The uses of storytelling in the classroom.* Cambridge, MA: Harvard University Press.

> *This book tells the story of a troubled child who continually disrupts the classroom. The teacher uses storytelling to help him become an effective classroom participant. This story will help you understand how flexible teachers must be to meet their students' unique needs.*

References

AAUW. (1992). *How schools shortchange girls.* Washington, DC: National Education Association.

AAUW. (1998). *Gender gaps: Where schools still fail our children.* Washington, DC: Author.

Ames, C. (1992). Classrooms: Goals, structures and student motivation. *Journal of Educational Psychology, 83*(3), 261–271.

Bartolome, L. (1994). Beyond the methods fetish, toward a humanizing pedagogy. *Harvard Educational Review, 64*(2), 173–194.

Bennett, W. (1998). A nation still at risk. *Policy Review, 90,* 23–29.

Blumenfeld, P. C., Puro, P., & Mergendoller, J. R. (1992). Translating motivation into thoughtfulness. In H. H. Marshall (Ed.), *Redefining student learning* (pp. 112–125). Norwood, NJ: Ablex.

Brophy, J. (1988). Educating teachers about managing classrooms and students. *Teaching and Teacher Education, 4*(1), 1–18.

Brophy, J. (1996). *Teaching problem students.* New York: Guilford.

Brophy, J., & Evertson, C. (1976). *Learning from teaching: A developmental perspective*. Boston: Allyn & Bacon.

Chandler, S. (1992). Learning for what purpose? Questions when viewing classroom learning from a sociocultural curriculum perspective. In H. H. Marshall (Ed.), *Redefining student learning* (pp. 86–99). Norwood, NJ: Ablex.

Comer, J. (1988). Educating poor minority children. *Scientific American, 359*(5), 42–48.

Dana, N. (1992). *Towards preparing the monocultural teacher for the multicultural classroom*. Paper presented at the 72nd annual meeting of the Association of Teacher Educators, Orlando. (ERIC Document Reproduction Service No. ED 350 272)

Doyle, W. (1986). Classroom organization and management. In M. Wittrock (Ed.), *Handbook of research on teaching* (3rd ed., pp. 392–431). New York: Macmillan.

Dryfoos, J. (1990). *Adolescents at risk: Prevalence and prevention*. New York: Oxford University Press.

Emmer, E., Evertson, C., & Anderson, L. (1980). Effective classroom management at the beginning of the school year. *Elementary School Journal, 80*(5), 219–231.

Epanchin, B. C., Townsend, B., & Stoddard, K. (1994). *Constructive classroom management: Strategies for creating positive learning environments*. Pacific Grove, CA: Brooks/Cole.

Fernie, D., Kantor, R., & Klein, E. (1990). *School culture and peer culture influences on adult and child roles in a preschool classroom*. Unpublished paper presented at AERA, Boston.

Garmon, A., Nystrand, M., Berends, M., & LePore, P. (1995). An organizational analysis of the effects of ability grouping. *American Educational Research Journal, 32*, 687–715.

Glasser, W. (1988). On students' needs and team learning: A conversation with William Glasser. *Educational Leadership, 45*(6), 38–45.

Good, T., & Brophy, J. (1999). *Looking in classrooms* (8th ed.). New York: Longman.

Graves, D. (1994). *A fresh look at writing*. Portsmouth, NH: Heinemann.

Green, J. L., Kantor, R. M., & Rogers, T. (1990). Exploring the complexity of language and learning in classroom contexts. In B. Jones & L. Idol (Eds.), *Educational values and cognitive instruction: Implications for reform* (Vol. II, pp. 400–422). Hillsdale, NJ: Erlbaum.

Hill, S., & Hill, T. (1991). *The collaborative classroom: A guide to cooperative learning*. Portsmouth, NH: Heinemann.

Jeneks, C., & Phillips, M. (Eds.). (1998). *The black-white test score gap*. Washington DC: Brookings Institute.

Jones, V. (1996). Classroom management. In J. Sikula (Ed.), *Handbook of research on teacher education* (pp. 503–524). New York: Macmillan.

Becoming a Teacher in a Field-Based Setting

Kounim, J. S. (1970). *Discipline and group management in classrooms.* New York: Holt, Rinehart &Winston.

Kuykendall, C. (1992). *From rage to hope: Strategies for reclaiming black and Hispanic students.* Bloomington, IN: National Educational Service.

Lepper, M. R. (1983). Extrinsic reward and intrinsic motivation. In J. Levine & M. Wang (Eds.), *Teacher and student perceptions: Implications for learning* (pp. 212–232). Hillsdale, NJ: Erlbaum.

Malhr, M., & Anderson, E. (1993). Reinventing schools for early adolescents: Emphasizing task goals. *Elementary School Journal, 93,* 593–610.

McCaslin, M., & Good, T. (1992). Compliant cognition: The misalliance of management and instructional goals in current school reform. *Educational Researcher, 21*(3), 4–17.

Noddings, N. (1995). Philosophy of education (dimensions of philosophy). Boulder, CO: Westview Press.

Olsen, L., & Mullen, N. (1990). *Embracing diversity: Teachers' voices from California's classrooms.* San Francisco: California Tomorrow Project.

Orenstein, P. (1994). *School girls.* New York: Doubleday.

Pappas, C. C., Kiefer, B. K., & Levstik, L. S. (1990). *An integrated language perspective in the elementary school: Theory into action.* New York: Longman.

Phelan, P., Davidson, A., & Cao, H. (1992). Speaking up: Students' perspectives on school. *Phi Delta Kappan, 73*(9), 795–804.

Pinnell, G. S. (1985). The "catch-22" of school discipline policy making. *Theory into Practice, 24,* 289.

Seeman, H. (1988). *Preventing classroom discipline problems.* Lancaster, PA: Technomic.

Slavin, R. E. (1987). Ability grouping and student achievement in elementary schools: A best evidence synthesis. *Review of Educational Research, 57*(3), 293–336.

Wehlage, G., Rutter, R., Smith, G., Lesko, N., & Fernandez, R. (1989). *Reducing the risk: Schools as communities of support.* London: Falmer Press.

Wiseman, D. L. (1992). *Learning to read with literature.* Boston: Allyn & Bacon.

Wlodkowski, R. J., & Jaynes, J. H. (1990). *Eager to learn: Helping children become motivated and love learning.* San Francisco: Jossey-Bass.

Zaharlick, A., & Green, J. L. (1991). Ethnographic research. In J. Flood, J. Jensen, D. Lapp, & J. Squire (Eds.), *Handbook of research on teaching the English language* (pp. 205–225). New York: Macmillan.

CHAPTER 8

Teaching Lessons in Today's Classrooms

*M*yths and their Meaning polished off, my SS class was given a collection of simple contemporary short stories; fortunately, there was a surplus in the Book Room. The first one dealt with a child who was allergic to sweets, his mother, who had admonished him never to eat them, and a good-hearted but misguided neighbor who believed the child's stories about his cruel mother and his deprivations, and who fed him sweets until he became violently ill. The mother threatened to sue the neighbor. End of story.*

The discussion I started in class—about good intentions and responsibility—proved so lively, that I decided to follow it up with a dramatization. I asked them to come prepared the next day to transform the classroom into a courtroom; and we would plead the case, as a sequel to the story. . . . I assigned the roles: mother, father, neighbor, child, prosecuting attorney, defense attorney, witnesses for the defense and the prosecution, even the doctor. I realized we had left out the judge. Through one of those swift moments of inspiration, I turned to Jose Rodriguez and asked him to be prepared to act the judge. A few in class snickered; Jose nodded; and I myself had no idea what to expect.

The following day he appeared in class in a cap and gown—a black graduation gown and mortarboard, borrowed or rented at what trouble or expense I could only guess, and a large hammer for a gavel. He bore a look of such solemn dignity that no one dared to laugh.

He sat at my desk and said: "The court clerk is supposed to say they gotta rise."

There was such authority in his voice that slowly, one by one, the class rose. It was a moment I don't think I will ever forget.

The class was directed to sit down, and the wheels of justice proceeded to turn. . . . When anyone spoke out of turn, Jose would pound on the desk with his hammer: "This here court will get quiet, or you will be charged with contempt."

He overruled every objection. . . . And when Harry Kagan challenged him on court procedure, he said, with quiet assurance: "I ought to know. I been."

The court ruled for the defense.

When the bell rang, Jose slowly removed his cap and gown, folded them neatly over his notebook, and went on to his next class; but he walked as if he were still vested in judicial robes.

I don't think he will ever be quite the same.

And that's it; that's why I want to teach; that's the one and only compensation: to make a permanent difference in the life of a child.

—Bel Kaufman, *Up the Down Staircase**

---

*From *Up the Down Staircase*, by Bel Kaufman (pp. 135–137). New York: HarperCollins.

Teachers are involved in making decisions every day. Decisions about what they should teach. Decisions about what materials they should use. Decisions about how to encourage learning in the classroom. Clarke and Peterson (1986) report that teachers make a decision on how to best affect student learning about every two minutes in the classroom. Many factors are considered when a teacher begins the planning process. This chapter will answer these questions:

- How do teachers decide what to teach?
- What resources are available to teachers?
- How can teachers use technology in the classroom?
- How is integrated instruction different from discipline-based instruction?
- How do teachers plan for individual lessons?
- How can teachers evaluate the success of their teaching?

Approaches to Classroom Instruction

It would take several books to describe all the different concepts, definitions, models, and approaches used to explain how teachers plan, organize, and implement their instruction. We will discuss two general categories, teacher-centered approaches and student-centered approaches, which provide a good overview of the choices available to teachers.

Teacher-Centered Approaches

Teacher-centered approaches hold the teacher responsible for all classroom activity. The teacher identifies topics of study, conceptualizes the goals, establishes the sequence of learning activities, presents the materials, and develops assessment procedures. The teacher explicitly identifies outcomes and controls and determines instruction. A common type of teacher-centered approach is direct instruction, during which the teacher relies on a structured process to direct students' thinking and participation. Instructional activities include whole group review, instructional input, and guided and independent practice. The teacher constantly checks for understanding and relies on drill and practice activities.

Direct instruction presents learning in small structured steps, requiring practice and structured feedback to make sure the student is learning. The teacher

Field-Based Activity 8.1

Talk to your mentor teacher about planning and writing a lesson, and discuss your mentor teacher's process for planning. What does he or she most enjoy, and what is the greatest challenge related to instructional planning? Share these responses with your classmates, and note the differences in how teachers approach their planning.

plays a major role and presents material, guides students, and provides students with extensive practice routines. This approach is especially useful when students are required to learn and master well-defined concepts and skills such as mathematics computations. Direct instruction illustrates many of the characteristics common to behavior learning theory (see Chapter 6).

Student-Centered Approaches

Student-centered approaches to instruction require a great deal of student participation and interaction between teacher and students and among students. Although the teacher facilitates and structures learning, students have a lot of responsibility and are delegated with a portion of the authority during learning activities. The focus of instructional strategies is on cooperation and class cohesiveness.

Student-centered approaches are also known as indirect methods because the teacher is involved less directly. Teachers are encouraged to shift from their traditional roles as information providers and toward a more facilitative, supportive role. The emphasis is on teaching students how to learn through peer and teacher interactions. Students are involved in goal-setting, and as a result of participation, they develop and share multiple opinions, question ideas and positions, and refer to multiple sources. Students may be asked to contribute personal experiences that offer information and clarify issues. Learning strategies are focused on the scientific or discovery method: gathering facts, hypothesizing, testing solutions, and revising solutions.

Student-centered approaches appear to improve students' attitudes toward learning, increase motivation, and develop social skills. There is some indication that student-centered approaches encourage higher level thinking skills, but critics of student-centered approaches maintain that basic skills learning is less emphasized in a total student-centered approach.

Establishing Goals for the Classroom

Goals and objectives are used by teachers to select the topics and activities for the day. Goals define what teachers expect students to learn if their teaching is successful. Ideally, all the materials, methods, and the climate of the classroom are manipulated to successfully attain these goals. Effective teachers not only understand these goals and how they fit into the larger framework of the total curriculum but make sure students understand them as well.

District, state, and national educational guidelines can begin to define a teacher's academic goals. According to Tyler (1974), goals establish priorities for what students learn and should be based on subject mastery, student needs and interests, societal concerns, community priorities, instructional theory, and research. Essential content for each grade level and learning objectives for each subject are often outlined by standards set outside the classroom. Standardized testing requirements also influence the curriculum content of the classroom, as teachers are often accountable for student achievement or mastery of test objectives.

State and National Goals

In recent years, several national teacher organizations, including the National Council of Teachers of Mathematics, the National Council for the Social Studies, the National Council for Improving Science Education, and the National Council of Teachers of English, adopted curriculum frameworks designed to develop learners who can think independently in real-world situations. These frameworks

TONY FREEMAN/PHOTOEDIT, INC.

Instructional approaches to classroom instruction should include opportunities to learn in a variety of ways. Students should experience a wide range of approaches including student-centered and teacher-directed learning opportunities.

shift the focus from curriculum based on isolated skills and memorization of basic facts to more complex thinking and problem solving (Falk, 2000). In the early 1990s, the president and the governors met to adopt six educational goals for the United States (see Table 3.1). Goals 2000 and the national curriculum focus on developing students who can think for themselves in a rapidly changing world and on maintaining high expectations for all students.

World Wide Web Sites

You can learn more about these national goals at:

http://www.odedodea.edu/2001_strategic_plan/research_study/goal.html

http://www.ed.gov/legislation/ESEA/Guidance/app-c.html

Address: Department of Defense Education Activity (DoDEA)
   4040 North Fairfax Street
   Arlington, VA 22203-1635

State educational guidelines also affect the goal-setting process of individual teachers in the classroom. State-mandated tests are often required at specific grade levels, and pressure to perform well can be intense. Figure 8.1 is a sample of instructional targets for mathematics for the Texas Assessment of Academic

Figure 8.1   Example of Objectives and Instructional Targets for the Texas Assessment of Academic Skills Test

Mathematics, Grade 4

DOMAIN: Concepts

Objective 1: The student will demonstrate an understanding of number concepts.
- Translate whole numbers (name to numeral/numeral to name).
- Compare and order whole numbers.
- Use whole numbers place value.
- Round whole numbers (to nearest ten or hundred).
- Recognize decimal place value (tenths and hundredths; using models).
- Use odds, evens, and skip counting.
- Recognize and compare fractions using patterns and pictorial models.

Objective 2: The student will demonstrate an understanding of mathematical relations, functions, and other algebraic concepts.
- Use whole number properties and inverse operations.
- Determine missing elements in patterns.
- Use number line representations for whole numbers and decimals.

DOMAIN: Operations

Objective 6: The student will use the operation of addition to solve problems.
- Add whole numbers and decimals (tenths and hundredths; using models).

Objective 7: The student will use the operation of subtraction to solve problems.
- Subtract whole numbers and decimals (tenths and hundredths; using models).

Skills test. Fourth-grade teachers in Texas, who know that they and their schools will be held accountable for their students' achievement in these areas, study these state guidelines and incorporate them into their curriculum to ensure student coverage of the material to be tested. Check the Web site of your state educational agency or other state educational resources to determine whether your state has guidelines or standards that you must incorporate in your lessons.

School districts also develop curriculum guides for teachers to use in planning. These guides often incorporate national and state standards and may be organized into subject matter units of study or around specific disciplines. School districts may also adopt special units of study, such as dental care or AIDS awareness, that teachers are required to teach at certain grade levels.

Assessing Curriculum Needs

Successful teachers serve as translators between the written curriculum and the needs of the students, constantly striving to define the written curriculum in a comprehensible, meaningful way for students. Bringing a written curriculum and preset curriculum goals to life in a real classroom, with a wide range of students operating at various levels of achievement, requires constant problem-solving and critical thinking skills related to assessment of the important need for curriculum and instruction.

At the beginning of any curriculum unit is the assessment of need. Need can be defined at several different levels. Subject matter and grade level needs are defined by the state and district curriculum guidelines, but interest and ability needs of students must also be considered.

Long-range planning decisions often occur before the semester or year begins. Teachers decide on broad topic areas or upcoming units of study based on what they want students to be able to do at the completion of the unit. Teachers estimate the time needed to accomplish their learning goals and plan a calendar for the year, knowing it will change constantly as students' interests and academic needs demand.

One technique for assessing what Pre K-12 students already understand and what they want to learn about a topic is by using a K-W-L chart (Carr & Ogle, 1987). The K column represents what students already know about a topic and reflects the need to link prior knowledge with new information, as discussed in Chapter 6. Students can work individually, in small groups, or with a whole class to discuss and record information they already know about the topic. Students then record or dictate the information to the teacher to complete the K column. The W column lists what students want to know about a topic. Questions are generated individually and in small groups and then reported to the class for recording and categorizing. This information can help teachers increase student motivation by making class topics interesting and relevant to students as they assist in goal-setting for their own learning. The last column on the K-W-L chart is for recording new learnings—what students learned about the topic. The K-W-L chart serves as a guide throughout the unit or lesson. Questions asked before the lesson are answered and crossed off the list as new learning occurs. New questions are added to the list, which may lead to extensions of a unit or topic.

After looking at goals set outside the classroom and at the learning needs of the students, teachers continue the individual planning process by reflecting on past experience. Based on previous experience with a grade or subject, teachers begin to establish short- and long-range goals. Retaining successful practices and redefining activities or processes that were unsuccessful, they learn to adopt high expectations yet are able to recognize unrealistic goals.

Field-Based Activity 8.2

Fill in a K-W-L chart, like the one shown below, for your own learning. Complete the first two columns now before you teach your lesson. Use the information you gained in field-based activity 8.1 to help you generate ideas for your first two columns. Discuss your charts in small groups, and then compile lists with the whole class. Fill in the last column after you have taught the lesson. Ask yourself these questions: What do I already know about planning and teaching a lesson? What do I want to know? What have I learned?

Topic: Planning and Teaching a Lesson

K	W	L
What I know . . .	What I want to know . . .	What I learned . . .

Short-range planning occurs every day in a variety of ways as teachers assess learning needs on a weekly or even an hour-by-hour basis. Short-range plans are constantly changing. For example, a math concept may prove to be more difficult than expected, and the lesson for the next period or for the next day may need to be adjusted. A writing activity may require more time than planned, and the activity may be extended into several additional upcoming class periods. Students may become very interested in a current event in the news, and the social studies unit may be modified to include this new topic of interest.

Creating, Selecting, and Adapting Resources

When students actively participate in acquiring new knowledge and are allowed to take some responsibility for their own learning, teachers must seek out many materials and resources to support the variety of classroom activities. Textbooks are supplemented with children's literature, reference materials, current periodicals, audiovisual aids, and computer software related to the topic. Needed materials can, however, be just as individual as the learning taking place in each classroom. Mr. Landmann, the third-grade teacher we met in Chapter 6, is constantly seeking out costumes and props suitable to portray the major characters in history so that when the third-graders present their research in a living history museum at the end of each six weeks they are properly attired. As a part of her unit on insects, one first-grade teacher worked to find live silkworms so that her students could observe them growing, spinning a cocoon, and eventually hatching into moths.

Using Technology

In most modern classrooms, technology is becoming an extension of the teacher's lesson plan, and students' thinking processes can be enhanced by using these new technologies (Jonassen, Peck, & Wilson, 1999). "Student motivation, attention and enthusiasm increase with technology in the classroom. Through technology, students become active participants, who are encouraged to creatively problem solve, explore and expand their horizons beyond the classroom" (Franzee & Rudnitski, 1996, p. 310). Let's examine some technological tools that provide a variety of modes for students to actively participate in their own learning and to construct new meaning.

- *Multimedia presentations.* When several senses (smell, touch, sound) are integrated to convey a message, multimedia is usually employed. Traditional instructional media include only the auditory and visual modalities, but new technologies available on multimedia software are engaging students in ways that were not possible in the past. Multimedia presentations now may include text, pictures, sound, video, and animation. Multimedia can also include record-based data, numeric data, and just about any form of communication that is possible (Jonassen, Peck, & Wilson, 1999). Such presentations can help students make learning meaningful and personal (Wilson, 1991), and students need to make these personal connections for learning to occur (Hawkins & Collins, 1992). Commercially or teacher-prepared multimedia presentations can be used in interactive ways, with students selecting the path of their own learning and moving through the material in ways that are individually meaningful to each student. Jonassen (1986) suggests that this nonlinear presentation of material is similar to

New technological innovations emerge at a rapid pace, requiring continuous learning on the part of the teacher and the students. Many students have access to computers at home and come to school with a wide range of technological expertise.

the way the brain stores information naturally and can encourage students to find relationships among the pieces of information presented. Students can also create their own presentations on the computer, manipulating new learnings into a creative presentation that reaches all the senses. These presentations provide a sense of ownership in producing a physical product as evidence of their understanding (Bruder, 1991).

• *Telecommunications.* With a computer, modem, and a phone line, classrooms are able to interact with the world. Students and teachers can take advantage of electronic mail, listservs, electronic bulletin boards, chat rooms, and videoconferencing. With Internet access, learners can communicate with other classrooms in different locations, contact experts in a field of study, and access resources in various libraries around the world. Electronic communication can occur synchronously or not at the same time, making it possible to hold conversations over days and weeks. Email is asynchronous, or delayed, communication. Chat rooms can carry on synchronous conversations where several people are online at the same time. New tools are becoming available almost daily, making telecommunications more and more viable for all classrooms and providing expanded instructional options.

- *Instructional games and simulations.* Games and simulations can provide practice, remediation, and enrichment for students in the classroom. Lessons introduced in a whole class setting can be expanded into individual or small-group practice in an instructional game provided by computer software. Some simulations are appropriate for use in a discovery lesson, enabling students to discover concepts and information first through their interaction with the computer, leading to later discussion and further instruction by the teacher.

- *Computer-assisted instruction (CAI).* One of the first ways computers entered the classroom was through computer-assisted instruction. CAI provides tutoring and practice with instant assessment and feedback capabilities. Drill and practice activities are not seen as the most innovative use of technology (Jonassen, 2000), nevertheless, they are still used in some educational settings. Students are presented with new material, and the computer assesses student responses and can provide immediate reteaching based on those responses. The level of difficulty is adjusted automatically by the computer so instruction is individualized to meet each learner's needs.

One issue associated with technology is how to provide equal technology access to all students. Most schools in high socioeconomic areas have no problem providing students with technology such as access to the Internet, but poorer schools may lack basic equipment such as computers (Wepner, Valmont, & Thurlow, 2000). In an effort to provide all students with access to technology, the federal government passed the Telecommunications Act of 1996, which established the University Service Fund Education Rate (E-Rate) to support educational use of the Internet. Schools and libraries can apply for government help to underwrite the cost of supplying Internet connections and hardware.

Creating Relevant Curriculum

Today's curriculum for students is often a sequential, skill-oriented continuum, involving direct teacher instruction, because many educators believe a fundamental set of basic skills must be mastered before moving on to more complicated higher level thinking activities. Mathematical concepts are taught as discreet skills, such as how to multiply a two-digit number or solve simple algebraic equations. Individual language arts skills might include how to decode a word with a consonant blend, divide words into syllables, or how to use capital letters correctly in a sentence. Skills are isolated and practiced until students are able to demonstrate understanding. There are benefits to this kind of instructional ap-

Interdisciplinary planning can be effective at any age level. When teachers plan instruction together, content areas such as English, social studies, and science are integrated with drama, art, and music.

proach (see behavioral theory described in Chapter 6). A list of sequential skills helps teachers diagnose specific learning weaknesses so a specific plan of remediation can be designed to address student needs. This diagnosis and remediation cycle allows for frequent feedback, rapid pacing, and repeated opportunities for practice. Teachers are able to assess students' achievement easily and to make adjustments as needed.

Even though test results can improve with such a planned approach to remediating student deficiencies, studies have found that this skills approach, which is more repetitive and less challenging, provides fewer opportunities for students to learn higher order skills (Allington & McGill-Franzen, 1989). A skills-based curriculum can keep traditionally low-achieving children from progressing to more challenging, meaningful activities and often results in a curriculum that fails to encourage problem solving, reading comprehension, and meaningful writing activities (Knapp, 1995). Children in such an environment often have difficulty making the connection between skills practiced in isolation and integrated, more meaningful tasks. Those students who already find school alien to their personal experience see little reason for completing isolated skill activities and end up falling further and further behind because they must master basic steps before they can move on to more challenging, and interesting, activities. By underestimating what students are capable of accomplishing, teachers may postpone more interesting work and keep students from having the chance to apply the skills they have been taught (Knapp, 1995; Knapp & Shields, 1990).

In contrast, some schools are looking at the strengths students bring with them to school rather than at the deficiencies. Children from poor and affluent backgrounds alike come to school with important skills and knowledge about the world around them—including sophisticated language abilities and numerical concepts. Instruction in advanced skills enables students to integrate prior learning in the process of knowledge acquisition and helps students build on existing basic academic skills. Instead of looking at what children do not know, a curriculum based on integrated skills acknowledges what children already know (Means & Knapp, 1991).

In mathematics, schools can offer a more challenging curriculum by emphasizing mathematical concepts along with computational skills. Students at all levels need frequent opportunities to apply mathematical concepts to real-life problems so that connections can be formed that help students draw on past experiences. Students may then be involved in solving complex, meaningful problems about issues they consider important. Computational skills can be embedded in the more global task of problem solving, enabling students to see the big concepts rather than spending the majority of their school time memorizing isolated and unconnected facts. Students learn basic mathematical skills as they are needed, connecting the skill with a meaningful purpose for learning the skill.

At the elementary level, a challenging reading curriculum is focused on comprehension, not just decoding skills. All skills instruction is focused on gaining meaning, giving students a purpose for using skills within the context of a story. Children's literature and reading material reflecting a diversity of backgrounds and cultures are integral to the reading program. Within such a reading curriculum, students are often encouraged to select their own reading material, increasing interest and building on prior experience. Teachers, and sometimes whole schools, implement a time of sustained silent reading, wherein students choose their own books and read silently for a set amount of time each day. At the secondary level, teachers can incorporate approaches to reading for knowledge in specific content areas that continue to build comprehension skills.

A strong curriculum for writing draws on the experiences and knowledge of students, with less emphasis placed on the mechanics of writing such as spelling, punctuation, and grammar and more emphasis placed on the process of writing. Students are encouraged to brainstorm for writing ideas using past experiences, write several drafts with input from teachers and peers, apply mechanical skills to revisions, and then produce a final piece of writing to share with others. Stories of experience, community, and family are shared in the classroom, and all students have the opportunity to bring their out-of-school experiences and culture into the classroom through shared writing. Students are consistently involved in reflecting on their own lives through autobiography and story. Written biographies of community elders or other influential adults in the community can also bridge the gap between home and school. Writing skills, formerly taught in isolation, are taught as a necessary part of the process as the need for understanding arises. Students are able to see the purpose of learning the skill when it is embedded in the writing process.

A strong curriculum for all students also emphasizes verbal communication, with constant dialogue as the central form of communicating knowledge. Teachers are no longer responsible for transmitting knowledge to a passive student. Students must be engaged in the learning process as a two-way communication between the teacher and the student or among students.

Just as skills are no longer viewed as isolated pieces within subject areas, individual subjects are also viewed as pieces of a larger integrated curriculum. Reading, writing, and mathematics are all combined across the curriculum. Readers comment on literature with written responses. Writers seek examples of style and tone through reading a variety of authors. Mathematicians write out answers to complicated problems in narrative form. Verbal communication is also important, and students are encouraged to talk about their solutions with teachers and other students in a variety of formats.

World Wide Web Site

If you wish to learn more about how teachers are connecting through the Web, you may do so at: http://www.teachnet.com

Integrated Instruction

Integrated instruction includes several important concepts. First, it can refer to how teachers approach skills instruction. Integrated curriculum embeds basic skills instruction into processes that demonstrate real uses of the skill. For example, elementary students learn the skills by using phonics and addition facts during reading and mathematic computations that resemble actual reading and mathematics calculations. The skills may be the focus of instruction when initially presented to the students, but their relevance to learning and understanding how to comprehend reading material or how the addition facts relate to mathematic computations is a formal overall goal of instruction. Secondary teachers may embed skills and facts in identified themes and issues such as communication or conservation (Clarke & Agne, 1996). Drill and practice of basic facts is used in integrated curriculum, but the skills learned are repeated and linked in the total process. Learning skills related to specific subject areas is more meaningful and relevant when integrated into real uses.

Second, integrated instruction has to do with overlapping the learning of different subject areas. There are times when different subjects are easily integrated for more meaningful instruction. For example, when studying a particular country in social studies, students can read literature presenting characters from the country's culture, use mathematic skills required for graphing population or determining distances on a map, look at art and listen to music of a specific culture, and review the types of animal and plant life associated with the country's geographic area, thus bringing many subjects together in one unit of study. Elementary teachers do this quite easily because they are usually responsible for more than one subject. Integrated instruction is somewhat more difficult for middle school and secondary teachers because these teachers must work together across content areas. However, participating in cross-content planning teams can help bridge traditional barriers between content areas.

Linking Disciplines

An integrated curriculum that links the disciplines throughout the day may be a preferred way of teaching for many teachers. As students get older and move into the more discipline-structured environment of secondary schools, integrated instruction becomes more difficult. Teachers who want to integrate subjects across disciplines often have to locate a willing partner in another discipline, and even then they face the further difficulty, when schedules cannot be coordinated, of not sharing the same students. Some secondary schools arrange their schedules to encourage cross-disciplinary teaching. They schedule classes such as math and science together in two- or three-hour blocks. The shared blocks of time for two different subject areas provide opportunities for students and teachers to work together across the disciplines. Some universities have integrated mathematics and science methods courses to set examples for future teachers.

Learners must continually search for connections between new learning and familiar concepts to make sense of the new information. An integrated curriculum can help in that process by making it easier for students to see patterns and connections between disciplines. By providing the brain with ways to connect and organize new information, students are able to understand the content more deeply and are then able to transfer this new information to other areas (Franzee & Rudnitski, 1996). "Because the learner is constantly searching for connections on many levels, educators need to orchestrate the experience from which learners extract understanding. They must do more than simply provide information or force the memorization of isolated facts and skills" (Caine & Caine, 1994, p. 5).

Some research has shown that the majority of teachers in the United States, especially in secondary education, are still following the prescribed written recipe of the textbooks with little deviation—students read the chapters and answer the questions at the end of the book (Goodlad, 1984; Sizer, 1984). However, some teachers are breaking new ground, developing curriculum that is student-centered and organized to help students make connections between subjects. Recent research has shown that such integrated techniques involving students in problem solving and critical thinking can lead to greater achievement and more meaningful learning (Aschlbacher, 1991).

Teachers who use an integrated approach often build classroom activities around problem solving and projects that incorporate higher levels of thinking (Jacobs, 1989). As students work to apply and demonstrate their knowledge, effective teachers begin to give students a greater voice in the curriculum, and the roles of teacher and student begin to change (Franzee & Rudnitski, 1996). Teachers who use a thematic or integrated approach to curriculum believe not only that subjects should be interrelated but that children should be part of the goal-setting process. No longer is the teacher seen as the source of all knowledge in the classroom, directing all classroom activities and learning. Today's teacher is seen as a guide and a resource for students as they need assistance in getting meaning from the curriculum.

Thematic Teaching

Thematic teaching is an effective strategy for helping students make connections between disciplines. Units of study may last only a week in the lower grades when students stay in the same classroom the whole day or six weeks or longer in upper grades. These units integrate learning objectives from many different subject areas under one thematic umbrella and are often selected from children's interests, a piece of children's literature, seasonal topics, or other material. Classroom space is designed with collaboration in mind. Children are expected to be active participants, and classroom areas are provided to encourage reading, writing, listening, and speaking. Secondary teachers may make a special effort to seek out colleagues who will collaboratively plan and participate in integrated thematic units across content areas. For example, English, history, art, and music teachers may collaborate on a Shakespearean unit focusing on appropriate literature, history, art, and music associated with a specific play.

Teaching for Multiple Intelligences

Many teachers have found Howard Gardner's (1983, 1991) theory of multiple intelligences useful when they are making decisions about content and activities for students in their classes. From this perspective, there are at least eight separate kinds of abilities or intelligences in which people may excel, but there is the possibility that there may be more (Latham, 1999). The eight intelligences discussed by Gardner include linguistic or verbal, musical, spatial, logical-mathematical, bodily-kinesthetic, interpersonal (an understanding of others), intrapersonal (an understanding of self), and naturalist (recognition of species and plants). Gardner bases his theory on several sources of evidence, including research that suggests that different abilities may be located in different parts of the brain. The existence of savants or prodigies who are gifted in a single area supports this idea. He situates intelligence in the human capacity for problem solving in different areas and in the creation of products that represent these eight abilities. Gardner's theory has been particularly popular in schools, but other theorists such as Robert Sternberg (1985, 1990) also offer approaches featuring more than one definition of intelligence that can be used to enrich classroom instruction.

One advantage of applying a theory of multiple intelligences in classrooms is that we begin to think about students in terms of abilities other than those traditionally emphasized in schools. Students can gain recognition for their ability to play musical instruments or to choreograph dances in a school play. The child who is constantly drawing elaborate sketches of battle scenes or comic book characters may be viewed in terms of his or her spatial intelligence and encouraged to develop these abilities. Students who assume leadership or facilitative roles in extracurricular activities may have well-developed interpersonal intelligence that can be utilized and rewarded in classroom settings as well. When teachers look for multiple intelligences rather than using the traditional definition, they increase the opportunities for student success in educational settings.

Another advantage of thinking about multiple intelligences is that it expands teaching strategies beyond the linguistic and logical ones traditionally used in classrooms. Although Gardner (1995) cautions against approaches that try to rigidly match instructional strategies to individual intelligences, increasing the variety of instructional strategies to represent eight ways of teaching results in a more interesting, creative classroom. Teachers can go beyond lecture and seat-work to include music, drama, creative movement, and art in their repertoire of activities. At the elementary level, centers built around storytelling, nature, or building can nurture various intelligences. At the secondary level, the use of portfolios with examples of artistic productions, musical recitals, collaborative projects, and self-assessments provide outlets and encouragement for different intelligences.

Including Cultural Diversity

Attention to equity and diversity should be included in every curriculum area, not just in special units of study (Banks, 1995). A two-week unit on African American leaders or on women's issues, although better than no mention at all, leads students to believe these issues are outside the mainstream of the normal curriculum. Every unit taught can have a story of a different culture in it. Examples that reflect the history of all groups should be integrated throughout the curriculum, not set apart as a special event to be studied in isolation at a special time of the year.

The materials a teacher selects for the classroom can have an impact on the success of all students. Diversity in the classroom should be reflected in the diversity of curriculum materials. Texts and other materials should reflect a variety of cultural backgrounds and be free of stereotypical language and characters.

Textbooks are often criticized for presenting history from a single majority viewpoint. For example, the stories of Thanksgiving and Christopher Columbus have long represented the European perspective on these events. As classrooms become more diverse, so must the perspectives of historical events. Textbooks also often use stereotypical images and language that can be nonrepresentative of students' background and culture.

Classroom libraries need to have a variety of multicultural books. No one book can represent one subject or one culture perfectly. Within each multi-cultural group are many different experiences and personalities. Although books may show some similarities among people of all colors, they should not make all characters talk and act the same regardless of color. Culture brings individual, distinct differences to characters and stories. Books also need to reflect changing times. Folktales from a particular culture can provide information on values and traditions of a group of people, but current stories from a variety of cultural backgrounds are also needed to tell the full story of how a culture has evolved.

Effective teachers are familiar with the cultural background of students in their classrooms. Such knowledge helps teachers learn to accept and respect students for their differences, realizing differences are strengths rather than deficiencies. Teachers learn to appreciate the variety of backgrounds and experiences that students bring with them into the classroom. Each person in the classroom, including the teacher, brings a unique perspective into the room. Each person has something to offer to the learning community. Good teachers encourage positive self-esteem when they recognize, validate, and respect each individual student's unique cultural background, making connections constantly with students' out-of-school experiences and cultures.

Instructional Guidelines

The content of the curriculum and the materials used to convey concepts are critical to the success of all students, but individual teachers bring their own personalities into the classroom as they seek out the best strategies for teaching the content. The selection of equitable instructional strategies is an important teaching responsibility. Several guidelines exist to help in this selection process.

- *Maximize time on-task.* Engage students in learning activities for the majority of the academic time. To accomplish this, teachers have to spend time planning and preparing learning activities before the instructional time. All necessary materials must be ready and organized for easy distribution so that students can begin work quickly with all the materials they need. Establish routines to make transition times move quickly and efficiently. The focus of the classroom and the majority of the time should be spent on meaningful learning activities.

- *Model thinking strategies aloud.* Effective teachers constantly model powerful thinking strategies—talking through their thought process as they explain solutions and responses. Every step of the learning task is modeled carefully to ensure success for all students. Students are routinely expected to follow the teacher's example and are often asked to "think aloud" so that others can learn the process they went through to solve problems.

- *Encourage multiple ways of solving problems.* Effective teachers encourage multiple approaches to academic tasks. Students are encouraged to come up with creative ways of approaching problems. The process of how students reach a solution is just as important, if not more so, as the correct answer. Teachers encourage students to use their own background and knowledge of the world to reach solutions unique to them. Problems must, therefore, be centered in the real world and applicable to the age group and interest of students.

- *Make dialogue an integral part of the teaching process.* Effective teachers make dialogue the central means for teaching and learning. Students are engaged in discussion about their learning, not only with the teacher but with each other, and are constantly called on to explain or justify their responses to others. Throughout the process, student language is not devalued.

- *Use cooperative learning activities in the classroom.* Cooperative learning is a way of promoting respect, understanding, and positive relations in a diverse classroom by encouraging students to work together in small groups to maximize their own learning and that of their peers (Johnson, Johnson, & Holubec, 1984). Cooperative tasks can encourage teamwork, intercultural understanding, and positive interactions when group members realize that they must combine their talents and abilities to complete the required task. Leadership responsibilities are shared, and students learn to help each other succeed.

Lesson Planning

An experienced teacher's lesson plans are usually little more than a written outline to follow. The lesson plan may describe the instructional goal, the behavioral objective, the activity, and the materials needed, but these plans usually serve as a means for teachers to organize their thoughts. Much more planning occurs in the teacher's mind than is ever written on the lesson plan.

For preservice teachers observing in an experienced teacher's classroom, this internalized decision making can be deceiving. Because extensive lesson plans are not specifically written down, some may think little planning was done prior to the lesson. When teachers are beginning to learn how to plan, clearly written lesson plans provide a necessary reminder of the thought processes that experienced teachers may have internalized through many years of practice.

There are many different formats for lesson plans, and teachers often experiment with several until they find one that works well with their particular style of instruction. Most lesson plans have some basic components in common as they guide a teacher through planning and teaching the important components of a lesson.

- *Objectives.* The learning outcome described in an objective is what students should be able to do on completion of the lesson. The language of the objective must be specific enough so that the learning can be measured and student outcome is observable. However, the often rigidly stated behavior objectives of the 1970s fit better with cognitive objectives. Objectives help teachers answer important questions about student learning. Were students able to achieve the objective? How did they demonstrate their understanding?

- *Motivation/introduction.* Starting a lesson and gaining the attention of the learner is a critical, and often overlooked, part of teaching a lesson. Each lesson should begin with an instructional focus that prepares the learner for active engagement in the lesson and should be designed to arouse curiosity and interest. Depending on the readiness of the learners and on the learning environment, this activity can be as simple as leading the class in a review of a previous lesson on insects or as complicated as a dramatic retelling in costume of the Gettysburg Address. Student motivation must be taken into account when planning a successful opening, and all students must be actively engaged in the lesson from the very beginning. In classrooms with young learners, this may mean physically moving students to a location in the room where they can focus on instruction. The introduction is also the time to inform students, in vocabulary suitable to the age group, about the objective of the lesson and what they will be required to do at the completion of the lesson to demonstrate understanding.

- *Teaching activities.* The direct instruction segment of the lesson is the time to help students recall past learning. Previously learned information can be recalled from past experiences outside of school or from the lesson the previous day, but the connection to past learning is critical. The actual teaching portion of the lesson can take many forms. A teacher can guide a whole class in a discussion of new concepts, or students can work together in small groups to discover new learnings. Whatever the format, careful planning is necessary to ensure maximum time on-task.

- *Student activities.* Students need the opportunity to interact with new concepts and learning materials independent of the teacher. Student activities provide necessary practice for students to achieve the objective. Activities can involve everything from independent seatwork or lab activities to creative writing and art demonstrations. Teachers monitor and provide feedback to students as they practice and interact with the materials.

- *Closure/evaluation.* At the close of the lesson, a teacher restates the learning objectives, summarizes the activities, and provides opportunities for students to demonstrate mastery of the objective. The closure of the lesson should have a direct relationship to the objective and the desired outcome. This component is one of the most difficult for beginning teachers because they often are unable to gauge how much time is needed for the other facets of instruction.

• *Classroom management concerns.* Teachers must provide a positive learning environment in the classroom where students feel safe from physical and emotional abuse—a classroom climate free of intimidation, insult, and criticism. Talking about respecting others is not enough. The environment of the classroom must encourage students to display responsible behavior and discourage abusive and disrespectful behavior. Effective teachers do not assume that students come to school with strong interpersonal and social skills. They teach these important life skills along with the academic subjects. Planning for classroom management concerns should be part of the lesson planning process. How should students move from one activity to another to ensure little wasted time? Which students might have difficulty working together? Where in the lesson might potential problems develop?

World Wide Web Site

You may learn more about creating lesson plans at:
http://www.ericsp.org/

Evaluation and Assessment

Structured evaluations, anecdotal records, interviews and interest inventories, and student self-evaluations are all examples of ways that teachers can be informed about their students' learning. A recent trend in assessment and evaluation is the use of a portfolio system. Traditionally portfolios have been used by artists, actors, and models to demonstrate their work and potential, but students can demonstrate their work and potential by collecting samples, examples, and responses to chronicle their learning, growth, and development. A portfolio is a collection of materials indicating an individual's thinking, problem-solving abilities, attitudes, beliefs, and knowledge acquisition. Portfolios are more than collections of responses to class assignments; they include self-reflections, summaries of work, and descriptions of students' work.

The lesson plan in Figure 8.2 was completed by a preservice teacher as part of a thematic unit on ecology and habitats for first-graders. Notice how carefully she planned out each part of her lesson—estimating the time needed for each part of the lesson, writing notes to herself on questions and content information, and anticipating possible classroom management concerns before they occurred.

Figure 8.2 Sample Lesson Plan

Week One, Day One

General Introduction, First Grade

OBJECTIVE (what students should be able to do after completing the lesson):

- The students will be able to define the terms *ecology* and *habitat* in their own words.

MATERIALS NEEDED (all the resources needed to teach the lesson):

- Word cards (ecology and habitat)
- *Professor Noah's Spaceship* by Brian Wildsmith

WHAT I WANT TO ACCOMPLISH (personal teaching goal for this lesson):

- I want the students to have a basic understanding of the terms *ecology* and *habitat* because the rest of the unit will build on these terms.

FOCUS AREA (If someone were observing this lesson, I would want them to help me by concentrating on the following . . .):

- Are the students on-task? Have I organized the discussion to ensure everyone the opportunity to participate?

Brief Outline of Lesson and Times (step-by-step description):

MOTIVATION/INTRODUCTION: **2–3 min.

- Show printed vocabulary word cards and ask students to predict their pronunciation and meaning. Record predictions.

TEACHING PROCEDURES AND STUDENT ACTIVITY: **5–8 min.

1. Show and pronounce the first word (*ecology*) and have students tell what they may already know about the word.

Once prior knowledge is activated, then add to definitions to provide a clear understanding. Ecology is the relationship between an organism and its environment. Different animals live in all different parts of the world and do different things to survive in their environments. The way humans treat these different places affects the health of the animals who live there. What are some things that people may do to prevent animals from being able to live in a certain place anymore? (pollute, litter, cut down trees, destroy environment)

Becoming a Reflective Teacher

Teachers who are effective in classes with a wide range of student differences are self-reflective about their own attitudes, beliefs, and actions. They constantly work to recognize and eliminate teacher expectations based on race, class, and gender

2. Repeat step one with the word *habitat*. **5–8 min.

Explain that the different parts of the world where animals live and grow are called habitats. As humans we need a special kind of habitat. What are some of the different things humans need to live and grow? Name them (food, shelter, clothing). What kind of habitat do we need? Could we live in the forest or desert? Because all animals are different and need different things to live and grow, all habitats are different. Think about all the different kinds of animals and where they live. Can anyone name some habitats? (desert, forest, swamp, rain forest)

3. Share book with students. **10–12 min.

Today I am going to share a book with you about animals that live in a forest as their habitat. They live there happily until something happens to their habitat. Listen while I read the book aloud and then we will talk about it.

4. Ask higher level thinking questions. **5–8 min.

- What part of the story could really happen? Could not really happen?
- Are the animals in our world in danger? Why or why not? Share pictures of panda bears and black rhinos.
- How can we help solve this problem?

5. Share information on chart tablet with students. **8–10 min.

Have one student read a part of this summary information and then discuss what the student has read. Have the class read this part chorally. Continue this process until all the information is shared.

CLOSURE/EVALUATION (How do students demonstrate new learning?):
    **5–8 min.

Return to the predictions of the meaning for habitat and ecology and have students decide what predictions were correct. Each student will then write or dictate a simple definition of each new vocabulary word in their own words.

CLASSROOM MANAGEMENT CONCERNS (Where can problems be anticipated and planned for?):

- Have all materials ready to share.
- Have brainstorming chart paper available.
- Watch the transition to and from floor—plan for orderly transition.
- Enforce good listening skills—raising hands.

and are continually asking questions at the completion of each lesson, looking for the strengths and weaknesses that will have an impact on future improvements. Here are some questions you can ask yourself after teaching your lesson:

- What was the most effective part of the lesson? The least effective?

Field-Based Activity 8.4

Using the following sample lesson plan, or one provided to you by your instructor, plan a lesson that you will teach in your field-based placement.

LESSON PLAN OUTLINE

   I. Objective

  II. Materials needed

 III. What I want to accomplish

 IV. Focus area

  V. Procedure

     a. Motivation/introduction

     b. Teaching procedures and student activities

     c. Closure/evaluation

 VI. Evaluation and assessment

VII. Classroom management concerns

- What were students most enthusiastic about and why?
- If you had the opportunity to teach this lesson again, what would you do the same? What would you do differently?
- Were there any surprises, and how did you handle them?

Reflecting on Learning

Successful teachers maintain high expectations for all students, and the influence of teacher expectations on student achievement is strong (Good & Brophy, 1999). Teachers' attitudes about students and resulting actions can help or hurt student performance. Teachers can perpetuate self-fulfilling prophecies in ways that influence their students' beliefs about themselves. Teachers' interactions with students reflect their expectations about performance. Eventually, students conform to these expectations, and teachers' beliefs become reality. Teachers can also influence student achievement by sustaining effects. In this case, a teacher expects a certain academic performance from a student because of past experience and fails to see any change in that pattern even when actual student behavior changes. Teachers translate their expectations in a variety of ways. Low-achieving students are often located farther away from the teacher in the classroom. Low-achieving students receive less time to respond to a teacher's questions, less attention, fewer opportunities to answer questions, and less feedback on responses. Self-reflection and careful monitoring of classroom response patterns can help teachers see when lowered expectations are keeping students from higher academic achievement.

Teachers must become "kid-watchers" and continually work to get to know each individual learner in a crowded classroom of diverse students (Goodman, 1977). Anecdotal records are notes teachers keep as they observe students' learning. They can be brief notes kept in a notebook or on index cards. Teachers might also record reflections in their lesson plan books about the success of a particular lesson and suggestions for future improvements. One teacher keeps a pad of sticky notes on her seating chart. As she walks around the room observing students, she records the information she observes on the note for that particular student. Later the notes are placed in the child's portfolio.

Anecdotal records readjust teachers' visions of who and where students are and sharpen teachers' insights into how students travel along the paths to learning. Only when we look as if with a magnifying glass can we see and hear individual and idiosyncratic child-based standards of growth, accomplishment, and failure (Mathews, 1992).

Peer coaching is defined as "the assistance that one teacher provides another in the development of teaching skills, strategies, or techniques" (Strother, 1989, p. 824). Teachers in peer coaching situations can observe in each other's classrooms, work together on classroom research, study current practices as part of a study team, or just work together to solve common problems. Peers—not supervisors or evaluators—work together to learn more about teaching and learning (Strother, 1989). Peer coaching is a form of direct assistance that helps teachers improve instruction: "The process is intended to examine the efficacy of the teacher's practices, not the teacher's competence" (Nolan, Hawkes, & Francis, 1993, p. 53). Peer coaching is a supportive, not evaluative, process that encourages professional, not social, interactions in a school and has a teacher-specified focus (Robbins, 1991).

Peer coaching requires training and preparation time to be effective. Teachers who will work together are identified and a structure for observation must be agreed on. The two teachers who are working together meet prior to the agreed-on observation time and identify concerns and a focus for the upcoming observation. One inviting teacher asked a peer coach to "map" her movements around the room when she taught to see if she was unintentionally ignoring any students. The observing teacher watched the lesson and drew lines on a seating chart to show the movement of the teacher around the room. Each time the teacher stopped, the observer marked an X on the chart. The observation chart was left with the inviting teacher so she could reach her own conclusions. The resulting observation report was clear—a table of students in the front was not receiving the same teacher attention as the rest of the class. In a conference after class, the inviting teacher and the observing teacher discussed possible ways to alleviate the problem and then discussed further areas for focused observation.

The Dynamics of Instructional Organization

Teaching lessons and delivery of instruction include long-term, deliberate planning as well as numerous fast-paced daily decisions. Effective teachers establish goals and make plans for an entire year, semester, or week. These plans serve as maps for daily instruction. Not all factors can be taken into account during long-term planning, so effective teachers question their instructional process as they teach, making changes based on how their students respond to what is presented.

Personal philosophy, beliefs, and recognition of students' needs result in unique approaches to day-to-day instruction. A great deal of what a teacher believes about students and teaching will be reflected in the lesson plans. Day-to-

---

Portfolio Reflections and Exhibits

Suggested Exhibit 8: Lesson Planning

Your lesson and personal reflection can be added to your teaching portfolio. There are several ways to illustrate your lesson planning and implementation in the portfolio. Possible representations include these:
- A lesson plan that you designed
- Samples of student work
- Feedback from your university or classroom supervisor
- Pictures of your students participating in the lesson
- Handouts, games, or other supplementary aids you developed to go with your lesson
- Audio and/or video tapes

To complete the representation of your lesson planning, include a self-evaluation and personal reflection about what you learned from presenting your lesson. What went well? What goals do you have for yourself the next time you have an opportunity to plan and teach a lesson? The lesson that you prepared and taught during your introductory class will serve as a benchmark to help you see how you contine to grow throughout your university preparation.

---

day lesson plans are one way that a creative teacher expresses individuality. The decision making associated with planning lessons is a dynamic and ever-changing process that keeps teaching alive and vibrant.

InfoTrac College Edition Extension

Log on to the InfoTrac College Edition Web site. To learn more about instructional planning in your content area, pair the term "lesson planning" with a specific content area such as social studies or mathematics and type in a search term similar to the following:

> lesson planning and mathematics

Or, if you are interested in finding out how to plan so that you encourage multiple intelligences in your classroom, type in the following:

> lesson planning and multiple intelligences

Related Readings

Armstrong, T. (1994). *Multiple intelligences in the classroom.* Alexandria, VA: Association for Supervision and Curriculum Development.
> *This book provides an overview of Gardner's theory and gives concrete suggestions to teachers for implementing the multiple intelligences approach in classrooms.*

Ladson-Bilings, G. (1994). *The dreamkeepers: Successful teachers of African American children.* San Francisco: Jossey-Bass.
> *This book talks about successful teaching and learning strategies used by African American teachers. The author allows the teachers in the book to tell their own stories, and, as a result, we are able to envision intellectually rigorous and culturally relevant classrooms. This book will teach you important lessons about teaching all children.*

Schaafsma, D. (1993). *Eating on the street: Teaching literacy in a multicultural society.* Pittsburgh: University of Pittsburgh Press.
> *This is an interesting example of some different ways culture can affect instruction. You will learn about cultural differences as you read this account of seven teachers who guided fifth-, sixth-, and seventh-graders to explore, interpret, and write about their community.*

Sternberg, R., & Grigorenko, E. (2000). *Teaching for successful intelligence.* Arlington Heights, IL: Skylights.
> *An easy-to-read book that includes specific lessons and units for building successful intelligence abilities.*

References

Allington, R., & McGill-Franzen, A. (1989). School response to reading failure: Chapter 1 and special education students in grades 2, 4, and 8. *Elementary School Journal, 89*, 529–542.

Aschlbacher, P. R. (1991). Humanitas: A thematic curriculum. *Educational Leadership, 49*(2), 9–16.

Banks, J. A. (1995). Multicultural education: Historical development, dimensions, and practice. In J. A. Banks & C. M. Banks (Eds.), *Handbook on research in multicultural education* (pp. 3–42). New York: Macmillan.

Bruder, I. (1991). Guide to multimedia: How it changes the way we teach and learn. *Electronic Learning, 11*(1), 22–26.

Caine, R. M., & Caine, G. (1994). *Making connections: Teaching and the human brain.* Palo Alto, CA: Addison-Wesley.

Carr, E., & Ogle, D. (1987). K-W-L plus: A strategy for comprehension and summarization. *Journal of Reading, 30*(7), 626–631.

Clarke, C., & Peterson, P. (1986). Teachers' thought processes. In M. R. Whitrock (Ed.), *Handbook of research on teaching* (3rd ed., pp. 255–296). New York: Macmillan.

Clarke, J. H., & Agne, R. M. (Eds.). (1996). *Interdisciplinary high school teaching: Strategies for integrated learning.* Boston: Allyn & Bacon.

Falk, B. (2000). *The heart of the matter: Using standards and assessment to learn.* Portsmouth, NH: Heinemann.

Franzee, B., & Rudnitski, R. (1996). *Integrated teaching methods: Theory, classroom applications, and field-based connections.* Albany, NY: Delmar.

Gardner, H. (1983). *Frames of mind: The theory of multiple intelligences.* New York: Basic Books.

Gardner, H. (1991). *The unschooled mind: How children think and how schools should teach.* New York: Basic Books.

Gardner, H. (1995). Reflection on multiple intelligences: Myths and messages. *Phi Delta Kappan, 77*, 200–210.

Good, T., & Brophy, J. (1999). *Looking in classrooms,* 8th ed. New York: Longman.

Goodlad, J. I. (1984). *A place called school.* New York: McGraw-Hill.

Goodman, Y. (1977). Kid watching: An alternative to testing. *Elementary Principal, 57*, 41–45.

Hawkins, J., & Collins, A. (1992). Design-experiments for infusing technology into learning. *Educational Technology, 33*(6), 26–31.

Jacobs, H. H. (1989). *Interdisciplinary curriculum: Design, development, and implementation.* Alexandria, VA: Association for Supervision and Curriculum Development.

Becoming a Teacher in a Field-Based Setting

Johnson, D. W., Johnson, R. T., & Holubec, R. (1984). *Circles of learning: Cooperation in the classroom.* Alexandria, VA: Association for Supervision and Curriculum Development.

Jonassen, D. (1986). Hypertext principles for text and courseware design. *Educational Psychologist, 21,* 269–292.

Jonassen, D. H. (2000). *Computers as mindtools for schools.* Upper Saddle River, NJ: Merrill.

Jonassen, D. H., Peck, K. L., & Wilson, B. G. (1999). *Learning with technology: A constructivist perspective.* Upper Saddle River, NJ: Merrill.

Knapp, M., & Shields, P. (1990). Reconceiving academic instruction for the children of poverty. *Phi Delta Kappan, 71*(10), 753–758.

Knapp, M. S., & others. (1995). Academic challenge in high-poverty classrooms. *Phi Delta Kappan, 76*(10), 770–776.

Mathews, C. (1992). An alternative portfolio: Gathering one child's literacies. In D. Graves & B. Sunstein (Eds.), *Portfolio portraits* (pp. 158–170). Portsmouth, NH: Heinemann.

Means, B., & Knapp, M. (1991). Cognitive approaches to teaching advanced skills to educationally disadvantaged students. *Phi Delta Kappan, 72*(4), 282–289.

Nolan, J., Hawkes, B., & Francis, P. (1993). Case studies: Windows onto clinical supervision. *Educational Leadership, 51*(2), 52–56.

Robbins, P. (1991). *How to plan and implement a peer coaching program.* Alexandria, VA: Association for Supervision and Curriculum Development.

Sizer, T. (1984). *Horace's compromise: The dilemma of the American high school.* Boston: Houghton Mifflin.

Sternberg, R. (1985). *Beyond IQ: A triarchic theory of human intelligence.* New York: Cambridge University Press.

Sternberg, R. (1990). *Metaphors of mind: Conceptions of the nature of intelligence.* New York: Cambridge University Press.

Strother, D. (1989). Peer coaching for teachers: Opening classroom doors. *Phi Delta Kappan, 70*(10), 824–827.

Tyler, R. W. (1974). Considerations in selecting objectives. In D. A. Payne (Ed.), *Curriculum evaluation: Commentaries on purpose, process, product.* Lexington, MA: D. C. Heath.

Wepner, S. B., Valmont, W. J., & Thurlow, R. (2000). *Linking literacy and technology: A guide for K-8 classrooms.* Newark, DE: International Reading Association.

Wilson, K. (1991). New tools for new learning opportunities. *Technology and Learning, 11*(7), 12–13.

CHAPTER 9

Outlining School Contexts, Organization, and Leadership

IN THIS CHAPTER
- **Community Contexts**
- **Organizational Contexts**
- **Leadership in Today's Schools**

*A*lphonse Laudato, the principal, arrived first in the morning and did not leave until
long after most teachers went home. During the day, Al roamed the hallways, a short man in an
oxford shirt with a clip-on necktie and, though in his forties, very trim. He had gone to college to play
baseball and football he said, and had drifted into education. He looked like an athlete. He rarely
stayed still.*

*Al belonged to Kelly School, and Kelly School belonged to Al. He once said, "I'm responsible for
every teacher who walks in this door. Not that I'm in charge of everybody, the only one in charge, but
I'm responsible. Come in, talk, and I'll decide if we're going to do it.". . .*

*On really important matters, he usually did what was best for the students. Somehow he always
seemed to find the money for new books or materials or field trips. She [Chris] thought Kelly's classes
remained small partly because of Al's clever budgeting. She gathered that Al sometimes fell out of*

favor on Suffolk Street, school administration headquarters, but she thought it significant that during the first crucial year of desegregation, Suffolk Street had sent Al to Kelly to soothe the white parents who had demanded proof that their children would be safe down in the Flats. Al, with a great deal of help from the chief secretary, Lil, kept the school running smoothly. The office of the Director of Bilingual Education for the city was situated in Al's school. At least once a year Al would pick a fight with that department over some small administrative matter. The director insisted though, that he could easily forgive Al because of the way Al ran Kelly School.

—Tracy Kidder, *Among Schoolchildren**

W hen you begin your formal training to become a teacher, you will probably focus primarily on the twenty-five children facing you in an elementary classroom or the one hundred to two hundred students that cycle through a secondary teacher's classroom in one day. Your attention to the classroom is not unusual. Beginning teachers are typically concerned about lesson plans, materials, and the classroom management techniques that will help them get through the day-to-day teaching process. They attend to their own classroom, planning for instruction and interacting with their students. Although it is important to understand the basics necessary to run a classroom, there is much more to being a teacher than what happens inside the classroom. Many other tasks and people are involved in teaching and learning. Interactions within an organizational structure and with the leaders of schools are important aspects of day-to-day teaching routines and activities. Teachers are part of a large, complex organization requiring numerous professional interactions.

The nature of teachers' professional interactions will be greatly influenced by the context of the school. The community and neighborhood where the school is located, the grade level of the classrooms, and even the arrangement of the school will make a difference in teachers' responsibilities and roles. The characteristics of city, suburban, and rural locations will interact with the grade level arrangements and contribute to the educational context.

---

*From *Among Schoolchildren*, by Tracy Kidder (44, 46). New York: Avon.

Voice of a Teacher

When I first heard I would have a student teacher and an intern in my classroom, I was ecstatic! Imagine the one-on-one instruction, collaboration, and general productivity in my classroom! I am an organizer and planner, so I planned for weekly meetings during which the three of us would brainstorm and structure lessons together. I provided dialogue journals for each preservice teacher as a quick communication tool during our hectic school days. Each preservice teacher had his or her own teacher desk, decorated with welcome signs from my students. I was ready for what I thought would be the best semester of my educational career.

But when Holly, the intern, came into our classroom, she felt "behind" Jennifer, the student teacher, and a little left out. She let me know this and I attempted to explain to her that both she and Jennifer were equally important to our classroom, although they held different roles.

I felt relieved to clear up this problem only to be presented with another. Holly essentially did not feel more comfortable after our chat and she was not very friendly toward Jennifer. This in turn made Jennifer feel uncomfortable and she came to me with her concern. What a mess! I never thought about personality dynamics not working or jealous feelings coming out of this experience. I guess I had the logistics figured out, but had not considered the human factors.

I finally realized I did not need to smooth things over between my student teacher and intern student. A feeling of mutual respect was fostered by being in a classroom where so much was happening and so many people were involved in the instruction. I feel that this is one of the greatest strengths of a Professional Development School. We learn from other educators and are exposed to other teaching styles and ideas. So many more solutions can be found by seeing actions rather than hearing words. Indeed, the semester turned out to be the greatest of my educational career, surprising me with wonderful learning experiences from the preservice teachers I worked with.

School leadership plays an important role in teachers' work and establishes the context of any school. Educational leaders have a great deal of responsibility not only to the students in the schools but to teachers, the community, and even governmental bodies. Educational leaders are responsible for establishing the vision, goals, and accountability systems for schools. The traditional expectations and requirements of school leaders such as superintendents, principals, and supervisors can be carried out in different ways depending on contexts, philosophies, and personal styles. The role of an educational leader is expanding and changing to meet the needs of increased student diversity in today's schools. Recently, school leadership has been expanded to encompass roles that many teachers play (Lambert, 1998).

One advantage of becoming a teacher in a field-based setting is that the experience provides immediate exposure to the whole context of a school and a school district. Preservice teachers in school–university partnerships who are formulating their professional identity will learn that teaching is more than an autonomous job with teachers and learners working behind classroom doors. They will learn about the organizational structures, leadership roles, and the multiple responsibilities of teachers that are routine in today's educational settings. In this chapter, we will examine these questions:

- What are some of the characteristics of schools in urban, suburban, and rural settings?
- How are schools organized?
- What leaders take responsibility for schools?
- What are some of the ways that teachers demonstrate leadership?
- How can preservice teachers demonstrate leadership?

Community Contexts

The location of schools and the size of the community affect teachers' day-to-day working conditions and environments. Small districts may serve fewer than five hundred students, whereas large metropolitan districts such as New York City, Los Angeles, or Chicago educate thousands of children. Smaller schools, such as Snook, Texas or Genoa, Illinois, may have only one superintendent and a single building for an entire Pre K-12 school. Large districts like New York City have multiple superintendents, school boards, and administrators and hundreds of buildings to maintain. Different schools across our nation have different organizational, administrative, and leadership systems, but all work with children and families who have diverse experiences, talents, and concerns. Urban, suburban, and rural schools develop educational contexts that reflect the values and expectations of the surrounding communities. Providing the best educational environments, meeting the challenges of a diverse society, and using available resources to their maximum benefit become the focus for any school setting no matter where it is located. Size and contexts are distinguishing characteristics of schools, but poverty, student diversity, and community identity establish commonalities and differences in various school settings.

Urban Schools

Because schools located in large cities interact with the environment, the problems faced by urban areas are also present in schools (Forsyth & Tallerico, 1993). Cities are often described as being in crisis. Instances of crime, deteriorating

Schools are located in many different settings. Their locations, whether in cities, towns, suburbs, or rural settings, provide different educational challenges and rewards.

school facilities, and teacher burnout are common portrayals of urban schools. Actually, reports about conditions in urban schools are somewhat ambivalent, presenting both negative and positive views of what it is like to be a student in a large city school.

On the negative side, the schools in our large cities have been associated with crisis for many years, and the statistics depicting their failures are often overwhelming. Urban schools are perceived as being plagued with insurmountable problems, often failing the children and young people who attend. Cities across the country regularly report dismal academic results (Rist, 2000). In 1990, only 10 percent of the tenth-graders in Chicago were able to read; graduating seniors in New Orleans were reading at levels lower than 80 percent of the graduating seniors anywhere else in the United States; and over half of Houston's elementary students were repeating grades because of unsatisfactory progress (Englert, 1993). Not only are the problems complex, they are long term. There is plenty of evidence to suggest that conditions in urban schools have worsened in the last twenty-five years (Englert, 1993; Rist, 2000). Historically, test scores of urban students have been lower than those of suburban students, and students in city schools have continued to achieve at levels lower than those in suburban and

Becoming a Teacher in a Field-Based Setting

rural schools (Ornstein & Levine, 1989). City schools typically report terrible attendance records (Maeroff, 1988) and are often associated with hopelessness (Kozol, 1991). Some cities report dropout rates as high as 75 to 80 percent (Hahn, Danzberger, & Lefkowitz, 1987).

On the positive side, during the past decade, urban schools have focused on improving student achievement and have achieved some degree of success and much improvement (Lewis, Jepson, & Casserly, 1999). Nevertheless, issues of diversity, economic conditions, and teacher quality continue to present major challenges for large school districts. One indisputable fact about teaching in urban schools is that there is a richness and variety of diverse cultures and ethnicities present. Minorities make up a large share of city dwellers and the numbers continue to increase. In 1997, nearly 90 percent of minorities lived in metropolitan areas (Population Reference Bureau, 1999), making urban school populations more ethnically and culturally diverse than those in other parts of the United States. Urban dwelling minorities represent a mix of racial and ethnic groups with no single group dominating. The makeup of urban school students is constantly changing. The percentage of African American students in central cities has been fairly constant for more than twenty years, but the number of Hispanic students has more than doubled. Furthermore, new waves of immigration from Middle Eastern and Asian countries continue to increase the cultural and linguistic challenges for urban schools (Crosby, 1999). Increased heterogeneity of the city populations has an impact on educational strategies and human relationships, making it crucial for teachers and school administrators to accept and understand cultural and ethnic diversity.

The diversity in city schools is exacerbated by the great range of socioeconomic statuses represented among families of students, but there are an especially high number of children from economically disadvantaged families. In fact, poverty has been identified as a fundamental issue related to the crisis associated with education and other social institutions in cities (see Chapter 5). Nearly 25 percent of all urban populations are living in poverty (Stromquist, 1994), so schools face the challenge of educating poor children. Poverty affects all aspects of children's lives, and educators often find themselves dealing with issues such as health and social services and housing to help provide the basics for students in their schools. Transportation and housing become major issues in urban students' lives. Children and young people who live in the city tend to have more health-related problems than young people in other areas. All the characteristics that poverty inflicts on families are important considerations in the education of city children.

In addition to the challenges emerging from diversity and economic challenges, city schools have difficulty identifying and retaining qualified teachers, especially minority teachers. This is particularly evident in subjects such as science and math. Salaries are not as high as they might be in suburban schools, and because of the conditions, city teachers combat high turnover and morale problems. "But it is the intensity of working for and caring about students in urban schools that makes effective urban teachers different from their counterparts in the suburbs" (Gordon, 1999, p. 304). Urban teachers must understand their students and deal with tough situations in a caring manner, all the while focusing on student achievement and high learning standards. The political, demographic, and economic diversity and the scarce resources of most urban school districts make it difficult to maintain the same learning standards as those in better equipped, well-funded schools in other settings (Urban Institute, 1995). Teachers often find themselves struggling with the inequities present in city schools.

Despite the grim picture, there are many examples of effective urban schools (Englert, 1993). Cities have long been identified with educational innovation and reform, and, as a result, there have been miraculous and confirming success stories of improving school conditions. Several cities, including Houston, Seattle, and Chicago, report recent improvements in conditions at their schools and increases in student achievement as measured by standardized tests. Teachers cite a number of benefits derived from teaching in city schools. The diversity of inner cities offers a richness and tolerance for a wide range of behavior. Greater population increases the political power and special interest group activity that provide support for educational issues. Large cities also offer a great number of economic, cultural, financial, religious, and noneducational resources to educational institutions.

One of the most hopeful signs that urban schools can meet the numerous demands of the setting is that educators are promoting smaller and more personal schools (Pipho, 1995). New York City has been in the forefront of this trend and has opened many high schools whose attendance ranges from 110 to 600 students. These schools are characterized by a great deal of interaction among parents, teachers, and students, and these small, creative learning environments offer some hope for success. Los Angeles is also considering breaking up its large high schools into smaller schools. Some inner cities are attempting to establish contracts with private companies to set up plans and programs to improve educational systems. Hartford, Connecticut entered into agreement with a private company to operate thirty-two of its schools and improve its curriculum, technology infrastructure, and physical plant (Pipho, 1995). This trend will be watched closely during the next decade.

Even though city school teaching has been identified as one of the most stressful career choices (Farris, 1996), many teachers feel that the rewards are great. Teachers who are socially oriented look forward to the challenges of inner-city schools. Curriculum is designed to encourage diversity of all kinds, enabling students to examine the social realities of their world and bring the richness of the urban setting into the classroom. Private schools also play an important role in the education of city students, and many new teachers choose to begin their careers in schools supported by churches or other nonpublic resources. Whether they teach in public or private schools, those who succeed in inner-city schools experience challenges and rewards not as evident in other settings, and these educators have a fierce commitment to urban school reform.

 World Wide Web Sites

You may learn more about urban school settings at the following Web sites:

http://eric-web.tc.columbia.edu/

http://www.cgcs.org/services/whatworks/

Suburban Schools

Suburban school districts are typically located outside of large cities. In many cases, urban dwellers have left the city and relocated to leave the problems associated with inner-city settings. Traditionally viewed as a middle-class white environment, more middle-class and affluent minority families have been moving to the suburbs, particularly those outside the largest metropolitan areas (Population Reference Bureau, 1999). Rising incomes among African American families and other minorities have enabled them to move to suburban settings where parents believe their children will have access to better schools (Richard, 2000). The new residents of suburban settings join the established middle-class families that have lived there for years, making suburban schools more diverse than they have been in the past.

The focus of middle-class, working professionals in suburbs results in the perception of more affluent neighborhoods and a school population coming from two-parent families, a mother in the home, and parents with more time and resources to spend with their children. But in reality, suburban schools vary in their makeup and approach to education. The number of children and young people living in poverty and other social problems may not be as great or as concentrated as in urban settings, but they are still present in suburban contexts. Some neighborhoods include low-income housing, whereas others are upscale and affluent, creating a great contrast between school settings in suburban areas.

Shuttered businesses and families living in poverty are evident in some older established suburban neighborhoods, but in most cases it is rapid, sprawling growth that is changing the nature of living in suburbia. Even the definition of suburbia is changing. Once considered to have strong links to a large city, new suburban developments are not as dependent on the cities near them, and many of these areas are developing as unique communities. But by far the most radical and far-reaching change in the future of suburban schools is the inevitable diversity of socioeconomic status, race, ethnicity, and age groups that accompanies fast population growth.

Urban students face the challenges of the inner city, but suburban school-children face problems associated with middle-class families. A high percentage of single or married working parents leave for work before their children go to school, and these parents arrive home long after school is out. In many households, children either are in childcare facilities or are latchkey children. Many schools offer before- and after-school programs so that students are not unattended when parents are out of the home.

Because suburban parents have higher incomes, the tax base provides resources and tax support not available to inner-city schools. Suburban schools are able to build and repair physical facilities, equip their schools with up-to-date technology, and pay their teachers well. Suburban schools usually have substantial flexibility in their curriculum and offer courses that prepare students for post-secondary educational opportunities. Furthermore, there are generally a wide range of extracurricular activities to accompany basic coursework.

Suburban teachers and administrators are more highly educated and better paid than their counterparts in urban and rural settings. Suburban schools are the settings where most beginning teachers imagine themselves teaching. Teachers experience different challenges in suburban schools than do teachers in urban or rural schools. Parents and students expect a great deal from their schools, and teachers are vocal if they do not feel their children are getting the education they deserve. The focus on test scores and entrance into college is a major concern of suburban families, and teachers must have the same expectations.

Suburbs must come to grips with dramatic changes in their communities and schools in the near future (Richard, 2000). School enrollment is growing rapidly, making it difficult for schools to meet the demands on their buildings, budgets, and teachers. Suburban schools are experiencing increasing diversity as Americans of different races and ethnic groups gain the means to purchase homes and live in new developments outside the city. Many suburban locations are becoming more international as immigrants bypass the cities and settle in the nearby communities. The changing nature of suburban communities will certainly have an impact on the educational context where teachers work and live.

Rural Schools

The U.S. government defines rural areas as nonmetropolitan communities with fewer than 2,500 inhabitants or fewer than 1,000 inhabitants per square mile (Herzog & Pittman, 1995). Since the 1800s, the population of the United States has moved from rural locations to urban and suburban communities. Nevertheless, there are numerous small rural school districts. Nationally, 51 percent of all school districts are small and rural (Schmuck & Schmuck, 1992), and nearly 25 percent of elementary and secondary students are educated in rural settings (U.S. Department of Education, 1998–1999).

Rural communities are changing as farming and other agriculture-related occupations continue to evolve. Large farming operations, fast-food, and nationally based retailers have had an impact on rural America. Many families have remained in the same community for decades, but family mobility is becoming more and more evident with the availability of low-rent housing and the lower living expenses in rural areas. A thirty-year decline in job opportunities has forced many students in rural schools to seek training that will take them away from their homes to work in more populated areas. The declining population rates in rural areas now seem to be reversing. In the 1990s the population of rural areas grew at the same rate or faster than other areas of the nation, and many communities experienced a rebirth of sorts (Huang, 1999). Many rural schools have benefited from these improved financial conditions and the steady income growth of families in these communities.

Rural communities offer a great deal of diversity and share many of the problems that urban and suburban schools have, although on a smaller scale. Problems of violence and crime are evident in small towns, but not at the same level as in more populated areas. Poverty is traditionally associated with inner-city settings, but a great amount of poverty is located in rural areas too, particularly in Appalachia and other locations in the South. Even though poverty has been somewhat alleviated by recent economic growth, more than one-quarter of rural residents live just above the poverty line (Huang, 1999). Other than central cities, rural areas have the highest rate of poverty in our country (Dewees, 1999). Such a large proportion of families having marginal income status has a great impact on the future of rural schools. As a result, rural schools are typically smaller and poorer than nonrural schools (Herzog & Pittman, 1995). Rural schools may have difficulty raising the resources needed to finance education, and it is difficult to maintain existing schools and build new facilities for growing school enrollments. Just as in city schools, poverty affects children's ability to learn, and educators are often involved in finding social services and support for low-income families.

Field-Based Activity 9.1

Identify some of the salient characteristics of your school. Where is it located? How does its location affect its context? Does your school have unique problems because of its location? Do the characteristics of your school reflect descriptions associated with urban, suburban, or rural locations described in this chapter?

Some of the positive stereotypes of rural communities, such as close connections with community and family, a slower pace of life, and close contact with agriculture and nature, suggest strengths associated with small community contexts. Schools are often the center of community life, with school activities such as Friday night football and basketball games the focus of the week's events (Farris, 1996). A sense of community, small businesses, and small settlements of people where everyone knows and watches out for one another are also positive aspects of rural contexts. A close-knit family feeling characterizes schools in rural areas, even though students and parents may be critical of the facilities and resources (Herzog & Pittman, 1995).

Rural settings are facing great challenges from socioeconomic issues that in the past have had an impact on both urban and suburban areas. Rural populations are predicted to grow at a faster rate than populations in other settings, and it is expected that diversity will increase in some areas. South Texas and the western states of Arizona, New Mexico, and California host large immigrant populations (Huang, 1999). By far the largest number of immigrants settling in rural environments are Mexican, but other immigrant populations are also increasing in rural areas. Rural schools that teach large numbers of immigrants must somehow determine how to increase their spending and include appropriate instruction for these concentrated immigrant populations.

Certain other characteristics are associated with rural schools. Historically, vocational and agriculture programs have been important in rural schools, but the decline in jobs associated with technical and agricultural professions has changed the look of rural education. Rural students have higher graduation rates than urban students, but fewer students from rural contexts attend postsecondary schools (DeYoung & Lawrence, 1995). Community colleges are becoming important options for rural students to pursue educational opportunities beyond high school.

One unique rural educational issue is the ambivalence of parents regarding educational experiences that prepare their children for work in cities and large urban areas. Rural young people who are educated tend to leave their community

Becoming a Teacher in a Field-Based Setting

to find work (DeYoung & Lawrence, 1995). Older community members believe rural life is preferable to urban life, and they feel that education takes young people away from the rural contexts. This belief may cause rural voters to reject referendums that would provide money and resources for rural schools.

Teachers and administrators in rural areas tend to be less experienced and lower paid than their counterparts in metropolitan areas (Herzog & Pittman, 1995), and rural schools often have difficulty attracting teachers. The slower lifestyle of rural communities and the isolation from cultural and recreational centers discourage beginning teachers from looking for jobs in small towns. Rural schools may not always be able to provide the range of courses offered in larger schools because they lack certified teachers for advance placement courses in foreign language or higher level math and sciences. To provide more choice of courses, rural teachers may need to teach a wider range of courses than they would in larger school districts. They often have more opportunities to assist with extracurricular activities such as coaching, cheerleading, or debate teams. Many rural areas are holding out hope that new technologies will offer a more flexible approach to offering courses not currently available. Teachers often choose to teach in rural schools because they find it easier to become part of the community and to interact with the families of their students. They also enjoy teaching a wider range of courses and having opportunities to become involved in leadership and school activities. Rural schools provide exciting challenges and offer teachers a career choice that is shaped by the small community context.

World Wide Web Sites

You may learn more about rural school settings at the following Web sites:

http://www.nces.ed.gov/surveys/ruraled/
http://www.ruralchallengepolicy.org

Organizational Contexts

Traditionally, school organization was rather simple. Most schools were divided into elementary, junior high, and secondary schools. Usually kindergarten through sixth grade classes were grouped together in elementary schools, grades seven through eight made up the junior highs, and ninth through twelfth grades were identified as high school. Innovations and new understandings have increased the options and acceptance for a number of different school organization patterns. There is no longer a standard arrangement for grade levels in elementary and secondary schools. Grade level arrangements are often determined by physical space needs, community traditions, and administrative decisions. School organizations provide configurations of grade levels that meet the needs of preschool, elementary, intermediate, and high school students and satisfy administrative needs for physical space.

Preschools

The growing acceptance of the importance of early education and the need for childcare have resulted in the emergence of educational programs for three-, four-, and five-year-old children (Bowman, Donavan, & Burns, 2000). Preschool education today certainly means more than childcare. Many preschool programs provide very young children with stimulating experiences and opportunities to develop language skills and other important concepts. Early childhood programs usually focus on language, social, emotional, and physical development, providing young children with a strong foundation for school learning. Even though preschool curriculum is flexible and includes time for play, reading aloud, naps, nutrition, and social interaction, important support for the developing young child is of the utmost importance.

One well-known successful early childhood education program is Head Start, a government subsidized preschool program that has existed since the 1960s. Head Start was designed to provide preschool experiences that would help children from low-income families succeed when they entered school. Its success has generated a great deal of support from parents and lawmakers and has evolved into an educational organization that supports the families of young children and collaborates with other service providers and community programs.

Early childhood programs vary in quality, content, organization, and relationship to public schools. Programs such as Head Start may be offered at a school or may be located in another community-based setting. Schools, particularly those in low-economic status communities, can obtain government funds to establish preschool programs within the school. Preschool programs may be combined with day care so that children experience structured learning. Many children attend private, church, or Montessori programs that provide them with experiences during their preschool years. There is a great deal of flexibility within the curriculum and the requirements for educators who work with very young children. Requirements for preschool teachers differ from state to state, and some states do not require teachers to meet the same certification requirements as kindergarten, elementary, middle, and high school teachers.

World Wide Web Sites

If you want to know more about programs for young children, these Web sites will provide additional information:

http://www.ed.gov/offices/OERI/ECI/

http://www.naeyc.org/

Elementary Schools

Elementary schools play an important role in the learning and development of young children from ages five to twelve. Most elementary schools are organized by grade level, and the classrooms are self-contained, with one teacher planning and delivering instruction for all subjects. Most early elementary school experiences are devoted to reading, writing, spelling, and mathematics, with smaller amounts of time designated for social studies, science, art, and music. In states with well-developed accountability systems and standardized tests, schools are increasingly focusing on basic skills before moving on to other subjects. They may departmentalize the upper grades with special teachers for certain subjects such as art, music, or physical education.

Traditionally, elementary school arrangements included kindergarten through sixth grade, but it is not unusual to see any number of grade arrangements in elementary schools today. Primary school arrangements may include preschool, kindergarten, and first and second grades in one building and the intermediate grades from three to five in another building. Arrangements may be based on space and other special needs of the school. Elementary schools have a full range of special education services, bilingual programs, and may include programs for gifted and talented students. Preschool programs, middle school arrangements, and programs for at-risk students have expanded the complexity and offerings at elementary schools, and extra space or special configurations may require the district to arrange grade levels in unique ways.

Elementary teachers are trained to understand the developmental needs of children and must complete a series of certification requirements before taking a position in a school district. The instructional roles and requirements of elementary teachers differ from school to school. Teachers may be rather isolated, working with the students in their classroom without many interactions with others, or they may be part of a teaching team that plans and teaches together. The working conditions, arrangements, and requirements for elementary teachers vary widely and offer a future teacher many choices.

Intermediate Grades and Middle Schools

The educational needs of older elementary children may be taken care of in several ways. Intermediate grade children may be part of an elementary school organization or attend a middle or junior high school. The more than five thousand middle schools and junior high schools in our country educate preadolescents, ages eleven to fifteen (Lewis, 1993). Intermediate grades and middle schools focus on children as young as ten or eleven and as old as fourteen or fifteen.

The term "middle school" refers to a school for adolescents only, and it provides a transition between the elementary and high school experiences. Middle school educational philosophy recognizes that the rapid physical and emotional growth apparent during the early teens requires a unique approach. A junior high school model more typically resembles a high school structure with a strong emphasis on individual subject presentation. The most common organization for middle schools is grades six through eight (Kellough & Kellough, 1999).

Middle level education is associated with a philosophy that incorporates instructional practices that meet the special needs of adolescents. Team teaching, common teacher planning time, and thematic teaching are all common characteristics of middle school teaching. Middle school incorporates elementary teaching methods to instruct specific content area material, preparing students for the subject-focused instruction of junior high and high school. Most middle schools are departmentalized but encourage interrelationships and connections across subjects in an interdisciplinary manner. The focus on content becomes greater with each successive middle school grade level.

Children establish life-long interests and develop their self-concepts during the middle school years. For this reason, exploration and encouragement are important. Middle school educational approaches attempt to reduce the competition in coursework and extracurricular activities so that adolescents will take opportunities to try activities regardless of their skill level. Making sure that all children feel a part of their educational experience is an important goal of middle school educators. Focusing on inclusiveness, middle school cheerleading teams may have as many as seventy-five members, and everyone who wishes can be a member of the basketball team. The great emotional and physical changes of young adolescents provide teachers with many challenges. Teachers at the middle school level must be highly student-oriented and enjoy the special challenges of adolescents who are straddling childhood and teenage years.

World Wide Web Site

You can learn more about middle school education at this Web site: http://www.nmsa.org/

Junior High and High Schools

The focus of junior high and high schools is on general subjects, college preparatory curriculum, and vocational training. Students usually have a wide variety of course offering options available. Junior highs may serve the same age group as middle schools and can include any combination of grades seven through nine. Junior highs, which typically do not offer the interdisciplinary approach of middle schools, are set up more like high schools and focus on individual subject areas. High schools commonly include grades nine through twelve, but some include only grades ten through twelve. Concerns about the transition to high school have prompted many districts to create freshman campuses or wings within existing high schools. There are also magnet high schools, which emphasize a particular area of study such as science or the arts.

High school students have many social pressures and must make decisions that will affect the rest of their lives. Growing independence from adults and strong peer relationships are the focus of adolescent emotional development. Behaviors and attitudes related to smoking, drinking, dating, and driving are established during this time. High school students also begin to develop interests and abilities that will influence their future career paths and lifestyles. Students can legally drop out of high school at age sixteen, and the dropout rate is a particularly troublesome issue for most high schools.

High schools have encountered great criticism for not meeting the needs of older teenagers. Recently there has been a great deal of pressure to change teaching and learning processes in high schools. Reduction in class size, more interaction between high school students and teachers, and a curriculum that is more relevant to issues and problems that teenagers face outside of school have been the focus of reform efforts. Some high schools are attempting to implement block scheduling (see Chapter 8).

High school teachers are trained as subject matter and educational specialists and usually major in a content area such as math, biology, or English. Their certification typically allows them to teach grades seven through twelve, but this may vary from state to state. Junior high and high school teachers are much more focused on the subject matter than are their elementary and middle school colleagues, and they may teach five or six daily classes in a specific content area.

World Wide Web Site

An example of some of the resources available for secondary teachers can be reviewed at this Web site: http://7-12educators.about.com/education/ 7-12educators/mbody.htm

Leadership in Today's Schools

In the past, definitions of school leadership implied that only administrators such as principals and superintendents were leaders in a school setting. More recently, school reforms and changing views have contributed to a different view of leadership that is much more complex and requires collaboration and contributions from multiple viewpoints. Districts and schools that embrace a more collaborative view of leadership have changed the definition of leadership to encompass teachers, staff members, parents, and the entire education community in decision making (Neuman & Simmons, 2000). This view of leadership directly affects teachers' roles, and in many schools teachers are required to participate in various decision-making processes related to teaching, learning, and policy making. Although traditional administrative roles are still present in most schools, there are plenty of examples of how educational leadership has become the job of the entire education community.

State Policymakers

State have the major responsibility for establishing and funding schools, and many leadership issues begin at the state level. Although states may have different requirements, boards or individuals who are appointed or elected establish educational goals and guide the state's educational process.

In addition to providing leadership for schools, principals play many roles during the school day. Charismatic principals are often recognized for creative and successful leadership.

State Governments   State governments have a great deal of influence on the educational opportunities available in individual districts. The state is responsible for the funding patterns that support its schools, and governors are often seen as leaders in educational reform efforts. Both former President Clinton, when he was governor of Arkansas, and President Bush, when he was governor of Texas, were viewed as strong educational supporters and gained political attention through their work in education.

States continue to exert a great deal of control over the schools (see Chapter 4). They may develop and require competency tests for both students and teachers, establish teacher certification regulations, develop state-adopted curriculum and textbook selection processes, set school year schedules, oversee special needs accommodations, and make rulings about many aspects of school life.

In most cases, the state has a direct impact on teachers and on what happens in individual classrooms. This is particularly obvious in states that emphasize mandated achievement tests. Most states develop standardized tests, establish test schedules, score and tabulate results, and respond to district performance on tests by awarding designations that indicate successful school achievement based on testing.

State Educational Agencies and School Boards   State agencies and school boards have official authority over schools, particularly in areas of high school requirements, student achievement testing, curriculum guidelines, teacher certification, and professional development of teachers (Myers & Myers, 1995). State agencies are made up of professional educators who work on establishing state guidelines and implement the policies of the state legislature and school boards. Their duties include assisting and ensuring that schools comply with state requirements, maintaining high standards for students, and conducting research that informs the public about schooling. The state agency also assists local school districts in interpreting new laws passed by the legislature.

Some states have both a state educational agency and a state school board, and the two entities usually work closely with one another. State school boards are most often composed of elected citizens or those appointed by the governor. They meet regularly to discuss school policy, review curriculum, and select state-adopted textbooks. In several states, the school boards accredit the teacher preparation programs and encourage the professional development of experienced teachers. School boards may also grant waivers to schools, enabling them to try innovations not covered by existing standards.

Teachers should be aware of the politics and policies established by state agencies and school boards because they can have a direct influence on important issues such as what and how teachers teach, when they teach, and how they and their students are evaluated.

Local Policymakers and Administrators

States make broad decisions about policy, curriculum, testing, and other issues related to education, but local school boards and administrators enforce and interpret these policies. In this way, local educational governance such as school boards, unions, and districtwide leadership directly affect the day-to-day working conditions and environments in schools.

Local School Boards   The local school board is a group of elected citizens who oversee the total process of schooling in the community. Depending on the state and the community, the school board may have a great deal of responsibility for leadership and advocacy for the educational process for young people (Cohen, 1990). It contributes to the development of long-range goals, attracts and retains high-quality personnel, and ensures that resources are directed to students with the greatest need. It oversees the implementation of goals and policies and checks to make sure intended efforts are being accomplished.

Voice of a School Board Member

When I won my election to the school board, I expected to help make decisions about textbooks, high school schedules, and budgets. I never thought that being a member of the school board in a small city would result in any kind of notoriety, but I soon found otherwise. About two years after I first became a member, the school board was asked to approve the name of a new elementary school after a famous state hero. Even though the historical figure was well loved in the state, he was a slave owner. I had very strong feelings against naming the school after him, believing that it would be offensive to some of the parents and children who attended the school. Instead, I favored using the opportunity to recognize a well-known female African American educator. I expressed my opinion openly at a school board meeting. I was not prepared for the reaction. Members of the board immediately became involved in a heated discussion. Once the nightly news and local newspaper reported the school board disagreement, the community immediately became embroiled in the discussion. It wasn't long before the state and national news agencies picked up the story. Imagine my surprise when the New York Times *printed a story about the school-naming incident. I was interviewed by television and radio commentators. In the end the school was named for the female educator. Serving on the school board does not always require that individuals stand up for their beliefs at the risk of causing long-term community controversy, but there is always the chance that might happen.*

A typical school board meeting addresses citizen and parental concerns as well as teacher and staff issues, approves building plans and budgets, and supports and suggests local educational efforts. Controversial issues such as sex education, role of prayer in schools, and censorship are often considered by the school board. The school board attempts to build policy consensus in school districts with factions and pluralistic differences. One of their big jobs is to interview, identify, evaluate, and supervise the superintendent. As a result, the superintendent's role can be greatly affected by the district's school board.

School board meetings offer a good example of the democratic process. Board members discuss and make decisions about issues that are reflections of societal concern. School boards that are attuned to their constituency listen to citizens and are influenced by what they hear. The most positive outcomes occur when decisions and solutions represent multiple constituencies in the community. Their decisions are usually made quietly and without a great deal of fanfare, but sometimes the entire community gets involved. Controversial decisions can produce an appearance of television cameras at board meetings, newspaper reporters at the schools, and citizens' debates in newspapers.

World Wide Web Site

This Web site provides additional information about the role of school boards in educational settings: http://www.nsbf.org/

Superintendents and the Central Office   The superintendent is the chief executive of an entire school system. As in most leadership and administrative jobs, the superintendent's role reflects the personality of the individual who assumes the role. Approaches to the demands of the job vary dramatically. A superintendent may be visible in school hallways, at community gatherings, or appear regularly in local newspaper articles. The accessibility of the superintendent depends on the individual's administrative style, but the influence of the superintendent is felt in all aspects of schooling in a community. The superintendent is usually the point person for the community in regard to educational issues and is responsible for the public view of the school. The community holds him or her responsible for establishing and maintaining a shared vision that reflects community values. In addition, the superintendent is responsible for overseeing the budget, conducting bond elections that raise money for the schools, working with the school boards, meeting state and local directives, and supervising and working closely with principals, curriculum directors, and other administrators in the district.

The amount of contact between teachers and superintendents will depend on the school setting. New teachers in a large city will probably seldom see their superintendent, whereas a small-town superintendent may know most of the teachers by name. There are, however, large-school superintendents who make it a point to walk the halls of their schools so that teachers are familiar with them and feel free to talk to them. The principal may serve as a liaison between the school and the superintendent, and in all but the very large districts the superintendent and the principals probably will know each other very well and have a strong working relationship.

A superintendent's office may be referred to as the central office or central administration. The central office is the hub of the entire district operation. Central offices in large cities may be housed in multiple buildings, but in small school districts, the superintendent and support professionals and staff are often located in one of the school buildings. In most cases, a physical complex is devoted to the administrative aspects of a school district. Central office administrators include curriculum directors, special program coordinators, teacher appraisal specialists, and personnel officers. Professionals in the central office assist

Field-Based Activity 9.2

Tour a district's central office. Arrange to have someone who works in the office explain what they do. Think about how a new teacher would depend on the support and resources offered by the office.

Note: Smaller school districts may not have a central office. Find out how the services typically provided by the central office are offered in smaller districts.

schools and monitor compliance with state and federal requirements. One group of educators who may support teachers at either the district level or on the school campus are the supervisors or curriculum directors. Assigned to oversee the instruction of a particular content or specialty area, these specialists operate at the district level or are assigned to a specific school. Schools also employ early childhood, special education, gifted and talented, and English as a second language supervisors who may be housed in the central office, visit school campuses regularly, establish professional development activities in their particular area, engage in problem solving with a teacher who is experiencing difficulty, or develop classroom innovations.

Supervisors and Curriculum Directors Teachers come in contact with district supervisors and curriculum directors during professional development sessions and curriculum planning projects. Professional development sessions may be conducted in afternoons after school, during the week or so before school starts, or for longer periods of time during the summer. These sessions are usually planned by supervisors and directors to introduce a new teaching approach or to work on instructional areas targeted by school goals and objectives (such as improving math scores on state achievement tests). Central office curriculum directors are responsible for guiding the development of new curriculum. They often identify representatives from individual schools and bring them together as a work group to design new guidelines for teaching and learning. Supervisors and curriculum directors are often outstanding teachers who have demonstrated a great deal of curriculum and instruction understanding, hold an advanced graduate degree, and also possess leadership skills to offer needed guidance and direction. They can be a great help to new teachers and will often be available to observe instruction and make suggestions for improvement. Some large school districts hire a supervisor for new teachers, and his or her job is to support beginning teachers during their first year.

School Building Administration and Leadership

Teachers work for and with many people—students, parents, school boards, communities—but principals and building level administrators develop a very close working relationship with teachers. Principals are the most immediate supervisors of teachers and serve an important leadership function in any school. The principal's role includes many responsibilities and has been identified as the primary factor contributing to excellence in public schools, regardless of the ethnic or socioeconomic factors of the school community (Task Force on Education for Economic Growth, 1983). The principal's main job is to oversee the day-to-day operations of the school campus, but he or she often performs a variety of other functions and extends leadership opportunities to others.

A review of a principal's day reveals the variety of activities that are a part of his or her job. The principal may arrive at the school before teachers. This may be the only quiet time he or she has in the day to go over budgets, write memos to the central office, or establish a schedule for the next school year. When teachers begin arriving for their day, they often stop to talk with the principal about one of their students, an encounter with a parent in the grocery store the night before, or their progress on curriculum development. On other mornings, teachers might want to talk about conflicts between two teachers, ordering more paper, or requesting a substitute teacher for a personal day of leave. As the early morning continues, the principal's office begins to fill with children arriving at school. Parents may stop by the office to compliment, complain, request, or greet the principal. As more children begin to arrive, the principal walks the halls greeting the children. He or she may stop to visit with students, interacting and commenting on their concerns. Once the bell rings and the school day starts, the principal divides the time between attending meetings at the central office, dealing with parental phone calls, meeting with local community groups, writing reports for state requirements, balancing the budget, ordering supplies, and meeting with small groups of teachers. At lunch, he or she may make an attempt to be present in the lunchroom or appear at the bus stop or on the playground during recess. As the school day continues, the principal may be called to fix the heat, help with a sick child, monitor a group of children while a teacher returns an important phone call, or talk to a parent. After the children leave, the principal may meet with teachers, conduct staff meetings, attend extracurricular activities associated with the school, or have an hour or two of paperwork to finish before the day is over. In the evening, the principal may attend school board meetings or other activities associated with the school.

Principals in secondary schools may have daily schedules similar to the one just described, but there are some differences. Their day starts early and ends late, but they may be working on larger budgets, ordering supplies for larger groups of teachers, and working closer with professionals from central administration. Secondary principals also work with assistant principals who supervise teachers and deal with individual student concerns. Supervisors and teacher team leaders take a great deal of responsibility for developing and implementing curriculum, but it is the principal's job to establish the vision, facilitate communication, and make sure standards are being met in all subject areas. Principals in larger schools may not have the same close, working relationship with teachers common in smaller schools, but they can be found supporting and attending sports events, concerts, drama productions, and other events that are part of the school's extracurricular activities.

Principals differ widely in the way they perceive their role (Leithwood, 1992; Riehl, 2000). Personal philosophies, personalities, idiosyncrasies and habits, administrative styles, personal interactions, and beliefs about student development all contribute to the uniqueness of leadership style. Some principals may be very reserved, whereas others are accessible and easy to approach. A supportive principal will remove obstacles, provide material and emotional support, manage details, share in the professional comradeship, and help establish the goals for the school (Sergiovanni, 1992). Principals have many tasks, but some are particularly important to new teachers or preservice teachers who are beginning their professional development. Let's examine a few of these important roles.

• *Establishing vision.* Principals are responsible for maintaining the school vision and for implementing the practical steps to accomplish educational goals and objectives. They help establish a "clear vision of short- and long-range goals for the school" (Sergiovanni, 1992, p. 7). A school's context and character reflect the goals and objectives established through the principal's facilitation. In one elementary school, the principal was the leader in recognizing the richness that accompanies the large number of international students in attendance at his school. The school hallways, curriculum, extracurricular activities, and pride became rooted in a focus on internationalism. The teachers and staff welcomed children from around the world and became known as a school that displayed a great deal of diversity. The same school faculty, under the leadership of the principal, accepted the preparation of new teachers as part of the vision and worked closely with a university to provide field activities. All the teachers in the school accepted the responsibility of preparing new teachers and became involved in a complex school–university partnership. The goals of internationalism and teacher education established a unique culture that influenced every teacher in the school.

The most important goal of any school is the success of all students, teachers, and professionals in the school. The achievement and happiness of students comes first in establishing a vision for the school, but principals must also have high expectations for teachers and themselves. A principal's way of administrating and leading can have a great impact on the potential success of all who work and learn in the school. Successful principals have figured out how to balance their focus among teachers, children, and the community.

• *Managing the school.* Principals are crucial contributors to schools and the way they operate. They manage the budget, oversee equipment purchases, hire teachers, and establish school schedules. Although they may distribute their managerial responsibilities to other professionals in the school, principals are ultimately responsible for administration. Schools that enroll a large number of students may hire assistant principals to be responsible for scheduling, student conduct, curriculum development, or other issues related to the complex process of school leadership. But when there is a problem to be solved, an issue to discuss, or teaching/learning expectations to uphold, it is the principal who must administer and guide the process.

• *Maintaining high standards for instruction.* The principal plays an important role in implementing and maintaining effective instructional programs within a school (Fullan, 1991; Hansen & Smith, 1989). The principal's beliefs about students' abilities to learn and teachers' ability to teach affect long-range and everyday teaching and learning processes (Greenfield, 1991). The principal is actively involved in decision making relative to instruction and must attend to instructional objectives as well as instruction strategies. The principal is also responsible for collecting information and using data in a manner that keeps everyone in the school well informed about the performance of teachers and students.

Principals have a great influence on the work of teachers. The way principals interpret what teachers do is of primary importance in the life of a teacher. Two examples of their direct impact on a teacher's career are instructional assessment and professional development activities. Consider that principals are responsible for observing and assessing teachers' classroom instructional behaviors. They provide feedback on teachers' instruction, interactions with children, and other important classroom procedures. They are responsible for providing ongoing professional development for teachers at their school. Effective principals work hard to build up the capacities of teachers and others so that they can take on some of the leadership in a school (Sergiovanni, 1992). They keep in touch with beginning teachers and provide support and advice for them. The principalship is a demanding and important role and one that influences each new teacher's professional development.

• *Facilitating shared decision making.* One impact of the reform movement of the last ten years is to involve as many people as possible in local school decision

Field-Based Activity 9.3

Ask the principal or an assistant principal to talk with you about some of the events or activities that occur during the work day. As the principal talks, try to determine which of the duties described in the text take most of the principal's time. Create a chart or graph that illustrates the principal's responsibilities.

making. Shared decision making, sometimes referred to as site-based management, reflects a less centralized approach to school leadership and requires a great deal of collaboration and trust (Midgely & Wood, 1993). Collaborative decision making means many things and takes many forms depending on the people involved in the process. It usually means placing as much decision-making authority as possible with the teachers, counselors, parents, and other professionals at individual school buildings (Myers & Myers, 1995). A team of decision makers typically includes the principal, teachers, other school staff, community representatives, and parents who work together to make decisions. These leadership teams can have an impact on who is employed at a school, what curriculum is implemented, and what textbooks are purchased.

One of the most common issues that arise with a site-based decision-making process is the sharing of power by those who have traditional leadership roles. Superintendents and principals must make dramatic shifts in their ideas about leadership to support shared leadership processes. Likewise, parents and others may not be familiar with decision-making responsibilities and may not possess the skills and time required to make good decisions about the school. Many districts are still experimenting with this concept, and as you begin your career you may see many levels of success with this process.

A school–university partnership usually illustrates a shared decision-making process. In most cases, a leadership team makes decisions about the teacher education process. School administrators, teachers, and university faculty are involved in making decisions for the students in the teacher education program.

Teachers as Leaders

Teacher leadership has been implemented in traditional roles such as department heads, textbook selection committees, and union representatives, but these traditional roles are limited compared to the leadership opportunities that are emerging. Teacher leadership roles involve teachers as mentors, team leaders, and

Voice of a Teacher

Some families are made up of doctors, lawyers, or dentists, and people who make money. My family has chosen a lifetime of poverty in exchange for the rewards of teaching. I'm the twelfth teacher in three generations. Most of my relatives have taught elementary school, with an occasional coach or high school math teacher thrown in. My mother has even taught special education classes in the Texas prison system. During my high school years, I fought the urging of my family. I was determined to be different, but after graduation I gave in to my destiny. I love teaching elementary children and have never regretted my decision. I would have been perfectly satisfied to teach third-graders for the rest of my life, not knowing that anything else was possible, but thanks to the Professional Development School program, I have experienced types of teaching that were never dreamed of by the previous teachers in my family.

Recently, I applied for and received a position as a co-teacher for a math methods course that was made available by the Professional Development School program. I wanted to teach this course because I knew that math was a weak area for me and I wanted to challenge myself as a teacher. I've been surprised by the changes I felt as a result.

Teaching this course, and working with college students, has helped me to acquire more information. I am a learner as well as a teacher. I feel more pride in what I do, which causes me to perceive myself differently. My role as a teacher has changed and expanded. I feel that my colleagues' perceptions of me have changed also, which increases my self-esteem. Whether these feelings are real or imagined on my part, the result remains the same. My teaching has improved.

It's a wonderful change of pace to work with college students. I feel the same joys when they succeed or learn a new concept that I do with my elementary students. The difference is the level of learning. We can deal with concepts and discuss topics that are far above my third-grade students. One of my favorite aspects of this class is when they come to me to discuss a problem or an idea that they have for a lesson. Many of their ideas are creative, and they are so enthusiastic about teaching that it's contagious. I've always felt that I touch the future when I work with my eight-year-old students, but now I also touch the future of all those children my college students will teach. What a phenomenal responsibility!

Teaching this math methods course and participating in the Professional Development School program has opened up a whole new world for me. It satisfies that part of me that needs to be different in a family of teachers and also that part of me that needs to teach.

curriculum developers. More innovative involvement in teacher leadership can come about as a result of participation in teacher-as-researcher or action research projects in which teachers collect data to answer questions about their own teaching or instructional practices. Also, instructional leadership, school–university partnerships, and staff development sessions provide many opportunities for teachers to provide leadership (Mendez-Morse, 1992).

Teachers have a great deal of insight and responsibility in decisions about teaching and can play an important role in providing instructional leadership. Instructional leadership focuses on decisions related to students and their learning and is guided by high expectations of students and teachers and an emphasis on instruction (Heck, Larsen, & Marcoulides, 1990). Instructional leaders also use the results of students' achievement, strengths, and challenges to make decisions about instruction. For example, in the role of instructional leader, teachers may identify the writing process as an area that needs strengthening in their school. They may recognize this need as a result of their students' test scores or because teachers have expressed a desire to become more knowledgeable in this area. The teacher leaders may arrange for a consultant to come to the school and work with small groups of teachers, present model lessons in classrooms, and expose teachers to innovative methods for teaching writing. The consultant and the teacher leaders might provide opportunities for teachers to participate in process writing workshops during the summer and work with groups of teachers to develop lesson plans for the coming year. As they implement their plans, they continue to monitor their students' writing development through test scores and the authentic assessment of portfolios.

Teachers can exercise their leadership talents in several ways. Teachers demonstrate instructional leadership when they become involved in planning and delivering professional development activities for the continuing education of their colleagues. Successful teachers can share their favorite strategies and innovative techniques with other teachers. When teachers plan, design, and deliver learning plans or activities for their school's professional development, the activities and processes they plan reflect concerns and interests of their colleagues and are more meaningful.

There are also opportunities for teacher leaders to facilitate the organization and management of their schools. Schools with more than one or two teachers at each grade level or within content areas usually have team leaders who are responsible for communication, announcements, decision making, and planning. The principal or their fellow teachers appoint team leaders. This small-group arrangement facilitates participation in decision making and provides a greater opportunity for all teachers to express their opinions.

The number of opportunities for teacher leadership is increasing and requires the modern teacher to consider a wider range of tasks related to the profession. Individuals in schools that work in a shared leadership manner must possess strong communication and listening skills (Mendez-Morse, 1992). They must recognize and appreciate the ideas of their colleagues and patiently hear everyone's ideas and solutions. It is not easy to assume new roles. Teachers who are in these roles must know how to deal with change, persuasion, and conflicts.

Field-Based Activity 9.4

Attend at least one team meeting or professional development session. Note the roles of the teachers that work at your school. Using the list provided here as a guide, determine which skills were most apparent.

group process	running meetings	visioning
enabling	advocacy	facilitation
conflict management	goal-setting	listening
budgeting	action research	network building
honoring dissenters	collaboration	consensus building
giving away power	cultural sensitivity	feedback

But most of all, teachers who take on new roles must learn how to use their time differently. Even with help, it is difficult not to feel stressed as the roles of teachers expand and change (Wasley, 1991).

Experienced teachers seldom view themselves as leaders (Bellon & Beaudry, 1992; Wasley, 1991). It is, however, becoming an increasingly important part of a teacher's career. There are a growing number of opportunities and situations in which teachers can become leaders. As this trend continues, you may have many chances to exercise your instructional leadership capabilities throughout your career. Take time now to complete the Self-Reflection exercise and to think about what you have learned.

Preservice Teacher Leadership

Preservice teachers rarely consider leadership opportunities during their training and in fact may be unconcerned about leadership roles because they view school leadership as the responsibility of superintendents, principals, and experienced teachers. Recognizing leadership responsibilities, taking part in activities that encourage leadership, and understanding the challenges of leadership in today's schools should be components of the preservice teachers' experiences.

Recognizing that leadership is part of the teacher's role is the first step to becoming a teacher leader. Teaching and leading are not necessarily separate processes. Several defining elements and skills are common to both teaching and leading. Day-to-day classroom routines require leadership skills. A teacher

Self-Reflection

LEADERSHIP PATHS

Read these statements about leadership, and circle the answer that reflects your view.

1. As a teacher, I expect to take part in making decisions about my school.	Yes	No
2. My principal will establish the vision and mission for my school.	Yes	No
3. It is not my role to question decisions my principal makes.	Yes	No
4. The central office, superintendent, and curriculum directors should establish the direction of my school.	Yes	No
5. It is important for teachers to collaborate and make decisions about school improvement.	Yes	No
6. If my school's test scores fall, the central office should set goals and objectives for my school.	Yes	No
7. It is the teacher's responsibility to understand and take into account parental goals and objectives.	Yes	No
8. Teachers should involve students in determining their needs based on results of standardized and in-class assessments.	Yes	No
9. New teachers need to understand how to collaborate with others.	Yes	No
10. Experts from the central office should determine the professional development needs for teachers.	Yes	No

Tally the number of yes responses you gave to items 1, 5, 7, 8, and 9. This gives you an indication of where you are on the path to shared leadership. Then tally the number of yes responses you gave to items 2, 3, 4, 6, and 10. This tally represents your traditional leadership. Now compare the two. Are you farther along on the shared or traditional path to leadership? Is this the path you want to take? If so, what kinds of questions would you ask principals when you are interviewing for teaching positions?

constantly assesses situations, develops strategies, and implements plans that solve problems. "Passion, meaning, and purpose" are the foundation for both leadership and teaching (Bolman & Deal, 1994, p. 3). "As a person learns to be a good teacher, he or she also learns to be a good leader" (Gardner, 1989, p. 18).

Good teachers develop strong leadership skills. Taking part in activities that encourage is an important component of preservice teachers' learning experiences.

Classroom interactions also require leadership skills. Teachers use skills related to problem solving, persuasion, and conflict resolution when interacting with children and young people. In addition, teaching and learning situations provide numerous opportunities for achieving goals set for yourself and for helping students achieve their goals.

Preservice training offers methods, concepts, and ideas to help you develop into a successful classroom leader. You may find opportunities to exercise your leadership skills within your university training processes. Whole class and small-group activities offer future teachers an opportunity to work with others and learn collaborative processes. Many future teachers take part in summer jobs, community or church activities, or volunteer efforts that require them to help make decisions and guide others.

Although it is easy to understand the connections between leadership and teaching, it is not always easy to recognize the more subtle aspects of leadership that exist in schools. Understanding the roles and differing perspectives of all those involved in the educational process and finding ways to exercise your own leadership capabilities can provide insights into the complexity of leadership in our schools.

Portfolio Reflections and Exhibits

Prepare a portfolio exhibit. Adapt one of the field activities completed in this chapter, create your own exhibit, or complete suggested Portfolio Exhibit 9 to represent the learnings and understandings developed in this chapter.

Suggested Exhibit 9: School Leadership

Your portfolio representation for this chapter should include:

1. A summary of the field-based activities you completed for this chapter.

2. The selection and explanation of the activity that was most important to your learning.

3. Develop a graphic (a web or some other relational graphic) to illustrate all the different types of leadership teachers can demonstrate. Use the text or other readings to support your observations. Describe each leadership role and some of the impacts of teacher leadership. Note which leadership roles can be developed during your preservice experience.

InfoTrac College Edition Extension

Log on to the InfoTrac College Edition Web site, and choose one of the following searches to expand your knowledge about school organization and leadership.

1. Using the PowerTrac option (choose the author index and the keyword index and type in the descriptors), find the work of educational researchers who have written about school organization and leadership. You may use someone mentioned in the chapter or try the ones listed here:
   au Michael Fullan and ke organization
   au Linda Lambert and ke leadership

2. The *Phi Delta Kappan* journal often has articles about school leadership. Using the PowerTrac option and the search term provided here, discover the kinds of articles about leadership the journal has featured recently:
   jn Phi Delta Kappan and ke leadership

Related Readings

McIntyre, D. J., & O'Hair, M. J. (1996). *The reflective roles of the classroom teacher.* Belmont, CA: Wadsworth.

This book presents the many roles of the teacher and encourages each teacher to develop those capacities. Leadership is one teacher's role, which is described by presenting realistic classroom scenes.

Sergiovanni, T. J. (1992). *Moral leadership: Getting to the heart of school improvement.* San Francisco: Jossey-Bass.

This book describes school leaders who understand that attending to "people" will create more effective and successful schools.

References

Bellon, T., & Beaudry, J. (1992, April). *Teachers' perceptions of their leadership roles in site-based decision making.* Paper presented at the annual meeting of the American Educational Research Association, San Francisco.

Bolman, L. G., & Deal, T. E. (Eds.). (1994). *Becoming a teacher leader: From isolation to collaboration.* Thousand Oaks, CA: Corwin Press.

Bowman, B., Donovan, M. S., & Burns, M. S. (Eds.). (2000). *Eager to learn: Educating our preschoolers.* Committee on Early Childhood, Pedagogy, National Research Council. Washington, DC: National Academy Press.

Cohen, M. (1990). Key issues confronting state policy makers. In R. F. Elmore (Ed.), *Restructuring schools: The next generation of educational reform* (pp. 251–288). San Francisco: Jossey-Bass.

Crosby, E. A. (1999). Urban schools: Forced to fail. *Phi Delta Kappan, 81*(4), 298–303.

Dewee, S. (December, 1999). *Improving rural school facilities for teaching and learning.* Eric Digest; ERIC Clearinghouse on Rural Education and Small Schools. [Available online: http://www.ael.org/eric/digests/edorc998.htm.]

DeYoung, A. J., & Lawrence, B. K. (1995). On hoosiers, yankees, and mountaineers. *Phi Delta Kappan, 77*(2), 105–112.

Englert, R. M. (1993). Understanding the urban context and conditions of practice of school administration. In P. Forsyth & M. Tallerico (Eds.), *City schools: Leading the way.* Newbury Park, CA: Sage.

Farris, P. J. (1996). *Teaching, bearing the torch.* Dubuque, IA: Brown & Benchmark.

Fullan, M. G. (1991). *The new meaning of educational change.* New York: Teachers College Press.

Forsyth, P. B., & Tallerico, M. (Eds.). (1993). *City schools: Leading the way.* Newbury Park, CA: Corwin.

Gardner, J. (1989). *On leadership.* New York: Free Press.

Gordon, G. L. (1999). Teacher talent and urban schools. *Phi Delta Kappan, 81*(4), 304–307.

Greenfield, W. D. (1991). *The micropolitics of leadership in an urban elementary school*. Paper presented at the annual meeting of the American Educational Research Association, Chicago.

Hahn, A., Danzberger, J., & Lefkowitz, B. (1987). *Dropouts in America: Enough is known for action*. Washington, DC: Institute for Educational Leadership.

Hansen, J. M., & Smith, R. (1989). Building-based instructional improvement: The principal as an instructional leader. *NASSP Bulletin, 73*(518), 10–16.

Heck, R. H., Larsen, T. J., & Marcoulides, G. A. (1990). Instructional leadership and school achievement: Validation of a causal model. *Educational Administration Quarterly, 26*(2), 94–125.

Herzog, M. J. R., & Pittman, R. B. (1995). Home, family, and community: Ingredients in the rural education equation. *Phi Delta Kappan, 77*(2), 113–118.

Huang, G. G. (1999). *Sociodemographic changes: Promises and problems for rural education*. ERIC Clearinghouse on Rural Education and Small Schools. Office of Educational Research and Improvement, U.S. Department of Education ED-99-CO-0027. Available online: http://www.ael.org/eric/digests/edorc987.htm.]

Kellough, R. D., & Kellough, N. G. (1999). *Middle school teaching: A guide to methods and resources*, 3rd ed. Upper Saddle River, NJ: Merrill.

Kozol, J. (1991). *Savage inequalities: Children in America's schools*. New York: HarperCollins.

Lambert, L. (1998). How to build leadership capacity. *Educational Leadership, 55*(7), 17–19.

Leithwood, K. A. (1992). The principal's role in teacher development. In M. Fullan & A. Hargreaves (Eds.), *Teacher development and educational change* (pp. 86–103). London: Falmer Press.

Lewis, A. C. (1993). *Changing the odds: Middle school reform in progress, 1991–1993*. New York: Edna McConnell Clark Foundation.

Lewis, S., Jepson, J., & Casserly, M. (1999). *Closing the achievement gaps in urban schools: A survey of academic progress and promising practices in the great city schools*. Washington, DC: Council of Great City Schools.

Maeroff, G. I. (1988). *The empowerment of teachers*. New York: Teachers College Press.

Mendez-Morse, S. (1992). *Leadership characteristics that facilitate school change*. Austin: Southwest Educational Development Laboratory.

Midgely, C., & Wood, S. (1993). Beyond site-based management: Empowering teachers to reform schools. *Phi Delta Kappan, 75*(2), 187–194.

Myers, C. B., & Myers, L. K. (1995). *The professional educator*. Belmont, CA: Wadsworth.

Neuman, M., & Simmons, W. (2000). Leadership for student learning. *Phi Delta Kappan, 82*(1), 9–12.

Ornstein, A. C., & Levine, D. U. (1989). Social class, race and school achievement: Problems and prospects. *Journal of Teacher Education, 40*(5), 17–23.

Pipho, C. (1995). Urban school problems and solutions. *Phi Delta Kappan, 77*(2), 102–103.

Population Reference Bureau. (1999). *America's racial and ethnic minorities.* [Population Bulletin No. 54, p. 3] [Available online: http://www.prb.org/pubs/population_bulletin/bu54-3/part5.htm.]

Richard, A. (2000). Remodeling suburbia. *Education Week, XX*(7), 1, 28–36.

Riehl, C. (2000). The principal's role in creating inclusive schools for diverse students: A review of normative, empirical, and critical literature on the practice of educational administration. *Review of Educational Research, 70*(1), 55–82.

Rist, R. C. (2000). Student social class and teacher expectations: The self-fulfilling prophecy in ghetto education. *Harvard Educational Review 70*(3), 257–265.

Schmuck, R. A., & Schmuck, P. A. (1992). *Small districts, big problems: Making school everybody's house.* Newbury Park, CA: Corwin.

Sergiovanni, T. J. (1992). *Moral leadership: Getting to the heart of school improvement.* San Francisco: Jossey-Bass.

Stromquist, N. (1994). Some trends and issues affecting education in the urban context. In N. Stromquist (Ed.), *Education in urban areas: Cross-national dimensions* (pp. 11–28). Westport, CT: Praeger.

Task Force on Education for Economic Growth. (1983). *Action for excellence: A comprehensive plan to improve our nation's schools.* Denver: Education Commission of the States.

Urban Institute. (1995). *Improving student performance in the inner city* [Policy and Research Report]. [Available online: www. urban.org/periodcl/prr26_1b.htm.]

U.S. Department of Education (1998–1999). *Number and percent of rural and non-rural public elementary and secondary students, by district locale and state: 1998.* National Center for Education Statistics, Common Core of Data, Local Education Agency Universe Survey. Washington, DC: Author.

Wasley, P. A. (1991). *Teachers who lead: The rhetoric of reform and the realities of practice.* New York: Teachers College Press.

CHAPTER 10

Collaborating with Families, Businesses, and the Community

IN THIS CHAPTER

- **Families as Partners in Education**
- **Community Involvement**
- **Business Partners**
- **Interprofessional Partners**
- **Churches and Religious Groups**
- **Challenges of Collaboration**

*T*here were plenty of other caring, responsible adults who did their best to see that all the children in the community were getting the attention they needed. From librarians to crossing guards to Scout leaders, adults looked out for us, made sure we had enough to do and a place to do it.

There was consensus among adults that they need to present a united front when dealing with children. Adult authority gave us both a structure to our lives and a target to rebel against....

Community resources were managed for the benefit of children. The land surrounding each school served as a park and playing field for kids all year round. The schools were open summer mornings for sports and arts-and-crafts programs run by teenagers....

For good or ill, our families and the environments in which we live are the backdrop against which we play out our entire lives. Families shape our futures; our early family experiences heavily influence, and to a degree determine, how we forever after think and behave. At the same time, our families are shaped by the forces at work in the larger society—and by the village, whether it is a suburb or a ghetto, in which the family lives. That is why it is important for us to try to understand the personal and social forces that formed our own families, and how they shaped—and continue to shape—both our lives and the village around us.

—Hillary Rodham Clinton, *It Takes a Village**

A teacher's work typically occurs in a single classroom characterized by daily lessons and learning activities. As you have seen in this course and as you observe in the schools, schooling goes far beyond the walls of classrooms and school buildings. When school is a collaborative endeavor, successful practices evolve from the team effort of many potential partners. Not all partners are educators. Partners from noneducational settings can create an expanded educational context.

Working with multiple partners may make the educational process more complex, but student success and achievement increases with additional partners. Depending on their roles, partners support teachers' daily work in different ways. Perhaps the most obvious, but also the most important, partnership is between school and family. Children, teachers, and schools all benefit when parents or other caretakers show an interest in their child's education. Other potential partners include professionals who work regularly with children and parents, health and human service professionals, businesspeople, community members, and university or other educational partners.

A teacher who is aware of the importance of home, community, agency, and business involvement plans and encourages activities that naturally involve partners. Some traditional partnerships, such as parents and schools, are expected; other collaborations, such as those between social workers and teachers, are less common but also beneficial. This chapter discusses the importance of collaboration and support in young people's school achievement and suggests benefits,

---

*From *It Takes a Village, and Other Lessons Children Teach Us*, by Hillary Rodham Clinton (pp. 26, 28). New York: Simon & Schuster.

Becoming a Teacher in a Field-Based Setting

barriers, methods, and techniques that encourage the involvement of parents, community, business, and health and human service professionals. The chapter answers these questions:

- What are the school's and the teacher's role in encouraging collaboration with parents and others?

- How can multiple partners be used to help children in today's schools, and what are the benefits of collaborative educational efforts?

- How can beginning teachers involve others to improve the success of children in individual classrooms?

- How do other professionals associated with children and young people see their connections to the schools?

The task of collaborating with educational partners to develop innovative and creative approaches to common problems is difficult. It takes time, commitment, and effective interpersonal skills. Connections to groups outside the school contribute to an expanded support system for children and to the likelihood that they will be able to reach the highest possible standards and successes.

Families as Partners in Education

Parents, family members, and other caretakers who provide the primary care to students make important contributions to their children's educational process. Recent suggestions that parental involvement in schools is of vital importance come from many different sources. During the past decade, the federal government has advocated family involvement. The National Goals 2000 report puts a great deal of responsibility on parent partners in educational activities, stating that "by the year 2000, every school will promote partnerships that will increase parental involvement and participation in promoting the social, emotional, and academic growth of children" (U.S. Department of Education, 1994, p. 2). This emphasis has persisted through the presidential terms of Reagan, Bush, Clinton, and now President Bush, indicating that the notion of parents as partners in the educational process is not a fleeting fad.

Evidence supports the importance of parent and family participation. Getting parents and other significant adults involved in school improves young people's attitudes toward school and contributes to their overall school success (Rasinski & Fredericks, 1989). Parental involvement in school results in clear gains in the achievement of children (Henderson, 1988). Involved parents have

Parental involvement in school activities has the potential to improve the school environment and student achievement. Schools should provide numerous ways for parents to take part in their children's education.

children with more positive attitudes about school and higher aspirations for the future (Epstein, 1993, 1995).

Parental and family involvement results in achievement gains and improved attitudes toward education for several reasons (Scott-Jones, 1988). Parents and primary caregivers are children's first teachers and have worked with their children for five or six years before teachers become involved. Parents know their children and continue to have a powerful influence on their attitudes and learning. Nevertheless, adult support does not provide the same influence in all situations. Parental attitudes toward their children can cover a wide range of responses from helpful and supportive to domineering and intimidating, to displaying indifference, or to demonstrating open hostility.

Family involvement tends to decline as children get older. For the most part, parents of elementary-age children control the environment and resources available to their children and have a great influence on children through the decisions and choices they make. Families continue to influence young people even as they begin to exercise their own independence in middle and high school, although this influence is not as obvious and direct. The changing relationship between families and their older children requires adjustments in expectations throughout the school years as students take on more responsibility for decision making.

Field-Based Activity 10.1

Write a short narrative about your memory of your own family members' experiences with the schools. What did they do? When did they come to school? Were they interested in and involved with your school experiences? Did their involvement change as you entered middle school and high school? If possible, contact your parents or other family members to determine what they remember about their involvement in your education. Share these stories with your peers.

The common decline in parental involvement at middle and high school can be avoided if parents and teachers consider and plan for the changing needs of students. All students, no matter what level, want their families to understand and be more knowledgeable about school (Epstein, 1995). When children are young, they are usually delighted to see parents and other family members at school. As students get older, they can take responsibility for engaging their family in school activities and communicating with them about homework and school decisions. In middle and high school, parental and family involvement may not be as explicit as it was in earlier years and may take different forms, but it is equally important.

There are benefits for teachers, family members, and children when parental involvement is successful (Spaulding, 1996). As family members and educators interact with each other, more understanding and acceptance develop among all involved. Parents' observations provide teachers with insights into the lives of students and give a different perspective on school behaviors. Sharing information about the child's situation at home or at school supports the development of successful learning that contributes to more effective classroom interactions and planning. Likewise, when families understand what is occurring at school, they can support students and become involved in school activities. Parents and family members involved in school activities recognize that teachers understand their children and know about their backgrounds, including any special circumstances in their history. Teacher expectations of children are often related to adult family members' involvement in school activities. Adults who work closely with the schools almost always perceive that teachers believe each child will succeed in school (Spaulding, 1996).

In addition to providing teachers with information about students, family members can become involved by visiting, volunteering, or working on projects at the school. The school can receive additional support from parents and family members when they add extra hands, additional ideas, untapped resources, and different perspectives to ongoing activities in the school. The presence of family members in the school and classrooms also means that community values are represented in the school. Family involvement in schools is one way to take advantage of a diversity of cultures and have the diversity represented in hallways, committee meetings, and school functions. At the same time, family involvement sends a signal to children and young people that learning and schools are important to the community and to the significant people in their families.

Characteristics of Family Involvement

Rioux and Berla (1994) and Flaxman and Inger (1992) point out that family involvement can take many forms, but certain elements of involvement characterize programs that are successful. Schools with successful family involvement programs share the basic assumption that collaboration with others provides benefits for children from elementary grades through high school. These schools encourage and nurture involvement and collaboration.

Children from low-income and minority families have the most to gain from parental involvement in the schools. Family participation in the education of these children enhances their achievement (Henderson, 1987). Despite this outcome, most collaborative programs have primarily attracted white, middle-class, English-speaking family members. Parents and other family members from all socioeconomic levels, but particularly from low-income and minority groups, may be intimidated by interactions with school personnel and be afraid the problems their child is encountering in school will ultimately be blamed on their inability to raise the child properly. In this manner, a child's difficulty in school can add to an already stressful home situation, leaving parents feeling like failures (Comer, 1994). In addition, some parents may relate school to their own past learning problems or bad experiences with school personnel.

Factors that Encourage Family Involvement

Parental involvement in schools sometimes depends on the ages and needs of the children. Family members may have every intention of being a partner with their teachers, and for some this comes naturally. Other family members may need to be encouraged and instructed on what will help their children and their teachers. Family involvement can be encouraged by the district or school administration or by individual teachers. More than any other strategy the school may employ, the teachers' interactions and encouragement build successful relationships between homes and schools. Teachers and schools can foster positive involvement by employing these strategies (Epstein, 1993; Fredericks & Rasinski, 1990).

- *Fulfillment of basic needs.* One of the first ways that families can be involved in the schooling of their children is to provide the basic needs for their children. A secure home that provides food, clothing, shelter, and school supplies contributes a great deal to school success. Teachers may take this obligation for granted, but some families struggle to meet even basic requirements. Teachers may need to obtain help in meeting student needs from other professionals, social workers, community health professionals, or others. When it appears that families are having a difficult time providing basic needs to their children, teachers can be catalysts for involving other professionals who can help the families.

- *Home–school communication.* Family involvement is encouraged when effective communication processes are established between home and school. Teachers and schools assume a great deal of responsibility for establishing lines of communication to parents. Positive communication helps family members learn about the nature of the school and the daily routines. When family members do not respond to school queries, teachers and administrators should investigate the reasons for communication failures and apply problem-solving strategies to encourage parental response.

- *Recognition of family differences.* Families demonstrate a wide range of comfort with school involvement. Many parents and family members take for granted that they will become involved in the ongoing activities of the school. They visit classrooms, attend school plays, volunteer for specific jobs, and participate in instructional activities or as guest speakers. Mothers, fathers, and other family members become involved through organized volunteer programs, which encourage individuals outside the school to become involved in school activities. Some family members may become familiar with the school and know the names of many children in the school. Other family members are more hesitant because they do not know how to become involved, need a great deal of encouragement to participate, or perceive that they lack the resources or time for involvement.

- *Home-based involvement.* Teachers may need to change their own definitions of family involvement. Involvement does not always mean that family members are visible at the school and participate in every opportunity available. Another way that busy family members can demonstrate their support of schools and the learning process is to participate in instruction at home. Well-planned, home-based activities provide a way for working parents and other family members to stay connected with school activities. Homework assignments provide one means for this, but a creative teacher might use television watching, Internet research, and reading together as part of a comprehensive plan to encourage students and family members to work together on school-related activities.

• *Schoolwide goals and objectives.* Schools that are most effective in involving parents have school goals and plans for regular parental involvement. Teachers might provide individual opportunities in single classrooms, but when family involvement is an overall goal of the school and accompanies a larger plan for increasing and maintaining parental involvement, it has more chances to be successful and long term.

• *Multiple methods of involvement.* There should be several ways to involve parents and family members. When families have several options for involvement, they can select ways to work with their schools that best suit their comfort, work schedule, talents, and abilities. Activities, meetings, and parent–teacher conferences should be planned at different times of the day so that parents who work can arrange schedules and care for their younger children. Different family values, abilities, and schedules should be considered when teachers and schools plan home–school connections. Providing interpreters for multilingual family members is another way to create a comfortable and welcoming environment.

• *Recognition.* Everyone likes to be recognized for contributing in a positive way. Family members who are recognized for a variety of activities indicating their involvement in schools and classrooms respond positively and enthusiastically. Positive reinforcement can result in parents who view their part in school activities as valued and recognized contributions to the child's academic career.

• *Children as recruiters.* Most parents will respond to requests of their children, particularly if children register a great deal of excitement and enthusiasm about their parents' involvement in school.

• *Inclusion of all significant adults.* Parental involvement can include other family or community members. Brothers and sisters, aunts and uncles, grandparents, regular caretakers, and good friends can all take part in classroom events. Families take many different forms and do not always reflect traditional mother-father-children units. Parental involvement activities should be flexible in nature to include all definitions of families.

• *Collaboration among families.* Involved families can work to recruit other families to participate in the classroom. Once family members understand routines in the schools, they can take over the training of new classroom volunteers. When a teacher forms teams of regular classroom supporters, these helpers can be engaged to explain to other parents how to read aloud, how to help children with their math, and how to help in other learning tasks.

• *Childcare provisions.* One way to encourage family involvement is to provide childcare for young children who are not yet in school. This encourages greater participation of family members who are caretakers to young children and assures that everyone who wishes to be involved in the school has the opportunity to do so.

In addition to the strategies described here, some schools use other techniques to make parents feel welcome. Employing volunteers from the community to serve as greeters of school visitors is one way to make parents feel more welcome. One school in Washington hired a parent to greet all visitors to the school. She was a member of the neighborhood, and almost all the parents recognized her and felt comfortable walking into the school when she was there to greet them. This particular greeter did not stay a stranger to anyone, and even people who had never visited the school before were greeted with a big hug and a warm hello. Everyone felt welcome at the school, and the school became a gathering point for the community.

Schools can develop a family-friendly attitude by providing physical space for families. Some schools provide a room for parents to gather. The family room becomes the hub of involvement activities and provides a community meeting place, a training center for parent and family education, and a place for families to meet their children. When schools provide a comfortable place for family members, it signifies a concrete commitment to the importance of partnerships in students' learning and school success. At the very least, the routine for parents and family members who visit the school to take part in activities should be readily recognizable so that they feel a part of the school instead of feeling left out.

Family Involvement in Elementary and Secondary Schools

Most family involvement techniques are appropriate for elementary school, but there is less experience with the family-centered approach with older students. Although family involvement is most common in the elementary years, communication with schools continues to be a high priority at the secondary level and has many positive results and benefits. Some of the most accepted practices associated with family involvement need to be reconstructed when adapting to middle school and high school. By the time children are in middle school, visits by parents must be carefully planned to support children who are generally pulling away from their parents and focusing on relationships with their peers. A parent's

Field-Based Activity 10.2

Talk to students in your classrooms about how they feel when members of their family visit the school or volunteer to work on school activities. Begin a list of tips and guidelines that reflect what students, family members, and teachers relate to your class about family involvement.

appearance in the hallway can cause extreme embarrassment, but at the same time a parent's absence at a sports event can be terribly upsetting. Middle school children like to know that their parents help plan behind the scenes and support them at home, but they do not necessarily want their parents' involvement to be obvious. By high school age, parental involvement is very different than it is with younger children. Older children want their parents to work with them to gain information, discuss important topics brought up at school, and help them make decisions about careers and college. High school students are usually comfortable having their parents attend a seminar on career choices or a band concert. However, they may feel very uncomfortable having parents show up during the school day to observe in their classrooms. Many high schools plan open-house events, which encourage high school students and their parents to go through the daily schedule together so that parents can have a better understanding of their children's school day.

Classroom Visits   One way to encourage parental involvement at the elementary level is to invite parents to visit the classroom. Having their parents or other adults the children know in the classroom to read, tutor, or help with a bulletin board can be exciting and comforting. The classroom should be open to parents, and each parent should feel comfortable visiting during instruction. Classroom visits can be arranged in several different ways and for differing purposes.

Observation of classroom instruction is the minimum level of parental activity in the classroom. A teacher may have a set time when family members are welcome to visit to observe specific teaching and learning activities. Visits that have no obligation other than observing in a friendly welcoming classroom encourage involvement by family members in other activities throughout the school year.

Classroom visits help familiarize family members with routines and procedures associated with teaching and learning activities. One of the simplest things for visitors to do when they visit elementary classrooms is to share favorite stories or reading material. Family members can be included in daily read-aloud sessions and can share their favorite books. Tutoring in math, helping with writing, or working with individuals and small groups are other things that can be accomplished during parent visits to the classroom.

Classroom visits with older children might not occur as regularly and might only involve very special occasions when there is a performance or guest speaker to which groups of parents attend. Some secondary teachers invite parents to talk to classes about their jobs or special areas of expertise related to course content. Classroom visits in middle school and high school are best planned and organized with a great deal of student input.

Family Members as Volunteers   The roles that parent volunteers can assume are endless. Many schools have parent volunteer programs that are regular support systems for school involvement. Family members may be responsible for an ongoing specific job associated with school routines. They may assist in elementary classrooms by listening to children read aloud, working as scribes for children, or helping children learn math facts. Family members can help in secondary schools by accompanying groups on field trips, selling tickets at sports events, and tutoring children who might be having trouble in content areas. In some schools, parents are morning greeters as the older children arrive at school, and they also walk the halls during class changes. The presence of family members provides teachers and administrators with needed assistance, and the practice has noticeably decreased rowdiness and negative behavior.

School Conferences   Teachers and family members interact about individual children during school conferences. Conferences are one way for teachers to measure the level of involvement of parents. Teachers get frustrated when family members do not appear, and they assume that families do not care for their own children when they fail to respond to school invitations. Ladson-Billings (1994) provides some insights about parental response from another perspective:

> One of the persistent complaints among today's teachers is that parents are not involved enough in the schools. Teachers lament the fact that more and more children come from households where both parents work. One statistic suggests that 75 percent of parents never visit their children's schools. I don't recall my parents going out of their way to come to school. Perhaps once a year they came for a conference or a student performance, but neither my mother nor my father was very visible. They were too busy working. They expected me to do what the teacher told me to do. However, if my teachers needed my parents for something, all they had to do was call. (pp. 39–40)

Teachers would do well to remember that perceptions of parents and family members may be very different from their own and that there may be numerous reasons for parents not to respond to invitations to conferences and involvement.

Many school districts require conferences with parents or other family members to communicate how children are doing at school. Unfortunately, most conferences occur as a result of children doing poorly at school. Because of this, family members often feel very insecure when they are scheduled to discuss their child's work with a teacher. If teachers also arrange contacts with family members to talk about positive events and behaviors, conferences will not be dreaded. Most family members enjoy talking with others about their children, and conferences give them an opportunity to discuss progress, strengths, and potential problems. Conferences provide information to both parents and teachers, making their respective jobs somewhat easier.

When family members arrive at school, the conference atmosphere should be comfortable and relaxed. It is good to have something concrete to discuss during the first moments of the conference. Work samples, writing folders, records of progress in content areas, and portfolios can guide the discussions, providing samples of work and anecdotes of classroom activity. Conferences provide an opportunity to interpret tests and help parents and others understand the results. Teachers alleviate many fears by discussing children's classroom responses and behaviors. Not only can teachers share information about students' classroom and school behavior, but parents can provide information about home behavior that may help teachers better understand their students.

Telephone conferences and home visits provide an important opportunity for parents to talk to a teacher in a more comfortable, less threatening environment. These types of contacts are most reasonable for working family members who cannot visit the school during the day.

Many levels of involvement can be expected from families, but the ultimate goal is to gain family commitment to the importance of active home–school cooperation. Parents, family members, and teachers should plan together for home–school involvement and work together to implement these plans (Rasin-

World Wide Web Site

The Center on Families, Communities, Schools, and Children's Learning can help you identify effective parent–school partnerships. You can learn about the five types of parental involvement at: http://npin.org

ski & Fredericks, 1989). Very few programs of family involvement ever achieve this level of cooperation, and, once achieved, it is very difficult to maintain. Even so, a high level of parental involvement should be the goal and desired outcome of each effort.

Challenges of Family Involvement

Family involvement in school activities makes sense, but it is not always as simple as it sounds. Parents and other family members do not always feel comfortable in schools, and educators often dismiss their views as unimportant to the educational task (Ayers, 1993). Certain attitudes and situations can interfere with interactions between parents and teachers. Sometimes school has a particular emotional impact on parents and family members. For example, parents may have experienced school failure themselves and feel uneasy when asked to become involved with their children's classroom activities (Wilson & Wilson, 1994). If parents have not finished school, do not speak English, or feel inferior to the teacher and other school personnel, it may be extremely difficult for them to be in the school setting and feel comfortable with their children's teacher. Parents' discomfort can increase if they do not understand what they are to do or if they feel they have nothing to offer in the school setting.

Parents and family members can also feel uncomfortable talking about their parenting skills, particularly if they are having difficulty providing some of the basic needs for their children. Family members may be embarrassed when they cannot provide basic supplies or pay for school lunches. When their children are exhibiting behavior problems or are not progressing in their schoolwork, parents feel may responsible. Teachers need to understand that caretakers may be very worried about their children but may not understand how to respond to the children's actions and behaviors that are causing concerns in school. If family members believe schools are being judgmental, they may avoid contact or view teachers' queries about their children's progress as attacks on their own competence as parents (Hamilton & Osborne, 1994).

Sometimes communication difficulties between the home and school create serious family and school discontinuities, discouraging parent–school linkages that provide support systems for students with limited English proficiency (Chiang, 1994). Immigrant parents who work long hours, encounter linguistic and cultural barriers, and lack familiarity with the U.S. educational system often avoid coming to schools and talking to teachers. Parents need to understand what to do and how to collaborate with the teacher to help their children succeed at school (Flores, Cousin, & Diaz, 1991). Unless parents, families, teachers, and

Field-Based Activity 10.3

Volunteer to work in an activity or project that includes parents and other family members. In the elementary schools, it might be decorating the school for a carnival or family night. In the middle or high schools, it might be working in a concession stand during a sports event or chaperoning a dance on Friday night. Share some things you learned about parents and families with your classmates.

administrators work together to build a supportive learning environment, students will not receive all the benefits available to them.

Transportation, time, energy, and childcare needs are all barriers that may prevent parents from participating in school activities. These barriers are particularly troublesome for low-income families who have few resources and less flexible job schedules (Hamilton & Osborne, 1994). At the same time, low-income families are in particular need of support and interactions that contribute to the education of their children. A good education is one way they can help their children have successful adult lives.

Teachers may contribute to noninvolvement of families by not understanding how to include them in the education of their children. Teachers may not have the skills or the experience to recognize the benefits of working with parents and families. Many teacher education programs do not emphasize working with families. Teachers may feel uncomfortable talking with families, and this may be more problematic for new teachers. The benefits of family involvement must be explicitly emphasized, and schools should encourage outside involvement. Otherwise, a teacher who has many tasks to complete may feel that parental involvement is just another intrusion that represents yet another time-consuming task. Research demonstrates that children's achievement and attitude about school can be influenced by parental involvement, so it makes sense to find ways to include parents as partners.

Teachers' Roles

Working with parents requires good interpersonal skills, and when conducted with respect, interactions with families will be successful in establishing the contact necessary for helping children do their best. The National Board for Professional Teaching Standards (1994), which seeks to create common standards for teachers throughout the United States, states in Proposition 5 that "highly accomplished teachers work to create positive relationships with families as they participate in the education of their children." Teachers need to develop skills and understandings to foster collaborative relationships between school and family. Basic interpersonal skills of communication and respect go a long way in establishing school–family relationships. However, at times, conversations with family members may involve difficult issues. Parents respond positively to reinforcement of their attempts to increase their child's well-being. Teachers who attempt to understand parents' actions will increase the number of positive interactions with parents and will enhance parents' and family members' perceptions of their own abilities. Teachers should be honest and direct when talking to parents, praising children and their efforts with sincerity.

One way to ensure that all voices are heard is to institute a school-based governance team with representatives from school and family groups. Together, this team, guided by the school principal, works to develop a school plan that includes strategies for a positive school climate and academic goals for all students. When a positive, inviting school climate is the goal of all participants, parent involvement can be built in as an integral and necessary activity (Comer, 1994). When the entire school supports and encourages parental involvement, it becomes easier for each individual teacher to work with parents in productive ways.

Community Involvement

Education should be everybody's business—"a common enterprise in which all adults of the community unite to protect, nurture, guide, and educate the young" (Hindle, 1993, p. 34). The community as a whole influences the way children feel about themselves and their attitudes toward education and is linked to student success in schools (Mattox & Rich, 1977). Explicit connections between schools and communities will affect children. Role models from all aspects of life demonstrate the importance of learning and the value of an education. If students see that everyone around them cares about what and how they do in school, it can have an impact on self-confidence, attitude, and achievement.

Accomplished teachers understand their school's community and use it as a powerful resource for learning by taking advantage of the many opportunities for enrichment and exploration. The community serves as a learning and resource lab for developing tolerance and civic responsibility and for understanding about human differences. Activities and events in the community can provide examples or starting points for discussions and classroom lessons. Experienced teachers will find community events and opportunities that are important to students and use them to build curriculum and classroom lessons.

Teachers effectively use available resources by understanding the community and how the environment affects the students and the school. The community's context, culture, and personality make up the fabric of its schools. The ethnic, religious, and cultural diversity, the economic and business settings, and religious and historical values are all important parts of the school. Using that knowledge to build classroom projects, activities, and lessons provides a relevant context for good teaching and learning.

Many valuable resources are offered by individuals in the community. Community organizations, such as churches, women's clubs, the NAACP, and fraternal groups, can provide important alliances to bring people and resources into the schools. Volunteers from these organizations may serve as mentors, tutors, or resources for lessons on specific cultural groups. More important, they can give critical advice on curriculum content. Senior citizens, parents, businesspeople, and local organizations can enhance and supplement teaching and learning activities. They can visit classrooms, tutor children, provide emotional support, and participate in governance and administrative activities. They can volunteer in the school and support school sports, music, and theater by attending events.

Involving the community in school activities produces citizens who understand and are supportive of schools and encourages good public relations between education professionals and those outside the educational setting. Informed and supportive citizens influence decisions in the schools by voting on school issues, participating on school boards, and supporting education experiences with their own work and leisure time. When schools involve and consider the community in educational endeavors, they receive needed support in times of bond elections and other endeavors that take resources to improve educational environments. Citizens who are familiar with the children and the school in a community support the efforts of educators. When schools lose the support of their citizens, schools suffer economically and are unable to generate the support they need for continued growth and progress.

Partnerships between schools and communities also are effective in working to solve some of our most difficult social problems. Communities and schools work together to curb violence, drug abuse, teen pregnancies, and other tough problems. Many effective community collaborations result in improved educational programs, changes in school climate, and an increase in family support systems (Epstein, 1995).

Communities include families and children but also include businesses, community services, health and human social services, city government, juvenile workers, and others. Educational experiences are enhanced when others who come from community settings become involved in the welfare and education of young people. Communities that encourage their agencies and institutions to collaborate to assist children and families are capable of building an effective support system that has the potential to enrich educational experiences. To develop an educated person, efforts must go far beyond the classroom. Without the help of those outside the classroom, even the best teachers will have difficulty educating their students.

Business Partners

The collaboration between business and education, focused on helping schools succeed, is developed in several different ways (Hindle, 1993). Business and public schools often collaborate to offer special programs to particular schools or to sponsor students for career exploration. Sometimes a three-way partnership is formed among businesses, universities, and public schools. Business–education collaborations are almost always formed under the belief that a broad-based alliance involving many sectors of the community is necessary for providing the best schools possible. Here are some ways that business supports education:

- *Resources.* Businesses can provide resources that go beyond the basic expectations of school support (Hindle, 1993). Businesses may provide money and equipment to support special programs such as summer tutoring, field trips, or college/career exploration. In the past few years, technology-based businesses have regularly supported school programs that feature technology. Computer companies have provided computers, scientific companies have donated lab equipment, and even school libraries have been stocked by companies.

- *Special programs.* Business supports supplementary programs that enhance students' educational experiences (Hindle, 1993). Special programs encouraging students' interest in math and science are one focus of business-oriented programs. Business-sponsored programs may occur in the summer, on Saturdays, or after normal school hours. Activities are planned to provide students with opportunities to serve as junior interns, office helpers, or lab assistants. Businesspeople develop mentoring relationships with individual students and have a great influence on attitudes about schools and career.

- *Expertise.* Businesspeople also offer their expertise to education professionals (Hindle, 1993). Specialists who use a particular group process or management technique may work with schools to suggest ways to improve decision-making

Businesses are very interested in helping schools in their communities succeed. School–business partnerships provide businesspeople with a way to contribute to their community, support special educational projects, and help students learn about careers and occupations.

processes, organizational approaches, and management. Total Quality Management is an example of a decision-making technique similar to site-based management that was adopted by many schools in the early 1990s.

• *Information.* Places of business provide students with a concrete lesson in understanding possibilities, skills, and requirements of potential jobs and occupations (Hindle, 1993). Summer internships for high school students, field trips to particular sites, and guest speakers provide needed information as young people make decisions about their future occupations.

• *Volunteers.* Businesspeople may be encouraged to become actively involved in school projects. Just as people from other walks of life do, people who manage and work in business volunteer, become partners, and work directly with schools to change and enhance educational programs. Some places of business give employees time off to help schools with activities.

Many of the activities sponsored by business and industry are specifically related to the focus of their work. The hope is that they will produce future workers who are prepared for their business. In other cases, businesses will partner with schools as a reflection of civic duty in the hope that they can support the community. There is often a very good match between the emphasis of particular businesses and the goals of schooling.

School-to-Work Programs

Business has recently been involved in the school reform debate, supporting changes in curriculum to more closely align learning with skills and knowledge needed by business. As a result, the School-to-Work Opportunities Act established a national framework to broaden the educational, career, and economic opportunities for all youth through partnerships between businesses, schools, community-based organizations, and state and local governments. The intention of school-to-work programs is to change the way teachers teach and children learn in schools. The basis of the change is to focus on identifying and classifying the skills workers need to perform successfully in the workplace and to coordinate curriculum developed from the skills of workers with school curriculum. Federal funds were allocated in 1994 to help establish these programs throughout the nation.

School-to-work programs encourage the involvement of state and national government, employers, educators, parents, labor unions, communities, and others in designing curriculum that will meet the specific needs of local areas. Proponents of the plan believe that all young people—whether they are college bound, career bound, or out of school, or whether they possess disabilities or are culturally and linguistically different—will benefit from collaboration between business, industry, and schools.

The school-to-work plan contains three core elements:

1. *Classroom-based learning that integrates work and school-based learning.* This learning incorporates knowledge or skills associated with certain jobs or occupations into the regular school curriculum.

2. *Work experience that includes training and mentoring at job sites.* This component is used to encourage high school students to work in business and industry during the summer, in the evening, or on weekends.

3. *Activities that interconnect school and work.* This component may involve the business or industry in the school day. Students attend class during the morning, studying a curriculum related to a particular type of work, and then work on-site at the business during the afternoon.

Field-Based Activity 10.4

Find out about the school-to-work efforts in your community. Take a field trip to where the efforts are located or bring in an individual who is involved to describe some of the activities. Identify the concerns and issues.

The school-to-work opportunities systems were designed to create a transition between classrooms and the workplace or other educational settings. Creative transition programs that many people are already familiar with (such as youth apprenticeship, cooperative education, and career academies) are the primary foundations on which school-to-work systems will be built.

Influences of Business

Business tends to have a greater influence over educational changes than other groups have (Myers & Myers, 1995). Businesspeople are usually active in government and have power in local and state decisions. During the last decade, business has had a great influence on educational curriculum and evaluation. Business directly impacts how schools spend tax money and the attitudes of the public toward education.

During the past decade, business and labor have paid particularly close attention to educational reform (Farris, 1996). Many believe businesses have the authority, as prominent community institutions, and the expertise to work in school reform efforts (Hindle, 1993). In some instances, business has leveled particularly harsh criticism at education, schools, and teaching. In particular, those in business question the effectiveness of school management and operations. They also support better teaching of basic skills. Most people associated with business believe it is in their best interest that teaching and learning produce students who are proficient, knowledgeable, and able to be successful in the workforce after graduation from high school.

Interprofessional Partners

There is no great mystery about what it takes to help a troubled child or family. In study after study, we find that two things stand out in the histories of kids who

Becoming a Teacher in a Field-Based Setting

make it against the odds. . . . The first fact is access to a second chance to succeed at something the person failed at before—going back to school, being helped to pass a class (as opposed to being either punished or excused for it). . . . The second is the intervention of just one caring person from outside the family . . . that person's role is . . . to get involved in the child's life. (Coontz, 1995, p. K16)

Children and young people often face personal and social difficulties that affect their academic achievement. Teachers commonly mention that the toughest problems they face when working with children and young people are related to social, personal, and health issues. Poverty, violence, drug abuse, and homelessness have become major problems in schools, and even the best teachers and the best-planned curriculum cannot overcome them. One way to combat social issues and the many demands that children and families face is to develop collaborative relationships between education and health and human services professionals. Nurses, doctors, social workers, community health professionals, and others are partners who focus on the welfare of children and can provide a wide range of social service activities and programs that help parents help their children. A collaborative effort between professionals who care about children is one of the best ways to offset at-risk behavior. Many feel that collaboration by professionals who work with children and families, called interprofessional collaboration, is one trend of the future that holds a great deal of promise for improving the lives of children and young people.

Many of the seventeen thousand organizations that offer community-based programs for children and youth are fragmented and address only one specific problem (Carnegie Corporation, 1992). The services designed to help troubled children and families and the red tape associated with support are overwhelming to even the most savvy person. When children and families need help, several agencies may need to be contacted before they can receive the help they need. The offices where the families could get help are often located in different parts of town and in areas that are unfamiliar to the adults and the children who need to access the services. Once individuals find where help can be provided, there are many forms to be completed, questions to be answered, and documents to be provided. The health clinic requires one form that asks a multitude of questions, the social worker asks for another form, the social security office requests still another, and so on. These documents and instructions are usually written in English that is difficult even for native speakers, much less for families who speak little or no English. Even when families finally access services, the services may be limited and may not accomplish what is needed or may require repeated visits. It is no wonder that children do not receive the services they need to do well in school.

Voice of a Parent

I am Maria Sanchez. I live with my husband and two children just up the block from the Family Center. I want to tell you about my experience.

I've been coming here (to the Family Center) for a year now. It is a great place to come and learn about resources around the community. Everything is in one place.

Let me tell you how I got started coming here. I used to walk my boys to the school cafeteria (adjacent to the Family Center) for free lunch during the summer. I had to walk by here and I noticed things going on. I peeked in and saw flyers telling about activities and meetings that were planned here in the Family Center. To be honest, I was bored and spent much of my time sitting in my apartment in front of the TV. It was summertime and it was hot. I had no air conditioning and this was a cool place to bring my children. I would bring my children here to the programs or to play with toys or read books or just to talk to people. I started coming a lot in the daytime. I came to CPR classes, jewelry classes, and the one I liked best was taught by the School District Parent Educator. It was a program about how to buy a house from the city. It raised my hopes for the future.

I am thirty years old now and I have been out of school for fourteen years. I don't know why I have not thought about doing anything much to improve myself, but I guess I just lacked the drive. Now I have completed and passed my GED and I have a job with the Family Literacy Program where I get to work with and help other parents.

If it hadn't been for the Family Center, I would not have my job. The Family Center Program Manager knew my capabilities and she recommended me to the Family Literacy people for this job. At the time I didn't have any intention to get my GED, but since it was a requirement for the job I went ahead and took the GED test. I passed right away. Now I plan to go back to school. I want to take courses at the Community College.

I love my job. As I said, I like working with parents. I get to plan trips to the library for parents. Let me tell you about one mother who had never had a library card before. It was a very exciting thing for her to get a library card. I made a xerox copy of her library card to keep in her file so that she could have a memento. It was so special.

And since I know about the Family Center I bring new people from the Literacy Program down here to see what's going on.

I want to add that since I have been coming here to the Family Center, and since I have joined Community Voices (neighborhood action group that meets at the Family Center), I have become more involved with my children's school. I feel more confident about just going to see what is happening.

Parents, especially those in low-income, high-risk neighborhoods, are often unaware of the array of social services available to them through the many different organizations working in the community. A school that strives to link social services and academic programs can meet many needs that can potentially improve academic achievement in the classroom. Through this link with family support services, schools can address not only the academic problems of students but also their social, psychological, and health problems. Serving as a center for social programs, such a school might offer after-school care for school-age children, day care for three- to five-year-olds, adult literacy classes, teen pregnancy prevention classes, and other services that address the needs of the community it serves.

Efforts that connect social programs and educational outcomes report success stories for children. "Schools, social programs, and caring individuals can compensate for stressful environments and troubled families" (Coontz, 1995, p. K17). Problems facing children and families seem overwhelming to parents and teachers. At the same time that parents are faced with troubled children, they may be having their own crises and cannot find the energy or resources to focus on their children's issues.

Interprofessional programs and activities provide needed support to children and families who find themselves in crisis. Teachers, social workers, community nurses, doctors, dentists, and juvenile workers are among those who generally collaborate to simplify processes. In some cases, police and judges are also involved in these endeavors. These professionals have various objectives, but improvement of children and family situations is at the center of their professional mission. Collaboration can begin by talking together. Collaboration among these groups must be learned, and even simple tasks linking health and human service agencies can take a great deal of time. In one town in Texas, professionals worked together for a year and a half to devise a single form that could be used in several social services. The result was that families and children could access services with a bit more ease than before the professionals sat down to talk.

The physical facilities supporting interprofessional activities may be based in schools or housing projects, community development corporations, or childcare centers. Sometimes collaborative efforts result in school-based clinics or family centers designed to encourage interprofessional collaboration. These efforts help parents and other interested adults promote their children's learning and give parents the training and self-confidence necessary to be involved in their children's educational processes.

Interprofessional activities such as job counseling and training, health care, substance abuse treatment, nutrition, housing, transportation, referral centers for family social services, and before- and after-school programs for working parents are examples of support systems that can aid learning and teaching. Activities that occur as a result of individuals from different professions collaborating together to provide integrated services may be called community-based services, school-based services, "one-stop shopping," or interprofessional activities.

Interprofessional collaborations focus on three major activities:

1. *Parent education and parent involvement in the education of their children.* Programs focusing on schools include the family, the school, childcare and youth programs, and health care agencies.

2. *Intersections between health and human service possibilities services.* The focus of these programs is to encourage parents to take greater responsibility for the primary health care of their children. Parents learn more about health care services, how to gain access to services, and how to make them work for the betterment of their children's lives. Efforts in this area work to assess health needs of children and youth, link families and health care providers, and help improve health education in the school.

3. *Professional training of teachers and other professionals.* The professional development of individuals who are trained to work across professions is crucial. University faculty involved in professional training of teachers, social workers, and other health and human service professions design curriculum and develop field experiences that help future professionals learn about this work.

Interprofessional work does not need to be embedded in a large, complicated program. Answers to some problems may not reside in these big programs. Intervention and help for individual children and their families occur when a teacher, a social worker, a community nurse, or a police officer talk and work together on one issue. In other cases, professionals may collaborate to share needed information.

The importance of interprofessional support is that public and private community resources and public school resources can be combined to focus on prevention and early interventions that address the needs of all students. Different professional groups work together to identify and remove unnecessary regulations and obstacles to coordinating efforts and to provide a strong support system to children. Professional collaboration increases students' access to social services, health care, nutrition, related services, and childcare services. The partnerships can help parents and families by locating such services in schools, cooperating service agencies, community-based centers, or other convenient sites designed to provide "one-stop shopping" for parents and students (U.S. Department of Education, 1994). To better understand this kind of collaborative effort, let's look at three examples in more detail.

Healthy Learners

One of the best-known examples of interprofessional collaboration is Healthy Learners, a community-based program in Miami, Florida (Briar, 1993). The program is a joint effort by Florida's public schools, a university, and the state's department of health and rehabilitative services. One of the most effective and critical components of the program is the Referral and Information Network (RAIN). Composed of a family advocate and a group of mothers who call themselves the Rainmakers, they visit families and children in the community and hold community meetings to help parents understand how they can better access the services offered in the community. Although it is difficult to assess the results of their work directly, positive indicators in the community demonstrate that changes for the better are taking place. Some of the indicators are fewer police sweeps, less graffiti, higher attendance in the schools, and fewer evictions from housing in the community (Corrigan & Udas, 1996).

Corridor of Success

Educators from Bronx Community College teamed up with local schools and began to develop collaborative relationships with city health and human services. The objective of the collaboration was to take back one school at a time and to develop a corridor of success in schools that were linked together by common neighborhoods and children. The initiative focuses on an evolving partnership among Bronx Community College (BCC), Intermediate School 82, and School District 9, and it includes representatives from human service agencies and other schools. BCC and IS 82 have served as a hub for the expanding efforts related to development of a Corridor of Success for children in District 9. Parents, teachers, school administrators, and health and human service professionals are collaborating to open lines of communication and link child and family services. The effort that began as a collaboration between BCC and IS 82 now includes schools that feed to Intermediate School 82 and a high school that many of the IS 82 children now attend. A cornerstone activity of the Bronx initiative is "Friday on the Campus," in which fifth-grade students spend their day at BCC being taught by university professors, working in science laboratories, and becoming familiar with the campus.

Field-Based Activity 10.5

Locate a community facility that has more than one service (social services, law officials, community health facilities) in one place. It will probably be a community or family center. Choose one of these activities to help you learn about the activities in the center: (1) interview the professionals and/or the children and families, (2) volunteer to help with a project, or (3) sit in the reception area of the facility and take field notes.

School Families

A middle school and a university in Texas developed a program to involve community volunteers, university professors, and teachers in a mentoring relationship that provided middle school children with support during the school day. A cornerstone activity at the Texas site has been the School Families program, which provides an academic and social support system for middle school children and provides opportunities for preservice and inservice teachers, school counselors, administrators, and community volunteers to collaborate. Once a week, five adults meet with one classroom, beginning with whole class discussion and then breaking into small groups where students and adults discuss social, academic, and personal issues.

Accomplished teachers participate in the coordination of services to students. They understand what is available to assist children and families who are under stress, and they know how to access support systems that will contribute to their students' classroom success.

Churches and Religious Groups

Even though there is separation between church and schools, students do arrive at the classroom with different ideas about how to act on their religious faith in the school setting. Teachers and administrators must understand the law and decide the application of the law in their particular setting (Myers & Myers, 1995). The role of the church as a partner in education is an issue in almost all school settings at one time or another. Churches provide an important community link. For many groups represented in classrooms, the church is an important component of family life. Church ministers are often considered members of the extended family and can be valuable in making school–home connections. In some communi-

Schools are part of the larger community in which individuals and organizations outside of school contribute to students' personal, social, and academic development. Religious leaders may serve as role models, teachers, and counselors for students.

ties, churches and schools are working together to provide day care and after-school programs, organize parent support groups, and improve education for their children (Freedman & Negroni, 1992; Lawson & Briar-Lawson, 1997). Constitutional law may prohibit churches from influencing public school curricular decisions, but their impact on families and their children must be considered as part of the context of schooling.

Challenges of Collaboration

Many potential partners may be involved in the complex job of educating our children. Collaboration is difficult, but when it is successful, there typically are payoffs to students. The challenges to developing broad-based community collaboration are many.

One of the factors that prevents collaboration from occurring among different professions is role-specialization. Professional specialists ranging from nurses to librarians are trained to understand a particular area and to control and manage different parts of the school system. Educators' roles usually are based on specialization and on understanding certain parts of the educational processes. Science teachers want to teach science, nurses are trained to provide health services, and social workers are experienced in social services. These professionals have not been exposed to ways of working together and connecting the work across professions. This specialization often results in a lack of understanding of the possible contributions of others. To begin this work, professionals will often have to learn how to work collaboratively, not worry about their own turf, and take the time to understand the context of other people and their professional lives. Collaborative work between schools, families, and communities involves a great deal of negotiating to ensure that an effective level of cooperation between professionals will occur.

The involvement of parents, family members, community, and health and human service professional personnel in the schools adds to the existing complexities and ambiguities. Involving others in the educational experience may seem an overwhelming task at first. However, if teachers and administrators view the involvement of others in the day-to-day routine of schools as vital to their mission and as a resource to supplement ongoing school activities, attitudes and approaches to collaboration with available partners will be viewed positively. The results of involving the community in children's learning are recognizable yet difficult to measure. It takes time to see differences from interventions that involve collaboration, and schools and business often lack the patience to support an initiative for the five to seven years it may take to note any differences. Nevertheless, the benefits of collaboration are worth the time and effort educators invest.

Beginning teachers can probably be convinced that working with families, the community, businesses, and other professionals is a good idea, but how to go about getting involved in collaborative efforts is quite another matter. It may take several years of teaching before you understand how you might develop your skills and make contributions in this area. The first step for beginning educators is to become comfortable with your students' families and the community where you work. Volunteer in community projects, serve on a citywide committee, or visit boys' and girls' clubs in the neighborhoods that surround your school.

A second step that you can take is to understand the potential and to be open and flexible to ideas that involve partners outside the school walls. Learning to talk and communicate with individuals from other professions is a first step toward developing the capacity for understanding how to collaborate. Participating in ongoing discussions and planning at school will help a new teacher understand the potential of partnerships. When new teachers see a way that they can become involved, they can participate in a way that seems appropriate in their own lives. Take the time now to complete the Self-Reflection exercise and to think about what you have learned.

New teachers need to develop the skills associated with good collaboration. Collaborative skills are useful in many areas of daily life and are skills that teachers usually already possess. Listening to others, rephrasing what others have said, remaining flexible, accepting new ideas, and realizing conflict will emerge when people work together are just a few of the valuable skills needed to collaborate with others inside and outside the school walls.

It is difficult to become involved with other individuals and professionals when you are learning about your own role as a teacher. Although a teacher cannot always single-handedly marshal resources on behalf of his or her students, there will be opportunities for new teachers to take part in discussions with

---

Self-Reflection

FAMILY AND COMMUNITY COLLABORATIONS

Read the following statements about activities that involve you with families and communities. Check any that you have done. If you have been involved in other activities not listed, add them to the list.

_____ 1. Visit local community centers

_____ 2. Work with boys' and girls' clubs

_____ 3. Coach a community sports team

_____ 4. Serve on neighborhood committee

_____ 5. Tutor in adult or child literacy programs

_____ 6. Attend community functions and celebrations

_____ 7. Tutor in an after-school program

_____ 8. Volunteer at a homeless shelter

_____ 9. Volunteer in low-income childcare facilities

_____ 10. Read to children at the local library

_____ 11. _____

_____ 12. _____

Count the number of checks you have. If you have three or more, you are well on your way to understanding and appreciating the potential contributions of family and community to your work with children. If you have very few checks, you may want to plan ways to learn more about the community where your school is located.

Portfolio Reflections and Exhibit

Review the field activities related to this chapter. Adapt and expand one of the activities, design your own exhibit, or complete this suggested portfolio exhibit to represent the learnings and understandings from this chapter.

Suggested Exhibit 10: Experiences with Families and Communities

Your portfolio representation for this chapter should include:

1. A summary of all the field-based activities you completed for this chapter.

2. Selection and an explanation of the activity that was most important to you.

3. A representation of your experiences and assumptions about the families of children in schools. Decide on the media you will use to represent your ideas. Review and summarize in writing your ideas about family involvement based on your own experiences. Add narrative explaining what the children and families at your school have taught you about family involvement. Finally, include a description of a community activity you have encountered. Draw a picture, make a collage, graph, continuum, or cut articles from magazines and newspapers that demonstrate your learning from this chapter. Limit this illustration to two pages.

others who may be able to help. Once new teachers gain information about what is available to help them teach and students learn, they can begin helping to plan cooperative ventures and participate with others to provide the best possible educational environment for their students.

InfoTrac College Edition Extension

Log on to the InfoTrac College Edition Web site, and use the skills you have gained throughout the semester to find the answers to these questions about collaboration:

1. What are the names of some journals that feature articles and research about collaboration between schools and other agencies or people?

2. Judging from the titles of recent articles in this area, what kinds of collaboration appear to be the most common?

3. What are some benefits and barriers to collaboration between schools and others?

Related Readings

Clinton, H. R. (1995). *It takes a village to raise a child.* New York: Simon & Schuster.
> *Mrs. Clinton describes her own upbringing and her view of raising children. She describes the responsibilities of communities and how it takes more than families to watch after children.*

Hechinger, F. M. (1992). *Fateful choices: Healthy youth for the 21st century.* New York: Carnegie Corporation, Council on Adolescent Development.
> *This book provides a sense of the complexity of the risks and opportunities of the adolescent years. The author believes that if adolescents are to make wise choices families and communities must provide support while they are making the transition from childhood to adulthood.*

Kralovec, E. & Buell, J. (2000). *The end of homwork: How homework disrupts families, overburdens children, and limits learning.* Boston: Beacon Press.
> *This book questions seriously the value of homwork in light of how it impacts overworked parents and discriminates against children who do not have computers, libraries, and well-educated parents.*

Lareau, A. (2000). *Home advantage: Social class and parental intervention in elementary education.* Lanham, MD: Roman & Littlefield.
> *Lareau illustrates how parents try to help their children succeed in school. She points out that working-class and middle-class parents differ in the type and number of resources they bring to the task. Her descriptions help us understand the many small ways parents act to make sure their children get a good education.*

References

Ayers, W. (1993). *To teach: The journey of a teacher.* New York: Teachers College Press.

Briar, K. (1993). *Response sheet: Program information on integrated services and interprofessional education.* Unpublished raw data. Florida International University, Miami.

Carnegie Corporation. (1992). *Matter of time: Risk and opportunity in the nonschool hours.* New York: Author.

Chiang, R. A. (1994). Home–school communication for Asian students with limited English proficiency. *Kappa Delta Pi Record, 30*(4), 159–163.

Comer, J. (1994). Home, school, and academic learning. In J. I. Goodlad & P. Keating (Eds.), *Access to knowledge: The continuing agenda for our nation's schools* (pp. 23–42). New York: The College Board.

Coontz, S. (1995). The American family and the nostalgia trap: Kappan special report. *Phi Delta Kappan, 76*(7), K1–K21.

Corrigan, D. C., & Udas, K. (1996). Creating collaborative, child- and family-centered education, health, and human service systems. In J. Sikula (Ed.), *Handbook of research on teacher education* (pp. 893–921). New York: Macmillan.

Epstein, J. (1993, April). Make parents your partners. *Instructor, 103*(1), 73–76.

Epstein, J. (1995). School/family/community partnerships: Caring for the children we share. *Phi Delta Kappan, 76*(9), 701–712.

Farris, P. J. (1996). *Teaching, bearing the torch.* Dubuque, IA: Brown & Benchmark.

Flaxman, E., & Inger, M. (1992). Parents and schooling in the 1990s. *Education Digest, 57*, 3–7.

Flores, B., Cousin, P. T., & Diaz, E. (1991). Transforming deficit myths about learning, language, and culture. *Language Arts, 68*(5), 369–386.

Fredericks, A. D., & Rasinski, T. V. (1990). Working with parents: Involving the uninvolved—how to. *Reading Teacher, 43*(6), 424–425.

Freedman, S., & Negroni, P. J. (1992). School and community working together: Community education in Springfield. In L. E. Decker & V. A. Romney (Eds.), *Educational restructuring and the community education process* (pp. 111–120). Charlottesville: University of Virginia.

Hamilton, D., & Osborne, S. (1994). Overcoming barriers to parent involvement in public schools. *Kappa Delta Pi Record, 30*(4), 148–152.

Henderson, A. (1987). *The evidence continues to grow: Parent involvement improves student achievement.* Columbia, MD: National Committee for Citizens in Education.

Henderson, A. T. (1988). Parents are a school's best friends. *Phi Delta Kappan, 70*(2), 148–153.

Hindle, W. R. (1993). The business–higher education link: Consider the possibilities. *Educational Record (Summer)*, 33–38.

Ladson-Billings, G. (1994). *The dreamkeepers.* San Francisco: Jossey-Bass.

Lawson, H., & Briar-Lawson, G. (1997). *Connecting the dots: Progress toward the integration of school reform, school-linked services, parent involvement and community schools.* Oxford, OH: The Danforth Foundation and the Institute for Educational Renewal at Miami University.

Mattox, B., & Rich, D. (1977). Community involvement activities: Research into action. *Theory Into Practice, 16*(1), 29–34.

Myers, C. B., & Myers, L. K. (1995). *The professional educator.* Belmont, CA: Wadsworth.

National Board for Professional Teaching Standards. (1994). *What teachers should know and be able to do.* Detroit: National Board for Professional Teaching Standards.

Rasinski, T. V., & Fredericks, A. D. (1989). Dimensions of parent involvement. *Reading Teacher, 42*(2), 68–69.

Rioux, W., & Berla, N. (1994). The necessary partners. *Education Week, 13*(17), 31.

Scott-Jones, D. (1988). Families as educators: The transition from informal to formal school learning. *Educational Horizons, 66*(2), 66–69.

Spaulding, A. M. (1996). The politics of primaries. In A. Pollard, A. Flier, & D. Thiessen (Eds.), *Children and the curriculum: The perspectives of primary and elementary school pupils* (pp. 132–148). London: Falmer Press.

U.S. Department of Education. (1994). *Changing education: Resources for systemic change.* Washington, DC: Author.

Wilson, S. M., & Wilson, J. D. (1994). Kentucky parents respond to primary education reform. *Dimensions of Early Childhood, 22*(2), 28–31.

Final Portfolio Reflections and Exhibits

You have completed Portfolio Reflections and Exhibits for each chapter and been involved in a series of field-based activities. The products that have emerged from these activities can become part of your professional portfolio. The exhibits and artifacts included in a portfolio should be carefully selected to help you describe your own teaching. However, a portfolio is more than a collection of work. A well-developed professional portfolio includes a carefully selected and presented group of exhibits or artifacts that represent your work and philosophy. Not only does a professional portfolio present artifacts or exhibits that illustrate your growth as a teacher, but it also provides an opportunity for you to demonstrate your own unique skills and creativity. Here are several suggestions that you may find helpful as you begin to develop your professional portfolio.

Establish the Purpose of Your Portfolio

Consider how and why you are creating a portfolio. You may want to develop a portfolio that will help you reflect on your learning or become the first step in documenting your professional growth. A portfolio can help establish a picture of you as a teacher and benchmark different developmental accomplishments. Perhaps it is a requirement of your program or of the course you completed; if so, be sure to review the established guidelines. Eventually, your portfolio may be helpful as you interview for teaching positions.

Reflect on Portfolio Exhibits and Artifacts

Determine what characteristics of your own teaching philosophy and practice you wish to convey, and select examples and artifacts that will present this view of your work. Review all the exhibits you have prepared during this course. Select one or two exhibits or artifacts that best represent what you have learned. Write a narrative explaining how they characterize your growth over the semester.

Use the exhibits to help you write a self-evaluation of your growth. What have you learned, and how do the exhibits demonstrate that knowledge? Write a narrative, produce a collage, prepare a graphic or an electronic representation that describes the growth you have experienced as you were introduced to teaching and education. The portfolio exhibits you select to represent this phase of your university program should describe the experiences and growth that have occurred as a result of this course.

Consider all of your experiences from the course, and select one that really made a contribution to your philosophy or view of teaching. Develop a representation of the experience, and illustrate how it is connected to your professional development.

Develop an Overview and a Table of Contents

A portfolio may be presented in a three-ring notebook, as a multimedia presentation, or on a Web site. Regardless of the type of presentation, you will need some organizational format that is easy to understand. Develop a guide for whoever might review your portfolio by providing an overview and description of the contents. By the end of your program, you may have several exhibits grouped in different sections or categories. As you continue to add to your exhibits, you will benefit from developing a table of contents.

Photo Credits

Index

flexibility, 198
guidelines, 242
leadership, 276, 279–282
materials, 211–213
objectives, 243
planning, 199
strategies, 191–192
Integrated curriculum, 237
Integrated instruction, 237–239
Interactive Seating Chart, 161
Intermediate grades, 268
Intermittent reinforcer, 152
Internet, 103, 233
Interpersonal relationships between teachers
and students, 194
Interprofessional collaboration, 308–315
Interstate New Teachers Assessment and
Support Consortium (INTASC), 73

J

Jefferson, Thomas, 36–37
Job opportunities for rural students, 265
Junior high schools, 269
Juvenile offenders, 126

K

Kennedy, John F., 46
Kentucky Education Reform Act, 62
"Kid watchers," 249
King, Martin Luther, Jr., 33, 46
Knowledge base, 11
K-W-L, 230–231

L

Lab activities in units, 244
Land Grant College Act of 1862, 41
Language differences in students, 119
Latchkey children, 116
Latin grammar schools, 36
Lau v. Nichols, 97
Law and education, 96–101

Leadership
classroom activities, 281, 284
communication skills, 281
multiple views, 277
school, 276
school–university partnerships, 279–280
teachers, 279–282, 284
Learning, 145–146, 160, 248–250
communities, 10
disabilities, 132
objectives, 243–244
repetition and practice, 162
specialists, 132
standards, 66–72
strategies, 169, 172
theory, 39
Learning to teach, 19
Lesson planning, 243–245
Lesson plans
components, 243–245
example, 246–247
outline, 248
Lifelong learners, 10, 12
Locke, John, 34
Long-range instructional planning, 230
Long-term memory (LTM), 166, 169, 170
Low-achieving students, 249
Low test scores, 86
Luther, Martin, 33

M

Magazines as instructional resources, 213
Males, classroom responses, 131
Management style of teachers, 183, 217
Mann, Horace, 38
Mathematics skills, 236
Memory
long-term, 166, 169, 170
modeling strategies, 167
short-term, 166, 169
Mental structures, 165

Stimuli, 147
Student
    accountability, 193–194
    group membership, 134
    success, 197–198
Student-centered approaches, 225–226
Suburban schools, 261–262
Success for All, 81
Successful educational programs, 83
Summerhill, 51
Superintendents, 274–275
Supervisors in public schools, 275
Supreme Court, 93, 96
Sustained silent reading, 236
Sylvan Learning Systems, 77

T

"Teach to the test," 66
Teacher career choices, 6–7
    career changes, 6, 18
    career cycle, 13
    career development, 12–19
    career exit, 18
    career states, 12
    childhood experiences, 3–4
    family tradition, 6–7
    love of children, 6
    negative perceptions, 6–7
    role model influence, 4
Teacher-centered approaches, 224
Teacher education
    formal experiences, 19
    induction into the profession, 16
    members of learning community, 10–11
    overview, 19–21
    partnerships, 22
    perservice, 19–21
Teacher-parent conferences, 299–301
Teachers
    academic freedom, 100

central office administration relation-
    ships, 274
characteristics of good, 7–11
childhood experiences, 3
commitment, 8
competency building, 16–17
cultures, 120
enthusiasm, 17
flexibility, 6
frustrations, 17
human relations, 109, 194–195
knowledge of subjects, 8
love of children, 6
moral endeavor, 104
negative perceptions, 6–7
personal philosophy, 26, 52
roles as mentors, 16
salaries, 62
satisfaction, 15–16
socialization processes, 18
stability in profession, 16
stress, 17, 62
testing, 64–66
transitions, 193
Teacher stress, 16, 17
    classroom management, 194
    urban settings, 258, 260
Teacher-student conferences, 206–208
Teaching
    as art or science, 142
    commitment, 9
    knowledge of subject areas, 9
    professionalization, 72–73
Technology, 45, 232–234
Teen pregnancy, 128
Telecommunications, 233
Television, 122
Tenth Amendment, 93
Testing, 64–66
Texas Assessment of Academic Skills, 228